Marx and Engels on Law and Laws

Marx and Engels
on
Law and Laws

PAUL PHILLIPS

BARNES & NOBLE BOOKS
TOTOWA, NEW JERSEY

First published in 1980 by Martin Robertson, Oxford.

First published in the USA 1980 by
BARNES & NOBLE BOOKS
81 Adams Drive
Totowa, New Jersey, 07512

ISBN 0-389-20120-0

Typeset by Oxford Publishing Services, Oxford.
Printed and bound in Great Britain by Billing & Sons Ltd., Guildford,
London, Oxford, Worcester.

Contents

Foreword

Contemporary discussions in the sociology of law cannot ignore the work of Karl Marx and Frederick Engels. As social theorists in their own right, and as progenitors of a received tradition, Marx and Engels remain important. For scholars who examine current problems of crisis and contradiction, and who research into historical processes, they must have an especial appeal. Despite their pre-eminence, and the possibility of gaining crucial insights from their work, however, the writings of Marx and Engels can often seem obscure as well as plainly difficult. This may result from the sheer quantity and scope of the writings — to read even a fraction of the total is a formidable task. The assistance provided by Phillips's book in understanding Marx and Engels on law is thus to be welcomed.

There are, however, more complex problems than those of mere scale in tackling the works of Marx and Engels. To begin with it is frequently difficult to separate Marx and Engels from *Marxism*. Such a notion might, at first sight, seem preposterous and certainly for those interested in Marx and Engels purely as originators of a political position and philosophy it no doubt is. Yet Marx sometimes found it necessary to distance himself from *Marxism* and that alone should warn us of the endless distortions and confusions that will occur if we are not clear in our ascriptions of theories and ideas. There are, of course, numerous *Marxisms* frequently diverging from one another. The various proponents can be bitterly hostile to one another's purposes and analyses, yet all claim to be legitimate interpreters of Marx and Engels. The contrasting and indeed shifting interpretations are refracted through lenses focused on particular political concerns and problems. *Marxism*, therefore, is a number of alternative political philosophies, continuously changing and adapting to new circumstances. This is not a criticism — indeed most Marxists would see the constant interplay of theory and action (praxis) as indeed fulfilling the dialectical method that is integral to the approach. It does, however, mean that theories of law provided by various *Marxisms* can be markedly different and can be distinguished (analytically at least) from what Marx and Engels said.

This book is about what Marx and Engels actually wrote about law. Clearly no account of their appreciations of law can be theoretically neutral, but Paul Phillips has gone to the original statements (and to considerable lengths) to allow the words to speak simply and directly for themselves. Of course, this might imply that understanding Marx and Engels on law will thus become straightforward. Unfortunately this is unlikely. The nature of law was never posed as a major theoretical problem by Marx and Engels. Further, in comparison with other nineteenth century social theorists such as Max Weber or Emile Durkheim, law was not used as a major element or category in their analyses. Occasionally law came into focus when it touched on particular political issues such as censorship. More typically, however, statements about law are embedded in discussions of broader compass. For this reason one cannot direct the student of law to a single book or central article on law by Marx and Engels. Rather their theories must be distilled or constructed from passages and references that are widely scattered and written over a long period of time.

As if this were not difficult enough it must be borne in mind that the corpus of writings, which is often treated as a single entity, was written by two people, not always jointly. It is not surprising, therefore, that inconsistencies can be found in the statements made about law (and other topics for that matter) by Marx and Engels. Such inconsistencies have previously been cited by those unsympathetic to the approach as evidence, if not proof, of its weaknesses. Equally they have often provided the departure points of different *Marxisms*. Thus the rediscovery of the early manuscripts stimulated a furore about 'new' interpretations. Initially this represented a parvenu humanist *Marxism*, and later an appreciation of a radical shift, or epistemological break, in Marx's and Engels' writings. What are less often noted are the differences discernible between Marx and Engels. The differences between the two men are hardly a matter of surprise. After all both produced early work independently, then worked together, although not always writing together and finally Engels continued to write after Marx's death. While some commentators have pointed to the importance of these different periods, and especially the fact that some of the concepts critical for some later Marxist–Leninist approaches belong to the final period, they are often ignored when discusing Marx and Engels on law. Paul Phillips's book has the great advantage that in collecting and making sense of the scattered and varied remarks and observations it pays due attention to this aspect.

In this difficult area for sociologists of law Paul Phillips has, then, provided a clear, simple and useful book. Anyone who has toiled through the difficult and often obscure original texts will know that this is no mean feat and they will understand how complimentary such epithets are.

C.M.C.
P.W.

ACKNOWLEDGEMENTS

I wish to thank the editors of the *Law in Society* series, Colin Campbell and Paul Wiles, for their help and encouragement in the preparation of this book. My colleagues in the Faculty of Law at the Queen's University of Belfast also gave much needed moral support. Finally, Miss Sandra Maxwell achieved wonders in typing the manuscript.

Extracts from *The Revolutions of 1848* by Karl Marx (edited by David Fernbach), *Surveys from Exile — Political Writings* vol. II by Karl Marx and *Grundrisse: Foundations of the Critique of Political Economy* by Karl Marx are reprinted by permission of Penguin Books Ltd., London, and Random House Inc., New York. Extracts from *Theories of Surplus Value* vol. 2 by Karl Marx, *Marx and Engels Selected Works in One Volume*, *Marx and Engels Collected Works* vols. I–X, *Marx and Engels Selected Correspondence*, *Marx and Engels Articles on Britain*, *Capital* vols. 1 and 3 by Karl Marx, *Contribution to the Critique of Political Economy* by Karl Marx, *Ireland and the Irish Question* by Marx and Engels and *The Peasant War in Germany* by Friedrich Engels are all reprinted by permission of Lawrence and Wishart Ltd., London.

LIST OF ABBREVIATIONS

MECW — *Marx and Engels Collected Works*. 12 Volumes, London: Lawrence and Wishart; Moscow: Progress Publishers, 1975–9.

ME Sel W — *Marx and Engels Selected Works in One Volume*. London: Lawrence and Wishart, 1968.

ME Sel Cor — *Marx and Engels Selected Correspondence*. Moscow: Progress Publishers, 1975.

On Britain — *Marx and Engels Articles on Britain*. Moscow: Progress Publishers, 1975.

Ireland — *Ireland and the Irish Question*. Moscow: Progress Publishers, 1971.

PSE — *Surveys from Exile*. London: Penguin and New Left Review, 1973.

PR1848 — *The Revolutions of 1848*. London: Penguin and New Left Review, 1973.

RhZ — *Rheinische Zeitung*

NRhZ — *Neue Rheinische Zeitung*

NRhZ POR — *Neue Rheinische Zeitung. Politisch-oekonomische Revue*

DFJ — *Deutsche Französische Jahrbücher*

NS — *The Northern Star*

NYDT — *New York Daily Tribune*

PW — *The Peasant War in Germany*. Moscow: Progress Publishers, 1969.

The Condition — *The Condition of the Working Class in England*

The Origin — *The Origin of the Family, Private Property and the State*.

Marx and Engels on Law and Laws

Introduction: Aims and Method

The objectives of this study are strictly limited. It is not an attempt to present 'the' Marxist theory of law or even 'a' Marxist theory of law. The principal objective is to present as wide a range as possible of the statements of Marx and Engels on 'law' and laws. Following from this, the study aims to examine the various explanations the authors give of how laws come into being and how they operate in actual practice. Finally, on the basis of these specific treatments, the study attempts to present the varying approaches advanced by the authors to the general question of the relationship between law and society.

The objectives of the study dictate the method adopted. With such objectives the only method possible is to go straight to the primary sources, i.e. the writings of Marx and Engels. The reader will not find in this work any reference to the writings of Lenin, Stalin, Trotsky, Althusser, Gramsci or any other theorist in the Marxist tradition. Given the aims of this work, secondary interpretations must be excluded, not the least because some of them suffer from distortion due to the non-availability of certain texts at the time the secondary author was writing, whilst in others the exigencies of the author's own praxis in his own historical configuration may have dictated an emphasis on some aspects of Marx's thought and the exclusion of others. The method adopted here, then, is to allow Marx and Engels to speak for themselves.

In regard to this method it is perhaps as well to make explicit an assumption that is quite evident in the actual study. The assumption is that since Marx and Engels were two distinct persons, each with his own different background, education and life experience, their thought will not be identical. The point may be illustrated by a topic outside the scope of this study, namely religion. Engels came from a family that apparently had a genuine commitment to Protestant Christianity and right up to his latest writings, e.g. 'Ludwig Feuerbach and the End of Classical German Philosophy' (1886), he pays more attention to the phenomenon of religion than Marx. (Since Marx's father abandoned Judaism in favour of Christianity for reasons of expedience rather than of conviction and since his mother deferred her own baptism until after her father's death, which occurred after Marx himself had been christened, it is scarcely likely that the home background would have inculcated Christianity at any great depth. In fact it could be argued that with such a background neither Judaism nor Christianity would be likely to have any great hold on the children.) Consequently, in this study it is accepted that there may be differences between the thought of the two authors, even differences of which the authors themselves were unaware. Where such differences do emerge in the expressions used, wherever possible a reconciliation is sought but only so far as this can be achieved without distortion either of the specific text or of other writings by the author that date from the same period.

This leads us to the second assumption the method makes, namely that neither Marx nor Engels was intellectually static. To put this in a positive way, it is assumed here that both authors grew intellectually. This may sound so obvious as to be trite, but closer specification of the possibilities envisaged here may not prove to be so readily acceptable. The concept of intellectual development adopted here does not entail, nor does it accept, that there was a unity throughout the thought of either Marx or Engels from the earliest writings to the latest. The concept of development used in this study embraces both the possibility of a complete change of direction in the author's thought and the possibility of unresolved conflicts between different elements in the author's thinking.

The desire to understand the authors' intellectual growth necessitates a close attention to the chronological order in which the works were written. This does not mean that one must present the writings in the order they were written, month by month, year by year, but it does involve the recognition of certain crucial points when the development took on some new aspect so that there is a substantial difference between the subsequent works and those that preceded the point. Without attempting to resolve the dispute over the issue of Young/Old Marx, it can be pointed out that certain Feuerbachian terms disappear from Marx's vocabularly after the writing of *The German Ideology*, as does 'the nature of the state' as a reason that explains particular phenomena. The period up to and including *The German Ideology* therefore almost marks itself out as distinct from the subsequent years. In Engels' writings a similar developmental point occurs around the time of Marx's death.

To conclude this Introduction it may be useful to give some account of the thinking behind the order of presentation adopted. As indicated above the period that concludes with the writing of *The German Ideology* is a significant one in Marx's intellectual development (as it is also in Engels'); the early works therefore form a fairly natural grouping. (For the benefit of readers who are not familiar with these early works or with German idealist philosophy it should be said that these works include some of the most obscure passages in all Marx's writings — I challenge anyone to produce a more difficult work in the whole of Marx's writings than the 1844 manuscript on 'Alienated Labour'. In the light of this warning such readers can choose for themselves whether to put in a hard, uphill slog at the beginning in the assurance that thereafter all will be (relatively) straightforward or whether to by-pass the early works in favour of the more mature works.) In Chapter 2,

'Law and Class Interests: England', the second section examines
Marx's accounts of English history in class terms and analyses
the uses he makes of the concept of a 'class'. The remaining
sections of Chapter 2 consider Marx and Engels' accounts of
the Reform Act, the Poor Law, the Corn Laws and their
repeal, the factory legislation. Chapter 3 centres on the events
in France between 1848 and 1852; since the specific pieces of
legislation referred to are closely tied in with the political
developments, e.g. the Constitution and the electoral law, the
analysis of the political events in terms of 'classes' and 'fractions' of classes is also subjected to scrutiny. Chaper 4, 'Crime
and Criminal Justice', is self-explanatory. In Chapter 5, 'The
Legal Regulation of Economic Institutions', the three such
institutions considered are industry, property and money; in
regard to property the focus is rather on the authors' views on
the development of the institution, since a full treatment of
Marx's ideas on property would virtually entail an account of
the whole of his economics. In Chapter 6 an attempt is made
to draw all these elements together and give some account of
the development and the range of views of Marx and of Engels
on the relationship between law and society, or, in their
terms, between the material/economic base and the legal
superstructure.

CHAPTER 1

Early Works

I. PHILOSOPHICAL TREATMENTS BY MARX

Preliminary

The primary source of our knowledge of Marx's early intellectual development, before he became a contributor to the *'Rheinische Zeitung'*, is his letter to his father of November 1837 when Marx was 19 (MECW I, pp. 10–21). In it he reviews the year he has just spent in Berlin. Initially, it appears that his position was one of idealism, which, as he says, he had 'compared and nourished with the idealism of Kant and Fichte' (p. 18). Significantly, in the light of his subsequent development, it was the opposition that idealist philosophy posited between the 'is' and the 'ought' that seems to have been at the centre of his dissatisfaction with idealism. he mentions the opposition twice in the letter, first in connection with his poetry and secondly as it affected his attempt 'to elaborate a philosophy of law covering the whole field of law' (p. 12).

Marx writes of both these works in terms that indicate that he regarded them as belonging to a stage that he had transcended. Of the poems he sent to his fiancée he says that they were 'marked by attacks on our times, diffuse and inchoate expressions of feeling, nothing natural, everything built out of moonshine, complete opposition between what is and what ought to be' (p. 11). The attempted philosophy of law grew to 300 pages before Marx abandoned it. He introduces his account of this work by saying: 'Here, above all, the same opposition between what is and what ought to be, which is characteristic of idealism, stood out as a serious defect, and

5

was the source of a hopelessly incorrect division of the subject-matter' (p. 12).

The overwork of this first term affected his health and on the advice of his doctor he withdrew to the country. It was here that in spite of his previous dislike of Hegel's philosophy he became converted to Hegelianism and 'got to know Hegel from beginning to end' (p. 19). At Stralow, too, he became acquainted with the Doctors' Club of which he was to be so prominent a figure on his return to Berlin. The main outcome of the remainder of Marx's stay in Berlin was his doctoral dissertation, 'On the Difference between the Democritean and Epicurean Philosophy of Nature' (MECW I, pp. 25–105), a work that even in its choice of subject reflects the pre-occupation with the effects of Hegel's system on philosophy. It has been suggested that the attraction of the subject lay in the parallel between the situation of philosophy in Germany after Hegel and the situation of philosophy in Greece after Aristotle. Typically, at the same time Marx also had other projects in mind, such as editing a literary review and co-operating with Bruno Bauer in editing Hegel's *Philosophy of Religion*.

Natural Law Tendencies

After concluding his doctoral dissertation, Marx continued to cooperate with Bruno Bauer on polemical works of the Young Hegelian, i.e. atheistic, tendency. It was not surprising, then, that the opprobrium of those works should also fall on Marx, so that when Bauer was deprived of his teaching post on account of his heterodox opinions, Marx's chances of obtaining a teaching post in a university virtually disappeared. In these circumstances Marx followed the course adopted by so many others and looked to journalism to provide a livelihood. For a while, until the paper was closed down, he found this in writing for and subsequently in editing the *Rheinische Zeitung*.

In the articles he wrote for this journal, and particularly in his articles on the censorship of the press, Marx's thought on law has a distinctly Natural Law cast. There seems to be implicit reference to a criterion of the validity of law other than either the purely formal criteria laid down by the constitution, e.g. as to what formal requirements must be satisfied for a rule to count as 'law', or the empirical criterion of whether the constituted authorities do in fact adjust their behaviour in accordance with the requirements of the rule. It is tempting to conjecture that the source of this strand of Marx's thought may derive from Aristotle since even in 1837 in his letter to his father Marx mentions a translation of part of Aristotle's *Rhetoric* as one of the endeavours with which he had occupied himself and even more so since the doctoral dissertation makes extensive reference to a range of Aristotle's works. Even in such late works as *Capital* Aristotle appears in the list of authorities. The exact extent of Marx's debt to Aristotle is, however, outside the scope of this work.

An outstanding example of this tendency is to be found in one of a series of articles written in 1842 'Debates on the Freedom of the Press' (MECW I, pp. 154–64). The article merits extensive quotation. The context is a comparison that Marx is making between a press law (apparently a statute under which the publication in the press of certain specific types of material was made an offence punishable by the ordinary courts) and the censorship law, under which the press was required to submit its material in advance to an administrative official to be vetted:

> The press law punishes the abuse of freedom. The censorship law punishes freedom as an abuse. It treats freedom as criminal, or is it not regarded in every sphere as a degrading punishment to be under police supervision? The censorship law has only the *form* of a law. The press law is a real law.
>
> The press law is a *real law* because it is the positive existence of freedom. It regards freedom as the *normal* state of the press, the press as a mode of existence of freedom, and hence only comes into conflict with a press offence as an exception that contravenes its own rules and therefore annuls itself. [pp. 161–21]

The exposition shortly develops into a consideration of law in general:

> Laws are in no way repressive measures against freedom, any
> more than the law of gravity is a repressive measure against
> motion . . . Laws are rather the positive, clear, universal
> norms in which freedom has acquired an impersonal, theore-
> tical existence independent of the arbitrariness of the indivi-
> dual. A statute book is a people's bible of freedom.
>
> Therefore the *Press law* is the *legal recognition of the free-
> dom of the press*. It constitutes *right*, because it is the positive
> existence of freedom. It must therefore exist, even if it is never
> put into application, as in North America, whereas censor-
> ship, like slavery, can never become lawful, even if it exists a
> thousand times over as a law.
>
> *There are no actual preventive laws*. Law prevents only as a
> *command*. It only becomes *effective* law when it is infringed,
> for it is *true* law only when in it the unconscious natural law of
> freedom has become conscious state law. Where the law is real
> law, i.e., a form of the existence of freedom, it is the real
> existence of freedom for man. Laws, therefore, cannot pre-
> vent a man's actions for they are indeed the inner laws of life of
> this action itself, the conscious reflections of his life. Hence
> law withdraws into the background in the face of man's life as
> a life of freedom, and only when his actual behaviour has
> shown that he has ceased to obey the natural law of freedom
> does law in the form of state law compel him to be free, just as
> the laws of physics confront me as something alien only when
> my life has ceased to be the life of these laws, when it has been
> *struck by illness*. Hence a *preventive law* is a *meaningless
> contradiction*.
>
> A preventive law, therefore, has within it no *measure*, no
> *rational rule*, for a rational rule can only result from the nature
> of a thing, in this instance freedom. It is *without measure*, for if
> prevention of freedom is to be effective, it must be as all-
> embracing as its object, i.e., unlimited. A preventive law is
> therefore the contradiction of an *unlimited limitation*, and the
> boundary where it ceases is fixed not by necessity, but by the
> fortuitousness of arbitrariness, as the censorship daily demon-
> strates ad oculos. [pp. 162–3]

The first point of note is the concept of law as the 'positive
existence of freedom'. This sounds heavily philosophical,
though whether Marx derived the idea from Hegel or from
Fichte is difficult to say (see Letter to his Father, MECW I, p.

12). Quite what the adjective 'positive' adds to the 'existence of freedom' is equally unclear; what would the 'negative existence of freedom' entail?

From a jurisprudential point of view, of far more importance is the distinction between 'real laws' and those that have 'only the form of law'. (There is, perhaps, a difficulty of translation in the passage, which asserts that censorship can never become 'lawful' even if it exists 'as law'; the ambiguity of the German word 'Recht', which means both 'law' and 'right', may be responsible for this apparent self-contradiction. On the other hand, however, it is possible that here, too, Marx was asserting the distinction between real and non-real laws.) The significance of this distinction is that it posits the existence of an order superior to that of mere man-made law and, to that extent, it is a Natural Law theory. The resemblance is strengthened by Marx's use of the expression 'the natural law of freedom', but even more so by the analogy he draws with the law of gravity. The context of the phrase 'the natural law of freedom' shows even more clearly the influence of Natural Law thinking on Marx at this time, since it regards it as a source of 'conscious state law'. The resemblance may be illustrated by comparing Marx's statement with some of the classic expositions of Natural Law, e.g. Cicero's — 'True law is right reason in agreement with nature', or Justinian's statement (in a passage subsequently quoted by Aquinas) — 'The law of nature is the law which nature has taught all the animals'.

The difficulty in maintaining Marx's distinction between 'real' and 'non-real' law is the same as that encountered by any Natural Law theory, namely the difficulty of assigning any valid meaning to a statement that a rule that satisfies the formal criteria of law, e.g. by being a statute duly enacted in the form laid down by the constitution, and that exists empirically in that subjects and/or enforcement agencies adjust their behaviour in accordance with its norms, is not 'real law'. The comparisons with the law of gravity and the laws of physics also betray the strong similarities with Natural Law thinking in that, as with most Natural Law theories, they tend to blur the distinction between 'law' as a description of what 'is', and 'law' as a prescription of what 'ought to be'. Since it was precisely this distinction that was one of the main sources of Marx's dissatisfaction with idealist philosophy (Letter to his Father, p. 12), it is not surprising that once he had broken with that philosophy he should be attracted by a line of thought in which that distinction could be claimed to be 'aufgehoben' (using this term in both of its senses — that of 'abolished' and that of 'raised to a higher level').

The argument against preventive laws equally calls for closer examination. Marx here seems to make an invalid transition from the empirical sphere to the normative. The assertion that law only becomes effective when it is infringed is, in effect, an empirical generalisation of a rather common-place or even trite character to the effect that law enforcement only occurs when there has been a breach of the law. (It may be noted incidentally that this bears a certain resemblance to the views of the contemporary jurist, Kelsen, who says that it is only in delict that the norm of the law stipulating the sanction becomes effective.)

It is at this point that the invalid step takes place. Either there is an empirical generalisation that preventive enforce-ment never happens, in which case Marx is assuming what he is trying to prove, or he is making a deduction from the facts concerning law enforcement to the facts concerning the mo-tives for obedience to the law, which is itself questionable, and thence to the normative sphere with his conclusion of the non-existence of preventive laws. In fact, is asserting that the law only intervenes when 'actual behaviour' has departed from the 'natural law of freedom', Marx implicitly denies the possibility that the existence of the sanction may operate to discourage the individual from breaking the law.

The second paragraph of this argument has a decidedly Aristotelian ring to it. The concepts of law as a 'measure' and of a 'rational rule' resulting from the 'nature of the thing' would not sound out of place in any of the classical Natural

Law theories. The argument by which Marx reaches the conclusion that a preventive law is 'the contradiction of an unlimited limitation' appears to entail a contradition of his earlier argument, in that he assumes that the object of a preventive law is the prevention of freedom whilst in the paragraph immediately preceding this his statement that law only intervenes when the actual behaviour of the individual has shown that he has ceased to obey the natural law of freedom implies that behaviour contrary to law is not 'freedom'; it is inconsistent to maintain that prevention infringes freedom whilst punishment compels a man to be free. Whilst the theoretical arguments by which Marx opposed censorship are not entirely convincing, when it came to practical reasons his own experience provided him with a range of telling arguments. In the passage quoted he refers to the daily experience of the arbitrariness of the censorship in practice.

In his next article on the subject (MECW I, pp. 164–70), he continues the contrast between a press law and a censorship law, but this time in terms of the contrast between a judge and a censor. Whereas the judge is independent, the censor is himself a government organ. Even more important is the argument that whilst the judge in administering a press law has the provisions of a definite offence before him, the censor makes the offence he punishes. Equally sound is the observation that '. . . no state has the courage to put in general legal terms what it can carry out in practice through the agency of the censor', (p. 166). (Even if recent developments in some legal systems have created offences far beyond the scope of anything that Marx would have envisaged as feasible, it is still probably true that the very governments that enact such measures are the ones that make most use of censorship.) The same point about lack of specificity is present in Marx's article of 1843 on 'The Ban on the *Leipziger Allgemeine Zeitung*', (MECW I, pp. 311–30), in the form of a claim that a person cannot be punished for his moral character or his political or religious opinions, as contrasted with his deeds (p. 327).

The practical arguments against the censorship are best

expressed in the articles of 1843 on 'Justification of the Correspondent from the Mosel' (MECW I, pp. 332–58, esp. pp. 349–5). and to a lesser extent in the 'Marginal Notes to the Accusation of the Ministerial Rescript' (MECW I, pp. 361–5). In the former of these, Marx demonstrates the stultifying effect that the practice of censorship has even in those areas where the censorship decree itself recognises the desirability of free and frank discussion. He points out that the free press is not simply the product of public opinion but itself produces public opinion. This develops into the positive argument for a free press, namely that such a press has the power to make a particular interest such as the distressed condition of the Mosel region into a matter of public concern. Substantially the same argument appears in the 'Marginal Notes to the Accusation of the Minsterial Rescript' in the form that the press can only participate in the development of the state if it is allowed to arouse dissatisfaction with the laws, since reform is only the result of criticism and the dissatisfaction thus aroused (p. 364).

Finally on the subject of legal regulation of the press, by 1848 Marx's views on the acceptability of press laws seem to have undergone a change. In his article 'On the Prussian Press Bill' (MECW VII, pp. 250–2) he inveighs against the bill as an attack on the freedom of the press. The provisions of the bill, e.g. making it an offence to accuse anyone of an action punishable by law, or to expose anyone to public contempt, or to insult an official in regard to the performance of his duties, differ little from the English law of criminal libel except that in the English offence even the truth is not a defence unless publication was 'in the public interest'. The important difference is, however, in the use made of such provisions. In England, prosecutions of the press for criminal libel have been increasingly rare since the beginning of the nineteenth century, whereas in Prussia at the time when Marx was writing such a bill was obviously not being promulgated as a purely academic exercise. Marx rightly feared that the bill would gag the press and thereby encourage abuses by bureaucrats who were thus released from public censure. Subsequent articles by Marx on the subject of censorship, e.g. 'Three New Bills', 'The Hohenzollern General Plan of Reform' and 'The Hohenzollern Press Bill' (MECW IX, pp. 50–4, 65–9, 125–32) show the same opposition to censorship but the treatment tends to be untheoretical; the imposition of censorship is explained by references to the wishes of the King but no attempt is made to relate these wishes to economic or any other social cause.

Theoretical Treatment of 'Customary Right'

The first major instance of the use of economic interests to explain a legal act is to be found in the series of articles 'Debates on the Law on Thefts of Wood' (MECW I, pp. 224–63), written in 1842. The Natural Law cast of thought is still evident in these articles, e.g. when Marx states that the legal nature of things cannot be regulated by law but rather the law must be regulated by the legal nature of things (p. 227), or when he makes a distinction between 'crime' and 'breach of police regulations' in a way that suggests that certain things are criminal by their very nature (p. 235).

The background to the law is quite simple. Traditionally, the poor had been allowed to gather dead timber from the forests for their own use. The agricultural crises of the 1820s had increased the numbers of the poor and also, perhaps, the rise of industrialisation had increased the commercial value of such timber. Consequently, the number of prosecutions for theft of timber had risen dramatically and the forest owners sought a new law that would be more effective in protecting their interests.

Before referring to Marx's explanations of the effects of the law, it may be useful to summarise the main provisions of the bill: s.4 provided that the valuation of the wood that was the subject of the charge should be made by the forest warden, s.14 awarded the money from the fine to the forest owner, s.19 allowed commutation of the fine to a sentence of labour in the forest, and s.20 allowed the forest owner to hand over the convicted person to the local authority so that his labour could be applied in discharge of the forest owner's obligation to provide labour on communal roads.

The whole tenor of the articles is that the effect of the law is to subordinate all to 'private interest'. One quotation will suffice to show the thought, although many more could be found since the idea permeates all the articles but especially the article of 30 October.

> Our whole account has shown how the Assembly degrades the executive power, the administrative authorities, the life of the accused, the idea of the state, crime itself, and punishment as well, to the *material means of private interest*. [p. 259].

An interesting aspect of these articles is that although the explanation refers to the economic interests at stake, Marx has not at this stage developed this into a class theory. In quoting from speeches by members of the Assembly, Marx frequently identifies them soley by reference to the estate to which they belonged — princely, knightly, urban or rural — but nowhere does he seek to attach any importance to the specific estate; all the members are present as equally subservient to private interest. The few references there are to 'classes' in these articles are all to be found in the context of a comparison of the 'customary rights' of the 'privileged classes' and those of 'the poor class' (pp. 230–1, 231–2 233–4). In the first of these cases it is not apparent that it would make any difference to Marx's meaning if the word 'estates' had been used rather than 'classes', and in the second case the word 'class' adds nothing to 'the poor'. In fact, the first reference to the latter group is to 'the poor' not 'the poor class', which again might indicate that Marx was not using the term here in the technical sense that appears in the later writings.

The exposition of 'customary right' has some interesting jurisprudential implications, although the terminology in which it is couched is highly philosophical, The exposition starts, in the first article, with the assertion that the 'so-called customs of the privileged classes are understood to mean *customs contrary to the law*' (p. 230) Marx appears to hold this view on the grounds that such customs derive from a period, e.g. the feudal era, when inequality was the rule, it being assumed that inequality = unfreedom and that the law is 'the positive existence of freedom' (see above, pp. 7–8).

> Mankind appeared to fall into definite species of animals which were connected not by equality, but by inequality, an inequality fixed by laws. The world condition of unfreedom required laws expressing this unfreedom, for whereas human law is the mode of existence of freedom, this animal law is the mode of existence of unfreedom. [p. 230]

Thus,

> When the privileged classes appeal from *legal right* to their *customary rights*, they are demanding, instead of the human content of right, its animal form, which has now lost its reality. . . [p. 231]

The significance Marx attached to the form/content dichotomy is not at all clear. In the very next passage (at the beginning of the second article) he uses the dichotomy in a way that appears to be the reverse of that just quoted:

> The customary rights of the aristocracy conflict by their *content* with the form of universal law. They cannot be given the form of law because they are the formations of lawlessness. The fact that their content is contrary to the form of law — universality and necessity — proves that they are *customary wrongs* and cannot be asserted in opposition to the law . . . [p. 231]

In the first of these quotations the customary rights of the privileged classes appear as the animal *form* of law (in contrast with the human *content*), whilst in the second it is the *content* of these rights that is contrasted with the universal *form* of law. It may be suggested that the use of the form/content dichotomy adds nothing to the general opposition to the privileges of the aristocracy.

The argument that universality is the form of law also creates difficulty in that it seems to deny the possibility of a legal right that is limited to a restricted class of holders. This is strange and does not accord with the fact that rights restricted to members of certain professions or to occupants of certain offices or inhabitants of certain localities are common among the various legal systems of the world. Before the reception of Roman law into Germany it can be argued that German private law was a mass of such particularistic customs and even after the reception it was open to a claimant to prove such a custom within certain limits, although the Prussian Landrecht adopted a more restrictive attitude towards customs that had not been adopted into enacted form. To deny such privileges the force of law one must either adopt a criterion of legality other than that arising from the empirical facts of law or one must re-interpret the concept of 'universality'.

Marx continues by arguing that since no one's action ceases to be wrongful merely because it is his custom, the 'customary rights' of the privileged classes should be abolished or even that their exercise should be punished. Whilst it is true that repetition does not make a wrongful act lawful, the whole question at issue in regard to customary rights is whether the action that constitutes the exercise of the right claimed is or is not wrongful. Marx may have been thinking along the lines of a German legal proverb that said that a hundred years of wrong can never be right, but the proverb is open to precisely the same objection as Marx's formulation.

The continuation of the passage is singularly obscure largely because Marx appears to have in mind specific concepts of 'law', 'legality', and 'right', although quite what these concepts are does not emerge from the article.

> At a time when universal laws prevail, rational customary right is nothing but the *custom of legal right*, for right has not ceased to be custom because it has been embodied in the law, although it has ceased to be *merely* custom, but it is enforced against one who violates it, although it is not his custom. [p. 231]

Perhaps the key to this passage is the expression 'universal laws'. If 'laws' is taken to mean enactments such as codes and statutes, and 'universal' is understood as referring to the range of subject-matter covered by such 'laws', then the first sentence would mean that once all law has been put in the form of an express enactment, 'rational and customary right' means the habitual observance of the law, since the enactment of the law adds to the quality of what is habitually observed but does not alter the empirical facts of the habitual observance. The difficulties with this interpretation of the passage are, first, that this meaning of 'universal' is quite different from the earlier use of the term where it appears to refer to the universality of the persons subject to the law not the universality of the subject-matter encompassed by it, and secondly, the distinction between customary right embodied in law and 'mere custom' appears to imply that before such embodiment the right does not have the force of law, which is legitimate jurisprudential position but not one which can be reconciled easily with the view of the relationship between law and society that Marx usually expressed: to make the *legality* of custom depend on its embodiment in law tends to give a greater significance to the law-enacting agencies vis-à-vis society, whereas Marx's usual emphasis is the reverse of this.

An alternative approach would be to interpret the language of the passage as Kantian terminology. Thus, the assertion that universality is the form of law would relate to Kant's distinction between the 'maxim' of an action, i.e. the subjective principle on which it was based, and the objective principle, which necessitates the will to action. When such an objective principle is valid for every rational being, i.e. is universal, it is a 'law'. This is expressed in the various formulations of the categorical imperative, e.g. 'Act as if the maxim of your action were to become through your will a universal law of nature'.* There are several difficulties with such an interpretation. First, it implies that Marx was still influenced by Kant long after the time that the Letter to his Father would suggest (MECW I, pp. 18 and 19). Secondly, since the categorical imperative is an ethical principle, the use of it as a

---

*H. J. Paton, *The Moral Law* (London: Hutchinson, 1969), p. 34.

standard against which to measure positive law entails a form of Natural Law thinking (as the formulation quoted indicates). Thirdly, Marx's use of the principle differs from Kant's; Kant defends the right of the state to abolish the privileges of the nobility but *not* on the ground that such privileges, in themselves, violate the universality of right.*

The next sentence is most difficult:

> Right no longer depends on chance, on whether custom is rational or not, but custom becomes rational because right is legal, because custom has become the custom of the state. [MECW I, p. 31]

First we have the implication that it is a matter of chance whether a custom is rational or not, without any reference to the purposes or standard in relation to which the custom might be judged rational or the reverse. Then it seems implicit in the text that only a right that arises out of a *rational* custom will be upheld. But, the assertion that custom *becomes* rational because right is legal comes close to the sort of position more commonly associated with the views attributed to Hegel by his unsympathetic popularising expositors, since implicit in it is the assumption that all that is legal is rational. (This is on the assumption that what Marx meant by 'legal' was 'belonging to the enacted law'). In any case, there is a problem in regard to the rationality of custom in the period before 'right is legal': if custom was rational before, then it cannot become what it already is, and if it was not rational before, then no mere enactment can make it so (unless, again, one assumes that all that is legal is rational).

The next sentence, however, indicates that there is a sphere of rationality open to custom outside the sphere of legal rationality:

> Customary right as a separate domain alongside legal right is therefore rational only where it exists *alongside* and *in addition to law*, where custom is the *anticipation* of a legal right. [p. 231]

Philosophy of Law. Transl. Hastie (Edinburgh: T. and T. Clark, 1887), pp. 253–4.

Perhaps the clue here is in the idea of the 'anticipation of a legal right'. If one were to construe the word 'rational' as being purely emotive, indicating approval of whatever it is applied to, then the sentence could be understood in some such sense as — 'The only acceptable form of customary right is that which is a primitive development of something that can be made into a legal right.' Some support for this interpretation may be derived from the conclusion Marx draws that one cannot speak of the customary rights of the privileged estates, as the law has anticipated all possible consequences of their right. Thus, as the law provides for the rational limits of the claims of these estates, all that is left to the realm of custom, *ex hypothesi*, exceeds rational limits.

Marx continues by contrasting these customs of the rich with the customary rights of the poor:

> But whereas these customary rights of the aristocracy are customs which are contrary to the conception of rational right, the customary rights of the poor are rights which are contrary to the customs of positive law. Their content does not conflict with legal form, but rather with its own lack of form. The form of law is not in contradiction to this content, on the contrary, the latter has not yet reached this form. [p. 232]

The problem raised by this treatment is how to reconcile the assertion that the customary rights of the poor are contrary to the customs of positive law with the assertion that their content does not conflict with legal form. A possible line of reconciliation might be to interpret the statement as an assertion that, although at present the customary rights of the poor transgress express legal enactments, these rights are such as *could* be embodied in law. Here again, in the attempt to set up 'rights' in the face of positive law, the Natural Law type of thinking is evident. There is a further difficulty with the passage, namely that of justifying the application of a different standard in dealing with the customs of the poor from that used in regard to the customs of other groups. It will be remembered that Marx claimed the customary rights of the aristocracy conflicted in their content with the form of law because they lacked universality; the same may, however, be said of the customary rights of the poor unless it can be said that the poor are a universal class. Here again the form/content dichotomy adds nothing to the clarity of the thought.

Marx then argues that the development of civil law has operated to the detriment of the poor. The development, as he saw it, consisted of raising existing rights to the universal level and abolishing particular customs. But, whereas the rights of the estates were arbitrary pretensions and therefore rightly abolished, the rights of the poor took the form of accidental concessions, e.g . charity from the monasteries. Whilst legislation sometimes raised arbitrary pretensions to the level of legal claims, it did not convert the accidental concessions into necessary ones. Thus, when the property of the monasteries was converted into private property, the monasteries received compensation but the poor did not. Marx explains that this happened as a result of the necessary one-sidedness of the legislation in that the customary rights of the poor were based on the indeterminate character of certain forms of property that were neither definitely private property nor definitely common. Since the claims of the poor arose out of this very ambivalence, the conversion of such property rights into definitely private property necessarily entailed the disappearance of the customary right of the poor.

The objection to this whole argument is that it is based on the assumption that the poor had a 'right' to charity from the monasteries. This raises the question of whether such a right, if it existed, was enforeceable and, if so, how, which is to examine the question that Marx ignores of what sort of right is involved such claims, a legal one or merely a moral one? It is possible, of course, that at this time Marx would not have accepted such a clear distinction between 'legal' and 'moral' right, which would indicate yet again the strongly Natural Law cast of his thought at this period. A further difficulty in describing the charity given to the poor by the monasteries as a 'right' is concerned with the actual behaviour of those giving of receiving such charity: did either of these regard the interaction as one in which the recipients claimed as a right against the donors who were under a duty to them to give such relief? In fact, almost by definition, the concept of 'charity' negates such as interpretation.

Hegelian Treatments of Law and the State

One noteworthy aspect of many of the early works is that in them Marx uses the concept of 'the state' much more frequently than in his later works. It would appear reasonable to attribute this to the influence of Hegel's thought on Marx at this time. The tendency is well illustrated in Marx's *Contribution to the Critique of Hegel's Philosophy of Law* of 1843 (MECW III, pp. 3–129). The work has comparatively little to say on the subject of law since Hegel's 'Rechtsphilosophie' itself is more concerned with developing the concept of the 'state' and its organs, the executive, the legislature and the administration, thus leaving 'law' as a somewhat imprecise expression to cover almost any output of the legislature and perhaps also outputs of the administration such as regulations. Marx's critique reflects this indirect treatment of law, and as his main purpose was to scrutinise Hegel's ideas one does not get from this work any clear idea of Marx's own views on law. Similarly, the references to law in the 1844 manuscript 'Critique of the Hegelian Dialectic and Philosophy as a Whole' (MECW III, pp. 326–46) do not convey any precise meaning of 'law'.

This tendency is apparent not only in Marx's treatments of 'law' in general but also in his consideration of specific instances of legislation. As we have seen (above p. 12) in the 'Marginal Notes to the Accusation of the Ministerial Rescript', Marx related the censorship law to the possibility of the press participating in the development of the state. Again, in the articles of 1844 'On the Jewish Question' (MECW III, pp. 146–74), in dealing with the possibility of repeal of the legal disabilities of Jews, Marx's focus is on the implications for the nature of the state in the existence/abolition of such disabilities.

The Hegelian phrasing of the political aspect is particularly clear in the 'Critical Marginal Notes on the Article "The King of Prussia and Social Reform" (MECW III, pp. 189–206). After reviewing various attempts at dealing with pauperism by legislative and administrative means, e.g. the English Poor Law, Napoleon's anti-begging law and the measures of the Convention in the French Revolution, Marx explains the failure of these measures by the nature of the state:

> From the *political* point of view, the *state* and the *system of society* are not *two* different things. The state is the system of society . . . Finally, *every* state seeks the cause in *accidental* or *deliberate shortcomings of the administration*, and therefore it seeks the remedy for its ills in *measures* of the administration. Why? Precisely because *administration* is the *organising* activity of the state.
>
> The *contradiction* between the purpose and goodwill of the administration, on the one hand, and it means and possibilities, on the other hand, cannot be abolished by the state without the latter abolishing itself, for it is *based* on this contradiction. The state is based on the contradiction between *public* and *private life*, on the contradiction between *general interests* and *private interests*. Hence the *administration* has to confine itself to a *formal* and *negative* activity, for where civil life and its labour begin, there the power of the administration ends. Indeed, confronted by the consequences which arise from the unsocial nature of this civil life, this private ownership, this trade, this industry, this mutual plundering of the various circles of citizens, confronted by all these consequences, *impotence* is the *law of nature* of the administration . . . If the modern state wanted to abolish the *impotence* of its administration, it would have to abolish the *private life* of today. [pp. 197–8]

It may be noted in passing that the view of the relationship between state and society expressed here appears to be uni-directional, of a kind that later developed in the direction of economic determinism. What is lacking is an appreciation of the relative autonomy of social institutions such as the state apparatus, by which they are able to diverge from the development of society in general and thus can interact with society and affect that development.

II. ENGELS' EARLY DEVELOPMENT

Hegelian Influences

Engels' early writings differ from those of Marx in that they show him to have remained a Hegelian idealist for longer than Marx who grew out of idealism whilst still an undergraduate. The general Hegelian cast of Engels' though at this time is clearly discernible in, for example, the article on 'Centralisation and Freedom' (MECW II, pp. 355–9), where the personification of 'history' is particularly revealing (pp. 356–7). The clearest example, however, is to be found in the article 'The Internal Crises' (MECW II, pp. 370–3). In commenting on the typical Englishman's rejection of the possibility of a revolution in England, Engel states:

> . . . this is the only possible opinion if one adopts the national English standpoint of the most immediate practice, *of material interests*, i.e. *if one ignores the motivating idea, forgets the basis because of the surface appearance*, and fails to see the wood for the trees. There is one thing that is self-evident in Germany, but which the obstinate Briton cannot be made to understand, namely, that the so-called material interests can never operate in history as independent, guiding aims, but always, consciously or unconsciously serve a principle which controls the threads of historical progress. [pp. 370–1; my emphasis]

The patent idealism of this passage requires no comment. The Hegelian cast of thought comes across even more strongly in the articles of 1844 on 'The Condition of England. The Eighteenth Century' (MECW III, pp. 469–88). One passage in particular calls for attention:

> The Christian state is merely the last possible manifestation of the state as such; its demise will necessarily mean the demise of the state as such. The disintergration of mankind into a mass of isolated, mutually repelling atoms in itself means the destruction of all corporate, national and indeed of

any particular interests and is the last necessary step towards the free and spontaneous association of men. *The supremacy of money as the culmination of the process of alienation is an inevitable stage which has to be passed through, if man is to return to himself, as he is now on the verge of doing.* [p. 476; my emphasis]

The sententence emphasised bears a remarkable resemblance to the thoughts that Marx was expressing at about the same time in his *Comments on James Mill'* (MECW III, pp. 211–28):

The complete domination of the estranged thing *over* man has become evident in *money*, which is completely indifferent both to the nature of the material, e.g. to the specific nature of the private property and to the personality of the property owner. What was the domination of person over person is now the general domination of the *thing* over the *person*, of the product over the producer. [p. 221; Marx's emphasis]

The theme of money (or the money economy) as the source of alienation recurs throughout the articles 'On the Jewish Question' (MECW III, pp. 146–74) as well as elsewhere in the *Comments on James Mill*. It may be observed in passing that Engels' use of the concept of 'alienation' appears in some ways to be closer to Hegel's use than Marx's does; the description of alienation as a 'process' in itself suggests this and Engels' situation of this in the context of man's 'return to himself' retains a feature that Marx rarely, if ever, emphasised.

Feuerbachian Influence

By January 1844 Engels had experienced the influence of Feuerbach. In that month he wrote for the *Deutsche Französiche Jahrbücher* a review article on Thomas Carlyle's book, *Past and Present*, in which in criticising Carlyle's pantheism Engels makes repeated explicit references to Feuerbach. The extent to which he had made the Feuerbachian critique his own is most amply indicated in the passage where he considers Carlyle's criticism of the rottenness of social institutions (MECW III, pp. 444–68). Engels traces the roots on contemporary 'soullessness' to religion itself and continues in the purest Feuerbachian manner:

> Religion by its very essence drains man and nature of substance, and transfers this substance to the phantom of an other-wordly God, who in turn then graciously permits man and nature to receive some of his superfluity. [p. 462]

The paragraph continues in this vein until Engel breaks it off with the interjection '— but why should I copy Feuerbach'.

Liberalism

A point of similarity between the early development of Engels and that of Marx is in the liberalism of their youthful approach. In Engels' case this is best testified in a series of items that he published in the *Rheinische Zeitung* in 1842 (MECW III, pp. 265–311, 355–67). The tone of these items is liberal but the content is of no great weight, e.g. 'The Liberalism of the *Spenersche Zeitung*' (pp. 300–1), which confines itself to disparagement of the newspaper in question, or 'The End of the *Criminalistische Zeitung*' (pp. 302–3), in which Engels shows his liberal preference for trial by jury, in contrast with the *Criminalistische Zeitung*, which opposed it.

More important is the article 'On the Critique of the Prussian Press Laws' (pp. 304–11). In contrast to Marx's articles on the same subject in the *Rheinische Zeitung* earlier that year (see above, pp. 7–12), Engels' approach is far less philosophical, more the common-sense approach of an intelligent, reasonably educated person who lacked acquaintance with specialised theoretical treatments of the nature of law. This is well illustrated by his criticism of s.15 of the Penal Code, which punished 'insolent, disrespectful criticism or mockery of the laws of the land and government edicts'. Engels regards it as a blunder to place 'insolent' and 'disrespectful' side by side on the ground that disrespect is a matter of negligence or omission whereas insolence presupposes malicious intent. He then continues by contrasting 'disrespect' and 'mockery' in the same way. The weakness of this argument lies in the assumption that words have a fixed meaning, whereas in practice it is usually open to a court to decide that, for example, in the particular context 'disrespect' required malicious intent and not mere negligence. The context of the provision in question would favour such an interpretation precisely because 'insolence' and 'mockery' entail malicious intent. Not having studied law, Engels would be unaware of the range of possible interpretations that are opened up by legal techniques of construction.

The case that Engels cites as proof of the harmful consequences of the inclusion of 'disrespectful' equally fails to establish his point. The verdict he quotes illustrates far more clearly the way in which a subservient court can find the malicious intent necessary to constitute 'insolence' in material that a more liberal approach would find innocuous (pp. 307–9). The case is thus an example of a tendency even of the courts in Prussia to subordinate themselves to what they took to be the wishes of the executive.

Later in the article (pp. 309–10), Engels briefly touches upon the point which Marx developed extensively, namely that the practical effect of such laws was detrimental since it made law dependent on the censorship. The following year in his article 'The Progress of Social Reform on the Continent' (MECW III, pp. 392–408) Engels refers to the practical effect of censorship in a way that is not free from ambiguity. On the one hand, he maintains that the censorship was pointless as the republican movement would have died in any case for lack of public support, whilst on the other hand he suggests that censorship is powerless to check the development of public opinion (p. 405).

The general liberalism of Engels' approach at this time is evident throughout the articles 'Frederick William IV' (MECW II, pp. 360–7) and 'Centralisation and Freedom' (MECW II, pp. 355–9) of 1843. In the former of these, the whole tenor of the article is that the direction in which the King was steering the nation was reactionary, aiming at the feudal past, rather than progressive, pointing towards the future. The latter article is an account of the failure of French liberalism to restrain the reactionary ways of the Guizot ministry. The main practical demands of the liberal platform are stated conscisely in the introductory remarks to the article, where Engels assert:

> The principle of popular sovereignty, of a free press, of an independent jury, of parliamentary government, have practically been destroyed in France. [p. 355]

These four principles might well be taken as the programme of mid-nineteenth century liberalism on the Continent.

III. THE GERMAN IDEOLOGY

Preliminary

It is singularly appropriate to conclude the examination of the early period of the writings of Marx and Engels with *The German Ideology* (MECW V, pp. 19–359). There are at least two reasons for this. First, it was the first major work written by the two in collaboration. The second reason is, however, far more important, namely the objectives the two authors were seeking to achieve in writing the book. In the Preface to the *Contribution to the Critique of Political Economy* (ME Sel W, pp. 181–5) Marx says of the work that, in it, he and Engels 'resolved to work out in common the opposition of our view to the ideological view of German philosophy, in fact, *to settle accounts with our erstwhile philosophical conscience* (p. 183; my emphasis). The work was thus intended by its authors to mark the conclusion of a period of their development.

Although the work is appropriate for the conclusion of this examination of the authors' early period, there are a number of difficulties involved in interpreting it. First, even if it were possible by examination of the manuscript or by the use of modern numerical techniques to establish which portions were written by each of the authors, the collaboration between them appears to have been so close that it would be impossible to say whether the ideas expressed derive from the same person whose words appear on the page. This leaves open the possibility that one of the authors may have adopted a formulation that embodies an approach more commonly exclusive to the other. Secondly, the polemical nature of the work imposes severe limitations on it as an exposition of the authors' own views. Thus, although there are frequent references and even whole sections devoted to 'Law', 'Right', 'Crime', 'Property', etc., these often prove to be purely negative — criticisms, for example, of the ideas of Stirner. (In passing, one may note that if Stirner's book was even a tenth as bad as it appears, it was not worth half the effort Marx and Engels spent in demolishing it.)

The third difficulty is that of deciding to what extent the authors were successful in achieving their aims. The continuing debate on the extent of Hegel's influence on Marx gives some indication of how serious this difficulty is. In regard to *The German Ideology* itself, it means that one cannot discount the possibility that, even in their criticisms, the authors may fall back into formulations derived from the very 'philosophical consciousness' they were trying to abandon.

Although the disappearance of the philosophical trends they were combating reduces the interest of much of the work, the book does contain several passages in which Marx and Engels advance the development of their thought on the topics in question. There are, for example, several important passages on the institutionalisation of law and the state. Less extensive, but significant, treatment is also given to the relationship between property and law, starting from the development of property. Finally, the authors describe the rise of the courts under the division of labour and the growth of legal ideology consequent on the emergency of legal experts. This will be the order in which the passages are examined although it is not necessarily the order in which they occur in the work.

The Development of Property

The development of property is treated in volume 1, part 1, section 4(11) 'The Relation of State and Law to Property' (MECW V, pp. 89–92). The exposition starts by asserting that in the Ancient World and in the Middle Ages the first form of property is tribal property. It continues:

> In the case of the ancient peoples, since several tribes live together in one city, tribal property appears as state property, and the right of the individual to it as mere 'possession' which, however, like tribal property as a whole, is confined to landed property only. Real private property began with the ancients, as with modern nations, with movable property. (Slavery and community) (dominium ex iure Quiritum). [p. 89]

Several aspects of this call for comment. First, the use of the adjective 'tribal' to describe a society that lives in cities and has developed the 'state' is to extend it beyond its usual range of application. Second, there appears to be some conflict between the idea that tribal property in *land* is the first form of property and the recognition that the tribal property of the ancient Germans was 'determined by the rearing of cattle', since the latter implies that the cattle were property. It is a pity that the authors did not consider the question of the ownership of cattle among nomadic or semi-nomadic peoples, as this might have led them to a totally different view of the relationship between property and law. In fact, it might have necessitated substantial modification, if not the complete abandonment, of their developmental framework. Third, if we follow Ehrlich,* the fact that an individual's claim to the land is a mere possessory one is not a consequence of tribal ownership of the land but rather an instance of what Ehrlich maintains to be the normal course of development, namely that the concept of 'possession' develops much earlier than that of 'ownership'.

Fundamental Principles of the Sociology of Law (Cambridge, Mass.: Harvard University Press, 1936).

The Relationship between Law and Property

After explaining the relationship between the modern state and modern private property in terms of the dependence of the state on the bourgeoisie, the authors consider the relationship between 'law' and 'private property':

> Civil law develops simultaneously with private property out of the disintergration of the natural community. With the Romans the development of private property and civil law had no further industrial and commercial consequences, because their whole mode of production did not alter. With modern peoples, where the feudal community was disintergrated by industry and trade, there began with the rise of private property and civil law a new phase, which was capable of further development. [p. 90]

The problem with this passage is to determine quite what the authors mean by the 'natural' community. If the 'natural' community is the tribal one, the difficulty is that private property can and does exist in such communities, e.g. cattle, without necessarily leading to the disintergration of the community. If, as the later sentence suggests, the 'natural' community is synonymous with the feudal one, then the problem is that feudal communities exist and thrive with private property not only in movables but also in land. It seems difficult, therefore, to accept that private property arises out of the *disintegration* of the 'natural' community.

The difficulties arising out of these treatments of tribal society are, perhaps, the result of a one-sided approach. Because of their basic concern with the relations of production, the authors were led to start their examination of law from the point of property. The result of this was that they overlooked the peace-keeping function of law, which is more fundamental and also, to some extent, comprehends the property function. The basis of the peace-keeping function of law is the logic of the situation, as Llewellyn demonstrated. Given that, unless restrained, the friction between individuals that is a normal part of any social context may easily be expressed in violence, which in turn provokes retaliation that may easily give rise to a blood-feud, the logic of the situation requires some framework of restraint to prevent such escalation; this is Llewellyn's 'law-job' of 'the relolution of trouble-cases'.* Regulations concerning rights of property fall within this framework inasmuch as property is a common source of disputes. The connection between invasion of property rights and breach of the peace is clearly demonstrated in the history of English law in the formal pleadings for actions of trespass; the pleadings alleged that the defendant had trespassed 'by force and arms and against the peace of our Lord the King', even if the only trespass complained of was that the defendant had walked across the plaintiff's field. Viewed in this light, law is a normal part of the community rather than an effect of the disintegration of it and the differences between institutionalised and customary law would be seen as deriving from the effectiveness of the non-specific sanction of social disapproval.

Although the authors' theory of the origins of law is open to question, which is perhaps the result of the inadequacy of the material available to them about tribal societies, when it came to the consideration of more recent developments their argument had a much sounder basis. The examples they cite — the development of maritime law in Amalfi, the first town to carry on an extensive maritime trade, and the adoption and adaptation of Roman law in Italy and elsewhere with the rise of trade and industry — illustrate their point tellingly (MECW V, p. 91). They note too that in all countries but England the 'real' development of law started on the basis of Roman law and claim that even in England Roman legal principles had to be introduced to further the development, particularly in regard to movable property. The difficulty with this is to establish a criterion for the 'real' development as opposed to any other: in England, for example, the law relating to land and much of

*The normative, the legal and the law-jobs' *Yale Law Journal 49*, 1940, pp. 1355–1400 at pp. 1373–6.

the law relating to chattels was developed in the twelfth, thirteenth and fourteenth centuries, so that the only aspect of the development that would fit the description would be the development of the Law Merchant by Lord Mansfield, who did draw on Roman principles.

The Institutionalisation of Law

The problem of the institutionalisation of law is first broached in volume 1, part 1. The authors explain how, because the development of productive forces is not subordinated to a general plan, it takes place unevenly with different areas, both geographic and economic, developing independently of each other, so that the different stages may co-exist in one society. They then continue:

> It follows from this that even within a nation the individuals, even apart from their pecuniary circumstance, have quite diverse developments, and that an earlier interest, the peculiar form of intercourse of which has already been ousted by that belonging to a later interest, remains for a long time afterwards in possession of a traditional power in the illusory community (state, law), which has won an existence independent of the individuals; a power which in the last resort can only be broken by a revolution. [p. 83]

A point of some interest in this explanation is whether any significance is to be attached to the use of the term 'interest' rather than 'class'.

In the third part of volume 1 they examine the relationship between individual and class interest. Although the account does not deal specifically with law, it would require little modification to extend it from the explanation of how class interests come to acquire independent existence to include the embodiment of those interests in law. The treatment is indirect inasmuch as it arises out of a criticism of Stirner's treatment of the relationship between individual interest and the general interest. The authors translate the question Stirner had asked into everyday language as follows:

How is it that personal interests always develop, against the will of individuals, into class interests, into common interests which acquire independent existence in relation to the individual persons, and in their independence assume the form of *general* interests? . . . How is it that in this process of private interests acquiring independent existence as class interest the personal behaviour of the individual is bound to be objectified, estranged, and at the same time exists as a power independent of him and without him, created by intercourse, and is transformed into social relations, into a series of powers which determine the subordinate the individual, . . .? [p. 245]

Their answers to these questions takes the form of pointing out what Stirner had overlooked:

Had Sancho understood the fact that within the framework of definite *modes of production*, which, of course, are not dependent on the will, alien practical forces, which are independent not only of isolated individuals but even all of them together, always come to stand above people — then he could be fairly indifferent as to whether this fact is presented in a religious form . . . [p. 245]

This does not answer the question but only shifts it. The answer takes for granted the independent existence of the forces of production and uses this to explain the development of the independence of class interests, but the real question is: how does any social element, including productive forces, come to be objectified so that it is independent of individuals and stands above them?

'Might' or 'Will' as the Basis of Law?

The most important treatment of law occurs later in volume 1, part 3, in the authors' criticisms of Stirner's views on law. The discussion arises out of a contrast between theoreticians who regard power as the basis of right and those who regard 'will' as the basis. Marx and Engels clearly range themselves with the former of these groups; in fact, in the first part of the volume they had already described the theory that reduces law to 'will' as 'juridical illusion' (p. 91). In the passage now under consideration, the authors treat of both the law and the state and what is said of one is applicable, *mutatis mutandis*, to the other:

> If power is taken as the basis of right, as Hobbes etc., do, then, right, law, etc., are merely the symptom, the expression of *other* relations upon which state power rests. The material life of individuals, which by no means depends merely on their 'will', their mode of production and form of production and form of intercourse, which mutually determine each other — this is the real basis of the state and remains so at all stages at which division of labour and private property are still necessary, quite independently of the *will* of individuals. These actual relations are in no way created by the state power; on the contrary they are the power creating it. [p. 329]

They then develop this to include the role of classes, particularly the ruling class, in the making of law:

> The individuals who rule in these conditions — leaving aside the fact that their power must assume the form of the *state* — have to give their will, which is determined by these definite conditions, a universal expression as the will of the state, as law, an expression whose content is always determined by the relations of this class, as the civil and criminal law demonstrates in the clearest possible way. [p. 329]

This is virtually identical with the view subsequently advanced in The Communist Manifesto that bourgeois jurisprudence is 'but the will of your class made into law for all, a will, whose essential character and direction are determined by the economical conditions of existence of your class' (MECW IV, p. 501). Whether the change from 'content' to 'character and direction' was a conscious limitation of the generality is uncertain. Clearly it would be far easier to maintain that the 'essential character' of law is bourgeois than to show that the whole of its content is determined by the relations of the bourgeoisie. In fact the latter view would conflict with their recognition of the independent existence of law (MECW V, p. 330).

The exposition continues in a way that touches upon a similar issue to that raised in the treatment of the relationship between individual interests and the general interest:

Their personal rule must at the same time assume the form of average rule. Their personal power is based on conditions of life which as they develop are common to many individuals, and the continuance of which they, as ruling individuals, have to maintain against others and at the same time, to maintain that they hold good for everybody. The expression of this will, which is determined by their common interests, is the law. [p. 329]

The continuation of the passage touches upon the problem of a conflict of interests between an individual and his class as a whole. The authors point out that on the basis of individual self-assertion the conduct of individuals is bound to be egoistical and therefore the law requires self-denial in the exceptional case, although in the average case it provides for the self-assertion of the individual's interest.

Legal Institutions

The account of the development of legal institutions occurs later. It relates this development to the growth of the division of labour:

The history of right shows that in the earliest, most primitive epochs these individual, factual relations in their crudest form directly constituted right. With the development of civil society, hence with the development of private interests into class interests, the relations of right underwent changes and acquired a civilised form. They were no longer regarded as individual, but as universal relations. At the same time, division of labour placed the protection of the conflicting interests of separate individuals into the hands of a few persons, whereby the barbaric enforcement of right also disappeared. [p. 342]

The difficulty with this presentation lies in the simple dichotomy between 'primitive epochs' and 'civil society'. As was mentioned above (pp. 30–1), there is a distinction between stages of development at which the law is not institutionalised and those in which it is, but this distinction is not the same as that between societies that have developed classes and those that have not. Since the anthropological evidence indicates that the division of labour may develop specialised agencies of law enforcement before 'classes' arise,* the transition posited in the text from 'factual relations' to 'class interests' as constituting right is inadequate.

The failure to recognise the possibility that the institutionalisation of law may precede that of economic interests into class interests also influences the authors' judgement on the historical importance of the courts. They state:

> It was just in the epoch between the rule of the aristocracy and the rule of the bourgeoisie, when the interests of the two classes came into conflict, when trade between the European nations began to be important, and hence international relations themselves assumed a bourgeois character, it was just at that time that the power of the courts of law began to be important, and under the rule of the bourgeoisie, when this broadly developed division of labour becomes absolutely essential, the power of these courts reaches its highest point [MECW V, p. 343]

This account is certainly not true of the development of English law. The centralisation of the royal courts and the extension of their jurisdiction at the expense of the local courts in the period after the Norman Conquest were important factors in the conflict between royal and baronial power.† The courts had thus already acquired an importance that made them a suitable instrument in the conflict between aristocracy and bourgeoisie, when it arose.

---

*See K. N. Llewellyn and E. A. Hoebel *The Cheyenne Way* (Norman: University of Oklahoma Press, 1967), pp. 99–131 — police; M. Glukman *The Judicial Process among the Barotse* (Manchester University Press, 1955) — courts; and generally R. Schwartz and J. Miller 'Legal evolution and societal complexity' *American Journal of Sociology 70*, 1964, pp. 159–69.

†See A. S. Green 'The centralisation of Norman justice under Henry II' in Commitee of the Association of American Law Schools (ed.) *Select Essays in Anglo-American Legal History*, vol. I (Cambridge University Press, 1907), p. 111–39.

Legal Ideology

The rise of the courts is accompanied by the growth of the legal professions, which in turn gives rise to the development of legal ideology. Marx and Engels explain the development:

> Within the division of labour these relations [i.e. of production], are bound to acquire an independent existence over against the individuals. All relations can be expressed in language only in the form of concepts . . . Besides this meaning in everyday consciousness, these general ideas are further elaborated and given a special significance by politicians and lawyers, who, as a result of the division of labour, are dependent on the cult of these concepts, and who see in them, and not in the relations of production, the true basis of all real property relations. [MECW V, p. 363]

Earlier, at the end of part 1, in explaining why ideology turns everything upside-down they had put it:

> In consciousness — in jurisprudence, politics etc. — relations become concepts; since they do not go beyond these relations, the concepts of the relations also become fixed concepts in their mind. The judge, for example, applies the code; he therefore regards legislation as the real driving force. [p. 92]

This latter passage is significant in that it offers a much more explicitly interactionist model of the process by which the inversion is achieved.

Conclusion

Three lines of thought about law emerge from this examination of *The German Ideology*. First, there are the authors' ideas on law in tribal society. Second, and of much more importance, is the theoretical treatment of the relationship between law and class interests. Finally, and also of major importance, there is the presentation of the independent existence of law and the consequent growth of legal ideology.

The treatment of law in tribal society is of least importance. As was noted in connection with the relevant passages, the inadequacy of the anthropological materials available to the authors fully accounts for any weakness of the treatment. It appears that the authors views were based on the examples of ancient Greece, ancient Rome and the ancient German tribal society and their knowledge of the latter may well have derived exclusively from the writings of classical authors. In such circumstances, it is not surprising that their theories both as to the development of property and as to the relationship between law and property in tribal society are open to question. Similarly, their ideas on the rise of courts might have been modified if they had had more extensive materials on primitive societies.

The centrality of 'class interests' to the subsequent thought of Marx and Engels is almost too obvious to be worth mentioning. Consequently, the demonstration of the conflict between egoistical, individual interest and the common interests of the ruling class and thus the necessity to express *as law* the will to maintain those common interests, is one of the most basic aspects of the theory. The passages in question are therefore of key importance. The doubt as to the adequacy of the explanation of how personal interests come to be objectified as class interests has already been noted (see above, p. 33). An interesting omission is the failure to relate the idea of law as an expression of the interests of the ruling class to the concept of ideology; the treatments of the ideological aspect of law are more concerned with the ideological function of law vis-à-vis professional lawyers rather than vis-à-vis subordinate classes in society.

The extensive treatment of the independent existence of law raises some major questions. First, how is one to reconcile the independent existence of law with the view the authors also put forward that law is merely a symptom of other relations? This obviously has implications for the relationship between law and property and thus the solution proposed will also affect the view of the relationship between law and class interests. As will appear later, the problem recurs throughout the authors' later writings. The second problem, which will also be more evident later, is why this insight received so little attention in their subsequent work until Engels redeveloped it in the 1980s (see below, pp. 209–23). Although, as was stated at the beginning of the section, the collaboration was so close as to make it virtually impossible to separate the contributions of the authors, it is tempting to surmise that this aspect derives more from Engels than from Marx. The strongly interactionist form of the explanation of legal ideology is more closely paralleled in subsequent writings by Engels — compare, for instance, his treatment of factory legislation with that of Marx (see below, pp. 85–109). However, this must remain at the conjectural level. The fact remains that in the subsequent writings the independent existence of law received comparatively little attention until a very late date.

CHAPTER 2

Law and Class Interests: England

I. INTRODUCTION

The classic statement of the class theory of law is to be found in *The Manifesto of the Communist Party* written in 1848 (MECW VI, pp. 477–519):

> Your very ideas are but the outgrowth of the conditions of your bourgeois production and bourgeois property, just as your jurisprudence is but the will of your class made into a law for all, a will, whose essential character and direction are determined by the economical conditions of existence of your class. [p. 501]

Marx and Engels applied this analysis to a whole range of nineteenth-century legislation such as the Reform Act, the Poor Law Amendment, the repeal of the Corn Laws and Factory Acts (especially the Ten Hours Act). Indeed, Marx in particular tends to group together the passing of the Reform Bill, the repeal of the Corn Laws and the passing of the Ten Hours Bill as stages in a continuing struggle between the bourgeoisie and the landed aristocracy. In some ways this approach might be argued to be closer to the presentation in *The German Ideology*, namely law as the expression of the average interests of the ruling class, rather than the above quotation, which concentrates more on the use of law by the ruling class against other classes. It is noticeable that even in regard to the various Factory Acts the emphasis tends to be on the internal relations of the ruling classes.

There are problems concerning the concepts of classes used by each of the authors and concerning the consistency of the explanations offered in different works. In Engels' case the conceptual problem is clearest in regard to the supporters of the Ten Hours Bill, whilst the problem of consistency is most acute in his explanations of the Reform Act. With Marx, the conceptual problem arises more from his consideration of pre-nineteenth-century legislation such as the Statute of Labourers 1349 or the Tudor Vagrancy Laws. The problem of consistency in Marx's explanations is tied in with the question of whether the industrial, commercial and financial interests comprise one 'class' or more than one and, if so, how many. Since the problem of the status of the industrial, commercial and financial interests also arises in connection with Marx's interpretation of English history, it is proposed to examine the whole question in the context of the pre-capitalist legislation. The problems of Engels' explanation will be considered in their relevant contexts.

II. PRE-CAPITALIST LEGISLATION

Marx's references to the Statute of Labourers and the Tudor Vagrancy Laws merit particular attention since they occur in the *Grundrisse* (1857–8) and in volume I of *Capital* (1867). In the *Grundrisse* the emphasis is on the Tudor legislation as a means of compelling the poor to work, and statutory regulations of wages and anti-vagrancy laws are considered together as being of the same character. The following passage illustrates the approach:

> Wages again regulated in 1514, almost like the previous time. Hours of work again fixed. Whoever will not work upon application, arrested. Hence still *compulsory labour* by free workers at given wages. They must first be *forced* to work within the conditions posited by capital. The propertyless are more inclined to become vagabonds and robbers and beggars than workers. The last becomes normal only in the developed

mode of capital's production. In the pre-history of capital
state coercion to transform the propertyless into *workers* at
conditions advantageous for capital which are not yet here
forced upon the workers by competition with one another.
(Very bloody means of coercion of this sort employed under
Henry VIII et al.) [*Grundrisse*, p. 736]

The passage continues with specific details of some of the
provisions to compel people to work. A later passage (p. 769)
refers to the various means by which this body of 'free' propertyless labourers was brought into being, e.g. the dissolu-
tion of the monasteries and the enclosure of common land,
and then again refers to the anti-vagrancy measures as means
by which the labourers were forced to become wage-
labourers.

In volume I of *Capital* the references are to be found in
Chapters 10 and 28. In Chapter 10 the treatment of the Tudor
Vagrancy Laws is compressed into a general reference to
'state-measures by which capital imposes a longer working-
day on labour' (p. 258). The first specific statute mentioned in
Section 5 Chapter 10 is the Statute of Labourers 1349. The
passage raises certain interesting questions and therefore is
worth quoting:

> The first 'Statute of Labourers' (23 Edward III, 1349) found
> its immediate pretext (not its cause, for legislation of this kind
> lasts centuries after the pretext for it has disappeared) in the
> great plague that decimated the people, so that, as a Tory
> writer says, 'The difficulty of getting men to work on reason-
> able terms (i.e. at a price that left their employers a reasonable
> quantity of surplus-labour) grew to such a height as to be quite
> intolerable'. Reasonable wages were, therefore, fixed by law
> as well as the limits of the working-day. [*Capital* I, pp. 358–9]

The first point of interest is the distinction made here between
the 'pretext' for legislation and its 'cause'. Whilst accepting
that the distinction is substantially valid as being the distinction between the reasons for the introduction of a law and
those for its continued existence, the terms in which Marx
makes the distinction are open to criticism. The substantial
distinction is not between a causal and a non-causal operative

factor but between causal factors operating at different stages of the existence of the law. Secondly, the word 'pretext' suggests that at least some of the leading actors knew and desired those subsequent consequences of the Act that Marx regards as its 'cause'.

In Chapter 28, Marx examines the Vagrancy Laws in much greater detail than is to be found in the *Grundrisse*. At the beginning of the chapter he examines the specific provisions of statutes of Henry VIII, Elizabeth I, James I and of comparable legislation in France and Holland. He shows that his use of the adjective 'bloody' to describe these statutes is not inapproptiate: whipping, branding and other forms of multilation were all provided for as sanctions under these Acts.

In this chapter (pp. 686–93) Marx advances a more systematically developed account of the reasons for such laws. Having shown in the previous chapter that the expropriation of the agricultural population from the land was a necessary condition for primitive accumulation, Marx shows here the part played by such laws in adapting those thus dispossessed into wage-labourers:

> It is not enough that the conditions of labour are concentrated in a mass, in the shape of capital, at one pole of society, while at the other are grouped masses of men, who have nothing to sell but their labour-power. Neither is it enough that they are compelled to sell it voluntarily. The advance of capitalist production develops a working-class, which by education, tradition, habit, looks upon the conditions of that mode of production as self-evident laws of Nature . . . The constant generation of relative surplus-population keeps the law of supply and demand of labour, and therefore keeps wages, in a rut that corresponds with the wants of capital. The dull compulsion of economic relations completes the subjection of the labourer to the capitalist. Direct force, outside economic conditions, is of course still used, but only exceptionally . . . It is otherwise during the historic genesis of capitalist production. The bourgeoisie, at its rise, wants and uses the power of the state to 'regulate' wages, i.e. to force them within the limits suitable for surplus-value making, to lengthen the working-day and to keep the labourer himself in the normal degree of

dependence. This is an essential element of the so-called primitive accumulation. [*Capital* I, pp. 688–9]

The remainder of the chapter deals with the statutory regulation of wages and with legislation against combinations of workers. The nature of wage legislation is illustrated by two of the examples Marx cites: first, although these laws laid down a maximum wage, Parliament never accepted the principle of a legal minimum wage, and secondly, although sanctions were provided against both the person paying wages in excess of the maximum and against the person receiving such wages, the punishment for the latter was heavier than for the former. Of the repeal of these provisions Marx says:

> Finally, in 1813, the laws for the regulation of wages were repealed. They were an absurd anormaly, since the capitalist regulated his factory by his private legislation, and could by the poor-rates make up the wages of the agricultural labourer to the indispensible minimum. The provisions of the labour statutes as to contracts between master and workman, as to giving notice and the like, which only allow a civil action against the contract-breaking master, but on the contrary permit a criminal action against the contract-breaking workman, are to this hour [1873] in full force. [*Capital* I, p. 691]

At this point we can examine the problem of how to reconcile the treatment of the Statute of Labourers and the Tudor Vagrancy Laws with a 'class' theory of law. At first sight it may appear straightforward: these statutes clearly promoted the interests of the employers, as Marx says. The problem arises when one attempts to assign these employers to a specific class. If one says that they were capitalists or industrial bourgeoisie, there is the difficulty of whether it is valid from a historical point of view to talk of either of these classes in the fourteenth century or even under the Tudors. Even if the historical difficulty is overcome, there is still a difficulty in explaining how the statutes come to be passed, since these people could not be described as the ruling class at such an early period without a revision of Marx's explanation of English history.

Marx had examined English history and explained it in class terms as early as 1850, in his review of Guizot's book *Why has the English Revolution been Successful?* (On Britain, pp. 89–95). In this work, Marx interprets the subordination of kingship to Parliament under William III as its 'subordination to the rule of a class' (p. 92) and ascribes the struggle between Charles I and his parliaments at least in part to his interference with free competition, which created difficulties for trade and industry and hence for the class(es) that Parliament represented. Later, he attributes the conservatism of the English Revolution to the permanent alliance between the bourgeoisie and the greater part of the big landlords (p. 93). He continues:

> . . . this class of big landed proprietors, which had allied itself with the bourgeoisie and which, incidentally, had arisen already under Henry VIII, was not antagonistic to but rather in complete accord with the conditions of life of the bourgeoisie. In actual fact their landed estates were not feudal but bourgeoise property. On the one hand, the landed proprietors placed at the disposal of the industrial bourgeoisie the people necessary to operate its manufactories and, on the other, were in a position to develop agriculture in accordance with the state of industry and trade. Hence their common interests with the bourgeoisie; hence their alliance with it. [p. 93]

After some criticism of Guizot's presentation of history, Marx goes on to show how the 'consolidation of the constitutional monarchy was precisely the thing that marked the beginning of the grand development and metamorphosis of bourgeois society in England':

> First, manufacture developed under the constitutional monarchy to a hitherto unknown extent, only to make room, subsequently, for big industry, the steam engine and the gigantic factories. Entire classes of the population disappear, and new ones with new conditions of existence and new requirements take their place. While the old bourgeoisie fights the French Revolution, the new one conquers the world market. It becomes so omnipotent that even before the Reform Bill puts direct political power into its hands it forces

its opponents to pass laws almost exclusively in *its* interests and according to *its* needs. It conquers for itself direct representation in Parliament and uses it to destroy the last remnants of real power that landed property retains. [p. 94]

The model presented here may be summarised in the following manner. Under Henry VIII a new class of landed proprietors arose, distinct from the feudal landed aristocracy. These allied themselves with the trading and industrial bourgeoisie. When Charles I interfered with the interests of this class (or classes) a struggle started that, ultimately, under William III led to the subordination of the Crown to Parliament, i.e. to the rule of the bourgeoisie. With the Industrial Revolution a new bourgeoisie arose that eventually, by the Reform Act and the repeal of the Corn Laws, established itself as *the* dominant class.

In 1855, in the article 'The British Constitution' (On Britain, pp. 219–22), Marx gave a somewhat different account:

> The British Constitution is, in fact, merely an out-of-date, superannuated, obsolete compromise between the bourgeoisie, who are *not officially* but actually *ruling* in all decisive spheres of bourgeois society, and the landed aristocracy, who are *governing officially*. Originally, after the 'glorious' revolution of 1688, only a section of the bourgeoisie, the *financial aristocracy*, was included in the compromise. The Reform Bill admitted another section, the *millocracy*, as the English call them, that is, the high dignitaries of the *industrial* bourgeoisie. This history of legislation since 1831 is the history of concessions made to the industrial bourgeoisie, ranging from the Poor Law to the repeal of the Corn Laws, and from the repeal of the Corn Laws to the death-duties on real estate. [pp. 219–20]

This account conflicts with the earlier one in two respects: first, it presents the Revolution of 1688 as a victory of the financial bourgeoise rather than the industrial, and second in regard to the power of the industrial bourgeoisie to secure legislation *before* the Reform Act.

There are several difficulties relating to the earlier stages of the development. First, it would be hard to treat any class other than the landed aristocracy as the ruling class in 1349; the explanation of the passing of the Statute of Labourers, therefore, needs to be amended either so as to relate the Act to the interests of that class or so as to show the relation between the interests of that class and the growth of manufacture. Secondly, the distinction between the 'old' class of landed proprietors and the 'new' class that rose under Henry VIII (and the later distinction between the 'old' industrial bourgeoisie and the 'new') is highly problematic. If the material interest is the basic definitional criterion of a 'class', in what way does the material interest of the 'old' class differ from that of the 'new' one? If, however, the difference lies not in the material interests but in the attitudes or ideas of the group, then there has been a significant departure from the materialist explanation, which is one of the features Marx and Engels claimed to be distinctive of their approach.

Marx approached this problem in the, tantalisingly, unfinished last chapter of *Capital*. The passage is so crucial as to merit extensive quotation:

> The first question to be answered is this: What constitutes a class? — and the reply to this follows naturally from the reply to another question, namely: What makes wage-labourers, capitalists and landlords constitute the three great social classes? At first glance — the identity of revenue and sources of revenue. There are three great social groups whose members, the individuals forming them, live on wages, profit and ground-rent respectively, on the realisation of their labour-power, their capital, and their landed property.
>
> However, from this standpoint, physicians and officials, e.g., would also constitute two classes, for they belong to two distinct social groups, the members of each of these groups receiving their revenue from one and the same source. The same would also be true of the infinite fragmentation of interest and rank into which the division of social labour splits labourers as well as capitalists and landlords — the latter, e.g., into owners of vineyards, farm owners, owners of forests, mine owners and owners of fisheries. [*Capital*, III, p. 886]

At this point the manuscript breaks off. The structure of the argument may be summarised thus: Marx raises the question, suggest *an* answer and then raises an objection to that answer. The logic of the passage suggests that the continuation was going to be the introduction of some element that would explain why wage-labourers, capitalists and landlords constitute the three great social classes and also why physicians and officials do not constitute separate classes. Unfortunately, we are left to speculate what that element was.

The last of the difficulties concerning the classes involved in the various developments is that of determining how many classes were constituted by the industrial, the commercial and the financial bourgeoisie. Marx's most explicit statement on the question occurs in Part II of the *Theories of Surplus Value* (1861–3):

> Hence Wilhelm Thukydides should see that the interests of the 'producing class', including the manufacturers, the industrial capitalists and the interests of the monied class are two very different matters and that *these classes are different classes* [my emphasis]. Furthermore, Wilhelm Thukydides should see that a battle between the industrial capitalists and the landlords was thus by no means a battle between the *'monied* interest' and the *'landed* interest'. [p. 123]

Here, quite explicitly, Marx treats the material interest as defining the class. The continuation of the passage examines the struggle over the Corn Laws. He states that in the struggle over the laws from 1815 to 1847 'the majority of the monied interest and some even of the commercial interest (Liverpool for instance) were to be found amongst the *allies* of the landed interest against the manufacturing interest' (p. 123). This suggests that by parity of reasoning the commercial bourgeoisie also constituted a separate class. This is suggested even more clearly in volume III of *Capital* where, in a footnote to an account of the backwardness of merchant capital, Marx says:

> In modern English history, the commercial estate proper and the merchant towns are also politically reactionary and in league with the landed and monied interest against industrial capital. Compare, for instance, the political role of Liverpool

with that of Manchester and Birmingham. The complete rule of industrial capital was not acknowledged by English merchant's capital and moneyed interest until after the abolition of the corn tax, etc [*Capital*, III, p. 327n]

The point that emerges from the examination of these differing approaches to the concept of 'class' is that there is an unresolved tension between the two. On the one hand, in some texts the material interests is *the* defining element whilst, on the other, some of the texts quite clearly posit an additional element to be included in the definitional criteria. It is a pity that Marx does not specify exactly what this element was. As has been noted above, if the element is derived from the consciousness of the members of the group, then there has been a significant departure from the materialist mode of explanation. Whether such a modification would answer the problem or simply shift it elsewhere is open to question, since the problem then becomes: how does one distinguish between elements of consciousness that may be used to define the class situation of the individual and those elements that are merely ideological? Basically, the problem we have here in regard to the definition of 'class' is simply a specialised form of the more general question of the relationship between the economic base of society and the various elements of the superstructure.

III. THE REFORM BILL

The immediate objectives of the Reform Bill were political, namely the revision of the franchise. It is not surprising, therefore, that the subject should have been of more interest to Engels than it was to Marx. The difference between the two authors' treatment of the Act may also reflect the different times at which they came upon the topic: Engels' major treatments are in 1844 and 1845, i.e. before the development of his collaboration with Marx, whereas Marx's references come later, which is probably explained by the simple fact that Marx first came to England after that date. Since Engels was

both the first of the two to examine the Reform Act and gave
it more extensive consideration, his treatment will be
examined first.

Engels' Analysis

Effects on the Tories/landed aristocracy

Engels' most extensive account of the Reform Act is in one of
his articles in *Vorwärts* of 21 September 1844, entitled 'The
Condition of England. The English Constitution' (MECW
III, pp. 495–7). The overall impression he gives in this article
is that the Act strengthened the Tories. First, the Bill increased the number of country members. As the electors in
the county districts were almost exclusively tenant farmers,
who were dependent on their landlords and thus afraid to vote
against them except in times of the greatest unrest, they could
normally be counted on to return a member who represented
the landed interest, i.e. a Tory.

Secondly, although the introduction of a property qualification (occupation of a house of at least £10 p.a. rental value and
payment of taxes such as the poor rate) gave the vote to the
middle classes in towns, in the smaller towns they were dependent to a large extent on the custom of the tenant farmers
and thus they, too, were subject to the influence of the landlords. Only in the large towns did the middle class really
achieve supremacy. In the smaller factory towns, although the
property qualification excluded the great majority of the
working class from the vote, the middle class were too few in
numbers and the country people had no significant influence,
so that the few enfranchised workers had a relatively greater
influence, with the result that these towns returned to Parliament, almost exclusively, Radical members.

Elsewhere, Engels presents the Bill as a defeat of the
landed aristocracy and as bringing the middle class to power.
Thus, in *The Condition of the Working Class in England*
(MECW IV, pp. 295–583) he asserts that the repeal of the
laws against combinations on workmen could never have

passed the House of Commons later 'when the Reform Bill had legally sanctioned the distinction between bourgeoisie and proletariat, and *made the bourgeoisie the ruling class*' (p. 503; (my emphasis). In 1845 in his 'History of the English Corn Laws' (MECW IV, pp. 656–61), he describes the Bill as bringing the monied middle class to power 'in principle' (p. 660), although in reality the Tories still retained a preponderance in Parliament. In his view, the repeal of the Corn Laws would deal a fatal blow to the political power of the landowners by liberating the tenant farmers from their dependence.

In the article on 'The English Ten Hours Bill' (On Britain, pp. 96–108), written in 1850, Engels gives quite a different picture. First, he contrasts the fate of the financial aristocracy in England with that of their French counterpart: in France, the July Revolution brought the financial aristocracy to power, whereas in England the passing of the Reform Act led to their downfall. The thought behind this assessment is that previously, because the aristocracy were so deeply indebted to the financiers, the financial aristocracy had held 'almost unchallenged sway in England', but when all the other sections of the bourgeoisie combined with the English proletariat and the Irish peasantry to defeat the landed interest, the financial aristocracy stepped down to avoid a revolution. Secondly, the article presents the Bill as giving the *industrial* bourgeoisie access to the field of parliamentary struggle with the result that they could not fail to win victory after victory.

After the death of Marx, Engels referred to the Reform Bill in two places. In the first of these, the article 'England in 1845 and in 1885' (On Britain, pp. 386–92), Engels says that the Reform Bill was the victory of the *whole* capitalist class over the landed aristocracy (whilst the repeal of the Corn Laws was the victory of the manufacturing capitalists over those sections of the capitalists, such as bankers, whose interests were bound up with the landed aristocracy) (p. 387). This is echoed in the 'Special Introduction' to the English edition of 1892 of *Socialism: Utopian and Scientific* (ME Sel W, pp. 379–98) when he states that the Reform Bill gave the bourgeoisie a recognised and powerful place in Parliament and the repeal of the Corn Laws settled their supremacy over the landed aristocracy (p. 393).

In comparing these explanations one can only conclude that no consistent explanation is given. The contrast between the Bill as a defeat of the landed aristocracy and the same Bill as increasing the parliamentary strength of the Tories raised the question whether, perhaps, Engels' account is lacking in some significant dimension. Similarly, the contrast between the Bill as admitting the monied middle class to Parliament and the Bill as leading to the downfall of the financial aristocracy also gives rise to doubts as to whether, in the light of the totality of the treatments of the Bill, the phenomena are explained at all. There is perhaps implicit in these ambiguities a similar problem in regard to the relationship between industrial and financial bourgeoisie as that which we have examined in Marx's treatment of pre-capitalist England.

Effects on the lower middle class

The discrepancies in the accounts of the classes which benefited from the Bill are at their most acute in regard to the effects of the Bill on the lower middle class. In 'The Condition of England. *Past and Present* by Thomas Carlyle' of 1844 (MECW III, pp. 444–68), Engels describes Chartism as the 'natural successor to the old radicalism which had been appeased for a few years by the Reform Bill' (p. 447), and since the 'old radicalism' was a petty bourgeois phenomenon it would appear that the Bill benefited that class. In 'The Condition of England. The English Constitution' also of 1844 (MECW III, pp. 489–513), his explanation of the Toryism of the smaller towns relies on the fact that the tenant farmers were the main customers of the 'tradesmen and craftsmen' (p. 496), which implies that they gained from the Bill, and in 'The English Ten Hours Bill' of 1850 (On Britain, pp. 96–108) he expressly states that 'The Reform Bill gave all the propertied classes in the country, *down to the last shopkeeper*, a share in political power' (p. 101; my emphasis).

On the other hand, in his account of the rise of Chartism in *The Condition of the Working Class in England* (MECW IV, pp. 295–583), Engels gives a contrary picture. He states that in 1835 Chartism was chiefly a movement of the working men, although it was not at that time sharply separated from the bourgeoisie. After associating the radicalism of the workers with that of the bourgeoisie, he continues by asserting that 'The lower middle class was just then in a very bellicose and violent state of mind in consequence of the disappointment over the Reform Bill and of the bad business years of 1837–1839' (p. 518). Unless the disappointment was that the passing of the Bill did not bring about the instant transformation of society in a way that the Radicals might wish or something of such kind, it would appear that in this passage Engels was excluding the lower middle class from those who benefited from the Bill. Even if the disapointment he had in mind was of such a kind, no explanation is given as to why they failed to derive the fullest of benefits from the Bill. There is perhaps here a conflict between the image of the petty bourgeoisie as a radical group and the picture of them as being essentially a group that was dependent on other, more important, classes.

Marx's Analysis

The most distinctive feature of Marx's references to the Reform Bill is that he rarely, if ever, considers that Act in isolation. Most commonly the passing of the Act is linked with the repeal of the Corn Laws, although there are some passages that include other pieces of legislation such as the Ten Hours Bill. The almost casual reference to the Reform Bill in the 'Speech on the Polish Question' of 1848 (MECW VI, pp. 545–9) is fairly typical of the approach:

> In 1789 the political question of the rights of man included the social question of free competition.
> And what then happened in England? In all questions from the Reform Bill until the abolition of the Corn Laws did the political parties fight about anything except changes in

propety rights, questions of property, social questions? [p. 546]

The clear implication here is that the political sphere is epiphenomenal, the substantive issues are the questions of property. In the light of such an approach it is not surprising that Marx found less interest in the specific detail of the effects of the Bill.

In 1852 Marx did give some attention to the political aspects of the Reform Bill in his journalistic writings for the *New York Daily Tribune*. In 'The Elections in England — Tories and Whigs' (On Britain, pp. 109–15), he examines the relations between the political parties and economic classes. Having stated that 'The Whigs, as well as the Tories, form a fraction of the large landed proprietary of Great Britain', he raises the question as to what distinguishes the two and answers it by saying that the 'Whigs are the *aristocratic representatives* of the bourgeoisie, of the industrial and commercial middle class' (p. 112). He then explains the political activity of the Whigs from 1688 to 1846 as having 'no other distinctive mark . . . but the maintenance of their family oligarchy' (pp. 112–13). He then makes the point that the 'interests and principles' that Whigs represented were not their own but were 'forced upon them by the development of the industrial and commercial class, the Bourgeoisie' and refers to their ability to unite with the monied interest in 1688 and the industrial one in 1846. He continues as follows:

> The Whigs as little carried out the Reform Bill of 1831 as they carried the Free Trade Bill of 1846. Both Reform movements, the political as well as the commercial, were movements of the Bourgeoisie. As soon as either of these movements had ripened into irresistibility, as soon as, at the same time, it had become the safest means of turning the Tories out of office, the Whigs stepped forward, took up the direction of the Government, and secured to themselves the governmental part of the victory. In 1831 they extended the political portion of reform as far as was necessary in order not to leave the middle class entirely dissatisfied. [p. 113]

The passage continues by explaining how the Whigs minimised the loss of privilege of the landed aristocracy involved in the passing of the Free Trade measures.

The implications of the article are highly significant. On the one hand, the Whigs are presented as a fraction of the landed aristocracy who are motivated, not by the interests of their class, but by the desire to retain office, whilst on the other, at least a suggestion is given that they looked after the interests of their class quite well. If one presses the development of the theory along the former line, it can lead to a recognition of the relative autonomy of the political sphere and even to the abandonment of the class model of explanation. On the other hand, if one follows the latter line, it might become necessary to modify the explanation of the development of class interests and their relation to and effect on the political sphere; it would almost certainly be necessary, for example, to abandon the idea of the reform movements having 'ripened into irresistibility'.

Marx returned to consideration of the problem arising from the phenomenon of the continued presence of members of the landed aristocracy in key positions of the government in 1855 in his article 'The British Constitution' (On Britain, pp. 219–22). In the passage already quoted from this article (see above, p. 46), Marx describes the Reform Bill as admitting the 'high dignitaries of the industrial bourgeoisie' into the compromise between the landed aristocracy, who rule officially, and the bourgeoisie, who actually rule. The article continues:

> If the bourgeoisie — even only the top layer of the middle classes — has been generally recognized as the *ruling class* in *political respects*, this has been done only on the condition that the entire administration in all details, even the executive functions of legislative power, that is, the actual legislation in both Houses of Parliament, should remain in the hands of the landed aristocracy. In the 1830s the bourgeoisie preferred the renewal of the compromise with the landed aristocracy to a compromise with the mass of the English people. [p. 220]

This concept of a 'compromise' between the landed aristocracy and the bourgeoisie raises some fascinating questions. If the landed aristocracy has been able to maintain a compromise successively with the financial bourgeoisie and then the industrial bourgeoisie, why should they be unable to continue that compromise indefinitely, i.e. is there any necessity for the bourgeoisie to take over completely? Is there any reason why the proletariat should not be included in such a compromise, either with the landed aristocracy or, if the landed aristocracy were to pass from the scene, with the bourgeoisie? The recognition of the possibility of a compromise between a class whose mode of production is no longer dominant and the class whose mode of production has replaced them does not fit particularly happily with the theory of class struggle, although Marx does occasionally describe the Reform Bill as a defeat for the landed aristocracy (e.g. 'Parliamentary Debates — The Clergy and the Struggle for the Ten Hour Day', On Britain, pp. 153–9 at p. 156).

Comparison of the Two Approaches

The major difficulty in explaining the Reform Bill in terms of class interest lies in its effect on the landed aristocracy. This problem affects both the authors' explanations, although in somewhat different ways. With Engels, the problem is how to account for the fact that the Bill strengthened the parliamentary position of the Tories, if the Bill was a defeat for the landed interest. In Marx's accounts, the problem arises from his recognition that the Whigs, who directed the parliamentary aspects of the Bill's passage, were themselves members of the landed aristocracy. There is, perhaps, a further problem in connection with the combination of the two accounts: if it was the Whigs who secured the passage of the Bill, how was it that the Tories gained from it? The most obvious answer to this, namely that both Tories and Whigs were drawn from the landed aristocracy, immediately creates difficulties for the idea of the Bill as a victory for the bourgeoisie.

The area of widest divergence between the two authors is probably in regard to the effects of the Bill on the middle classes. There are two aspects of this divergence: (a) in regard to the lower middle class and (b) in regard to the financial aristocacy. As we have seen, in some places Engels treats the Bill as benefiting the lower middle class (although in others he takes the opposite view); Marx, on the other hand, never refers directly to this group and his reference, in 'The British Constitution' (see above p. 46) to the Bill as admitting the 'high dignitaries of the industrial bourgeoisie' or 'only the top layer of the middle classes' to the power compromise, implicitly excludes the petty bourgeoisie from those who gained from the Bill. The conflict in Engels' accounts of the effect of the Bill on the financial aristocracy coincides to a large extent with the development of his collaboration with Marx; in the earlier works he presents the Bill as bringing the monied middle class to power, whereas in the works written when the collaboration was fully developed the Bill appears as a victory of the industrial bourgeoisie (which agrees with the explanation most favoured by Marx). The account Engels gave in the works written after Marx's death, viz. that the Bill was a victory for the whole capitalist class, conflicts with this and, incidentally, re-opens the question of the exact status of the financial, industrial and commercial bourgeoisie.

IV. THE POOR LAW AMENDMENT ACT 1834

The Poor Law Amendment Act of 1834 was one of the major examples of the reforming trend of Victorian legislation. One might have thought that the very nature of the Act and its objectives would have inspired extensive consideration from Marx. Similarly, the controversy to which the Act gave rise might have been expected to attract Engels. Again, the opposition to the Act in the North of England and the Act's total inadequacy to deal with the industrial unemployment consequent on trade crises and the eventual merging of the Anti-Poor Law movement into Chartism, all would seem to be themes that would be expected to have come in for detailed examination by Marx and Engels. This was not the case

however. Each of the authors did make a significant examination of the Poor Law — Marx in 1844 in 'Critical Marginal
Notes on the Article, "The King of Prussia and Social Reform"'
and Engels in 1845 in *The Condition of the Working Class in
England* — but after 1845 the Act is rarely mentioned.

Marx

As the title suggests, Marx's 'Critical Marginal Notes on the
Article, "The King of Prussia and Social Reform" by a
Prussian' (MECW III, pp. 189–206) are a response to the
earlier article. The background events that form the basis of
the articles are the military suppression of an uprising of the
Silesian weavers and the Cabinet Order issued by the King of
Prussia which, apparently, was an order 'to display concern
for the poor'. The French newspaper *La Réforme* had interpreted the Cabinet Order as being promoted by the King's
'alarm and religious feeling' and Arnold Ruge, writing under
the nom de plume 'Ein Prusse', had disputed this on the
ground that the unpolitical nature of Germany was such that
the significance of the proletariat had not yet been realised
and therefore the uprising caused no alarm. Marx, in turn,
took issue with Ruge's interpretation on the ground that the
political antithesis of the King was liberalism not the proletariat, and hence the actions of the proletariat were not a
source of alarm to the monarchy. He attacks Ruge's explanation of the reason for the misinterpretation of the distressed
state of the workers by referring to the example of England:
unlike Prussia, England was not an 'unpolitical' country but in
England just as in Prussia the causes of pauperism were
misunderstood.

Marx's treatment of the Poor Law arises as an illustration of
the misunderstanding by the English bourgeoise of the
'general significance of a universal state of distress' (p. 193).
He lays the foundations for the discussion by explaining the
system of Poor Law established by the poor Relief Act 1601.
Under that Act each parish was obliged to support its poor,
which was done by levying a rate on property. He then inter-

prets the reforms of the administration of poor relief that the Poor Law Amendment Act enacted as indicating that Parliament 'explains the frightful increase of pauperism by 'deficiencies in the administration' (p. 194). He continues by examining how the Poor Law itself came to be seen as the *cause* of pauperism. He does this by showing how the charitable approach of the old Poor Law was regarded as contravening or interfering with the (Malthusian) law of nature. The Malthusian approach was embodied in the workhouses, which were designed to deter the poor from applying for relief. The argument is summarised in the following paragraph:

> At first, therefore, England tried to abolish pauperism by *charity* and *administrative measures*. Then it came to see in the progressive advance of pauperism not the inevitable consequence of modern *industry*, but, on the contrary, the consequence of the *English poor rate*. It regarded the universal distress merely as a *specific feature* of English legislation. What was previously ascribed to a *lack of charity* now began to be attributed to an *excess of charity*. Finally, poverty came to be regarded as the fault of the poor themselves, and consequently they were punished for it. [p. 195]

The paragraph that follows the one above concludes the argument by asserting that the administration had given up the attempt to abolish poverty at its source but was content to discipline and perpetuate it (p. 195).

Later in 1844, in the manuscript on 'The Antithesis of Capital and Labour' (MECW III, pp. 283–9), Marx again refers to the Poor Law. The context is a discussion of wages:

> Wages, therefore, belong to capital's and the capitalist's necessary *costs*, and must not exceed the bounds of this necessity. It was therefore quite logical for the English factory owners, before the Amendment Bill of 1834, to deduct from the wages of the worker the public charity which he was receiving out of the Poor Rate and to consider this to be an integral part of wages. [p. 284]

In itself this account presents no problems. Where it does give rise to difficulty, however, is in regard to the presentation

Marx gave in 1855 in his article 'The British Constitution' (On Britain, pp. 219–22). There, Marx says:

> The history of legislation since 1831 is the history of conces-
> sions made to the industrial bourgeoisie, ranging from the
> Poor Law to the repeal of the Corn Laws, and from the repeal
> of the Corn Laws to the death duties on real estate. [p. 220]

If the poor relief given under the old Poor Law acted as a reduction in wages, how was the alteration of that system a 'concession to the industrial bourgeoisie?

The puzzle as to the relative lack of treatment of the Poor Laws is most evident in the references in *Capital*. In Chapter 37 of volume III of *Capital*, which is the Introduction to Part VI, 'Transformation of Surplus-profit into Ground-rent', Marx says:

> The inquiries into the level of wages by the parliamentary
> investigating committees, which were appointed before the
> passage of the Corn Laws in England . . . proved convin-
> cingly and beyond a doubt that the high rates of rent, and the
> corresponding rise in land prices during the anti-Jacobin war,
> were due in part to no other cause but deductions from wages
> and their depression to a level that was even below the
> physical minimum requirement; in other words, to part of the
> normal wage being handed over to the landlords. Various
> circumstances, such as the depreciation of money and the
> manipulation of the Poor Laws in the agricultural districts,
> had made this operation possible at a time when the incomes
> of the tenants were enormously increasing and the landlords
> were amassing fabulous riches. [*Capital* III, p. 627]

This casual references to the Poor Laws, simply as one of 'various circumstances', occurs in the middle of an extensive examination of the Corn Laws. It is intriguing that the return to the 1844 insight on the effect of the Poor Law on wages should appear in such a context and not in Part VI of volume I; in the whole of Chapters 19 to 22, which constitute the part on 'Wages', there is no reference to the Poor Laws. The most extensive mention of the Poor Laws in volume I is again in the agricultural context, in Chapter 27, 'Expropriation of the Agricultural Population from the Land', in relation to the

effects of the Reformation on the process of forcible expropriation of the people. Marx quotes Queen Elizabeth I's
observation on the ubiquity of poverty and continues:

> In the 43rd year of her reign the nation was obliged to
> recognise pauperism officially by the introduction of a poor-
> rate. 'The authors of this law seem to have been ashamed to
> state the grounds for it, for (contrary to traditional usage) it
> had no preamble whatever.' By the 16th of Charles I., ch. 4, it
> was declared perpetual, and in fact only in 1834 did it take a
> new and harsher form. [*Capital* I, p. 672]

The assertion that 'the nation' was obliged to pass the Act is a
sufficiently unusual departure from the class model of explanation to provoke questions.

The other references to the Poor Law in volume I of *Capital*
tend to be concerned not with the passing of the Acts but with
the operation of the workhouses. In section 5 of Chapter 10
Marx quotes from Ferrand's speech in the House of
Commons, 27 April 1863, for the purpose of making a comparison between the slave trade and the labour market. After
quoting Ferrand's belief that in the ninety years of its existence the cotton trade had destroyed nine generations of
factory operatives, Marx continues:

> No doubt in certain epochs of feverish activity the labour-
> market shows significant gaps. In 1834, e.g. But then the
> manufacturers proposed to the Poor Law Commissioners that
> they should send the 'surplus-population' of the agricultural
> districts to the north, with the explanation 'that the manufac-
> turers would absorb and use it up'. [*Capital* I, p. 254]

He continues quoting Ferrand's description of how the system
operated until in 1860 the manufacturers found that the
surplus population had been absorbed. Chapter 31, 'Genesis
of the Industrial Capitalist', also describes the transfer of
people from the workhouses of the south to the industrial
north (*Capital* I, p. 709); the only difference is that Fielden,
from whom Marx quotes in this passage, refers to the workhouses of Birmingham and London rather than those of
Dorset and Wiltshire.

By way of a conclusion of this examination of Marx's treatments of the Poor Law we may examine some of the possibilities of fitting these laws into a class model of explanation. The old Poor Law, i.e. the Act of 1601, might be explained in terms of the interests of the new class of capitalist farmers except for the fact that the poor rate was levied on property; it appears that that Act was an attempt to alleviate the consequences of a process of expropriation that was already well under way rather than a means to accelerate that process. If the old Poor Law could be manipulated so as to reduce agricultural wages, this could give the tenant farmers (and possibly, through them, the landowners) a vested interest in preserving that law unless pauperism increased to such a point that the saving on wages was off-set by the cost of the poor rate. At that point the landed interest would gain by the deterrent philosophy of the Poor Law Amendment. If the manufacturers did treat the poor relief as an integral part of wages, this would give them a vested interest in preserving the old Poor Law, particularly since the burden of the poor rate was likely to fall on the landowners. The advantage to the manufacturers in the new Poor Law would be in the use of the workhouses as instruments to channel the surplus population into industry; the problem here is whether such a potential could have been or was seen and intended before the system came into operation. If it was not foreseen but was merely an unintended consequence of the Act it cannot explain why the Act was passed.

Engels

Engels' treatment of the Poor Law is confined almost exclusively to *The Condition of the Working Class in England* (MECW IV, pp. 295–583). His focus differs from that of Marx in that the contrast between the old and the new Poor Law is central to his presentation. This focus necessarily entails a much closer examination of the interests involved on each side of the debate. Another noticeable difference is that Engels' account is much more abundantly provided with illustrations of the working of the Poor Law in actual practice; the picture he paints of the conditions in the workhouse is truly horrific.

The first mention of the Poor Law in *The Condition* is the chapter on the agricultural proletariat (pp. 548–62). The explanation offered there of the reason for the replacement of the old Poor Law is in terms of the effects of the introduction of large-scale farming. Large-scale farming abolished the old patriarchal relationship in agriculture between man and master and also made redundant large numbers of the workforce. Since these workers were now day-labourers, nominally independent of the farmers, they were eligible for parish relief. The increased burden on the poor rates that this caused was a major factor in promoting the new Poor Law.

Later, in the chapter on 'The Attitude of the Bourgeoisie towards the Proletariat' (pp. 562–84, esp. pp. 571–8), Engels attributes the change to the action of the bourgeoisie who had just come into power through the Reform Bill and reformed the Poor Law according to their own point of view. Since he continues this explanation by relating how the Commission appointed to investigate the administration of the Poor Laws discovered that 'the whole working-class in the country was pauperised and more or less dependent upon the rates, from which they received relief when wages were low' (p. 571), there is a problem with this interpretation. As the rates were levied on property ownership, the onus of increased demand for poor relief would have fallen heavier on the landowners than on the industrialists (and this would apply even more if by 'country' Engels meant 'countryside' as opposed to 'town', rather than 'country' = 'nation'). In this case it is difficult to see why the industrialist should be so sensitive to the interests of the class they had just defeated, particularly as the poor relief in effect subsidised the wage bill.

In explaining this 'point of view' of the bourgeoisie, Engels compares the philosophy of the old Poor Law with that of the new in terms very similar in substance to those that Marx had used earlier in 1844 (see above, p. 59). Of the old Poor Law, which derived from the Act of 1601, Engels says:

> [It] naively started from the notion that it is the duty of the parish to provide for the maintenance of the poor. Whoever had no work received relief, and the poor man regarded the parish as pledged to protect him from starvation. He demanded his weekly relief as his right, not as a favour, and this became, at last, too much for the bourgeoisie. [p. 572]

He continues by quoting from the Report of the Poor Law Commissioners what they regarded as the harmful consequences of the old Poor Law. This brings him back to a theme he had touched on earlier, namely the new Poor Law as a practical expression of Malthus' Law of Population:

> Convinced with Malthus and the rest of the adherents of free competition that it is best to let each take care of himself, they would have preferred to abolish the Poor Laws altogether. Since, however, they had neither the courage nor the authority to do this, they proposed a Poor Law constructed as far as possible in harmony with the doctrine of Malthus, which is yet more barbarous than that of *laissez-faire*, because it interferes actively in cases in which the latter is passive. We have seen how Malthus characterises poverty, or rather the want of employment, as a crime under the title 'superfluity', and recommends for it punishment by starvation. The commissioners were not quite so barbarous; death outright by starvation was something too terrible even for a Poor Law Commissioner. [p. 572]

Having explained the motivation behind the Act of 1834, Engels then considers the operation of the Act. The next few pages are filled with case after case illustrating the abuses and horrors of the workhouses, from which Engels rightly concludes that the Poor Law Commissioners had attained their object. At the same time he points out the unintended consequence of the new Poor Law, namely the intensification of the hatred of the working class against the property-holders, and explains the political effects of this hatred:

> The bourgeoisie has formulated so clearly in this law its conception of its duties towards the proletariat, that it has been appreciated even by the dullest. So frankly, so boldly has the conception never yet been formulated, that the non-

possessing class exists solely for the purpose of being exploited, and of starving when the property-holders can no longer make use of it. Hence it is that this New Poor Law has contributed so greatly to accelerate the labour movement, and especially to spread Chartism; and, as it is carried out most extensively in the country, it facilitates the development of the proletarian movement which is arising in the agricultural districts. [p. 577]

He concludes this by referring to the application of the Poor Law to Ireland, observing that the reason why it had not attained such an importance there was that it only affected 80,000 out of the 2½ million proletarians in that country.

In the examination of the Poor Law Amendment Bill of 1844, which follows these passages, Engels makes some important observations on the support for the new Poor Law. He explicitly states that the Bill of 1844 'did not originate with any one section of the bourgeoisie but enjoys the approval of the whole class' (p. 578), and refers to the parliamentary debates of 1844 for proof. He then shows how both parties, Liberals and Conservatives, supported the Bill. This would seem to imply that, in this context, Engels was including the landed aristocracy within the 'bourgeoisie', which differs from his treatment of the Tories in regard to the Reform Bill, the Corn Laws and the Factory Acts. This conclusion is supported by the footnote that Engels appends to the paragraph: there his list of 'the few members of the bourgeoisie who have shown themselves honourable exceptions' expressly includes 'philanthropic Tories'.

Engels' later reference to the Poor Law, in 'The English Ten Hours Bill' of 1950 (On Britain, pp. 96–100), is simply a casual assertion, almost in passing, that the Poor Law sacrificed the paupers to the industrial bourgeoisie once they had gained access to parliamentary power, just as the abolition of the tariffs had sacrificed the landowners to the same class (p. 101). This is the nearest Engels comes to mentioning the use of the workhouses as a means of channelling the surplus population of the agricultural districts into the industrial areas.

To conclude this examination of the Poor Laws I shall briefly compare the approaches of the two authors. A central theme that Marx and Engels share is that of the Malthusian inspiration of the new Poor Law. In regard to the old Poor Law there is a slight difference in that Marx tended to refer to it in terms of 'charity' whereas Engels expressly states that it was seen as a 'right'. As far as the operation of the Act goes, it is Engels who gives the detailed picture of the actual operation of the workhouses whilst Marx shows their function for the industrial system. Finally, neither author really ties up the class interests involved in the transition from the old to the new Poor Law; both give materials that show an interest of the landowners but neither provides a satisfactory statement of the motives of the industrialists for supporting the change (and Marx even shows an interest that might lead to opposition).

V. THE CORN LAWS

The Corn Laws are a very important example of Marx and Engels' explanation of the role of law. As may have appeared already, they frequently couple the abolition of the Corn Laws with the passing of the Reform Act as stages in the 19th century struggle between bourgeoisie and landed aristocracy in England. (The third stage in this struggle, the passing of the Ten Hours Bill, will be examined in the next section.) The Corn Laws, however, are important for another reason, namely that they are an example of an attempt to interfere, by legislation, with economic forces. The operation and repeal of these laws is therefore relevant in regard to the authors' theoretical explanations of the relationship between law and economy. The order of presentation to be followed here will divide the treatments into: references to the introduction and effects of the Corn Laws; examinations of the campaign for their repeal; the results of the repeal. The works of the two authors will be considered separately under each heading.

The Introduction and Effects of the Corn Laws
Engels

Engels' most comprehensive account of the background to the Corn Laws is in an article in the *Telegraph für Deutschland* of December 1845 under the title 'The History of the English Corn Laws' (MECW IV, pp. 656–61). The account starts with the change that occurred in English agriculture in the middle of the eighteenth century by which England, from being a grain exporting nation, became an importer of grain: the low price of grain led to the conversion of arable land into pasture and this, together with the increase in the population, created the need to import grain. The twenty-five years of war against revolutionary France had the same effect as a protective tariff in restricting imports with the result that grain prices, and consequently ground-rents, rose. The increased income of the landlords tempted them to adopt luxurious styles of living, which soon led them into increasing indebtedness, so that when the wars ended they were unable to respond to the reduced price of corn with a reduction in rents. The only possible solution, therefore, was to introduce a tariff.

Although the major effects of the tariff on corn might be expected to be felt in the agricultural sector, a high price of corn would also affect the industrial sector through its influence on the price of bread. In the agricultural sector three groups must be considered — the landowners, the tenant farmers and the agricultural labourers. In the article Engels shows how the initial measure failed to achieve its objective: the tenant farmers were unable to cover their production costs since the price of corn remained low (p. 657). It was not until the sliding scale which Canning and Huskisson invented was introduced, in 1828, that the price of corn became high enough to enable the tenant farmers to cope with their high rents (p. 675). The effect of the laws on the agricultural labourers is examined in *The Condition of the Working Class in England* (MECW IV, pp. 295–583) in the chapter on the agricultural proletariat (pp.

548–9). There Engels explains the agricultural distress as due first to the decreasing ability of industry to absorb the surplus population of the rural districts and secondly to the ending of the artificial prosperity that the wars with France had given to agriculture, and he continues:

> The farmers had to sell their corn at low prices and could, therefore, only pay low wages. In 1815, in order to keep up prices, the Corn Laws were passed, prohibiting the importation of corn so long as the price of wheat continued less than 80 shillings per quarter. These naturally ineffective laws were several times modified, but did not succeed in ameliorating the distress in the agricultural districts. All that they did was to change the disease, which, under free competition from abroad, would have assumed an acute form, culminating in a series of crises, into a chronic one which bore heavily but uniformly upon the farm labourers. [p. 549]

This seems to imply that the Corn Laws at least had the effect of preventing the reduction of agricultural wages to a crisis level.

It is common-place throughout Engels' treatments of the Corn Laws, from the very earliest (MECW II, pp. 375–7 and 380–2) — in the *Rheinisch Zeitung* of December 1842 — that the landowners benefited from the Corn Laws. In fact, in the second of these articles he suggests that the repeal of the Corn Laws would reduce the property of the aristocracy by 30 per cent (p. 380). Though this explanation appears, at first sight, to be adequate, closer examination reveals a deficiency: if the Corn Laws gave no benefit to the tenant farmers until 1828, how did the landed aristocracy benefit from them in that period? The advantage to the landlords must follow from the benefit to the tenants, unless one assumes that there was always a surplus of potential tenants who would pay the rents even though the low price of corn rendered farming at those rents uneconomical. If one makes this assumption, however, the only effect the Corn Laws could have, as far as the landlords were concerned, would be to increase this surplus.

The effects of the Corn Laws on the industrial sector are so obvious that Engels does not spell out the full argument in

'The History of the English Corn Laws' but simply refers to the higher wages necessitated by a high price of corn as the reason for the opposition of the industrial middle class to these laws (MECW IV, p. 657). The full argument is as follows: a high price for corn results in a higher price for bread; if bread is expensive,either another foodstuff must be used in its place, e.g. the potato, or the minimum wage must rise; an increase in wages leads either to higher prices, which in a competitive market is not possible, or to a reduction in profits.

Marx

Marx first examined the Corn Laws in 1845 in his draft of an article on Friedrich List's book *Das Nationale System der Politischen Oekonomie* (MECW IV, pp. 265–93, esp. pp. 288–9). He confirms the view of the development of English agriculture that Engels put forward, citing writers of the sixteenth, seventeenth and even the first two-thirds of the eighteenth centuries as still regarding the export of grain by England as the main source of wealth. He then states that the old English industry, e.g. the woollen industry, was wholly subordinated to agriculture and continues:

> Later, when the factory system proper developed, already in a short space of time the necessity for customs duties on corn began to be felt. But they remained nominal. The rapid growth of the population, the abundance of fertile land which had yet to be made cultivable, the inventions, at first, of course, raised also the level of agriculture. It especially profited from the war against Napoleon, which established a regular system of prohibition for it. But 1815 revealed how little the 'productive force' of agriculture had really increased. A general outcry arose among landowners and tenant-farmers, and the present Corn Laws were enacted. [p. 289]

His account of the effects/ineffectiveness of the Corn Laws come earlier in the same article as part of an argument against the idea that rents are *produced*:

> In England, high land rents were ensured for the landlords only through ruining the tenant-farmers and reducing the

farm-labourers to the level (of real beggars) of an Irish Poverty. All this in spite of the various Corn Laws, and apart from the fact that the landlords in receipt of rent were often compelled to allow the tenant-farmers a remission of one-third to one-half of the rent. Since 1815, three various Corn Laws have been passed to improve the position of the tenant-farmers and to encourage them. During this period, five parliamentary committees were appointed to establish the existence of the distressed state of agriculture and to investigate its causes. The continual ruin of the tenant-farmers, on the one hand, in spite of the total (full) exploitation of the farm labourers and the utmost possible reduction of their wages, and, on the other hand, the frequent necessity for the landowners to forego part of the rent, are themselves proof that not even in England — in spite of all its manufacturing industry — have high land rents been produced. [p. 288]

The account of the effect of the Corn Laws that Marx gave later in the third volume of *Capital* is similar:

. . . the Corn Laws of 1815 . . . had indeed the effect, excluding cases of a few extraordinarily rich harvests, of maintaining prices of agricultural products above the level to which they would have fallen had corn imports been unrestricted. But they did not have the effect of maintaining prices at the level decreed by the law-making landlords to serve as normal prices in such manner as to constitute the legal limit for imports of foreign corn. But the leaseholds were contracted in an atmosphere created by these normal prices. As soon as the illusion was dispelled, a new law was passed, containing new normal prices, which were as much the impotent expression of a greedy landlord's fantasy as the old ones. In this way, tenants were defrauded from 1815 up to the thirties. Hence the standing problem of agricultural distress during this entire period. Hence the expropriation and ruin of a whole generation of tenants during this period and their replacement by a new class of capitalists. [*Capital* III, pp. 626–7]

This version differs from the earlier one in two ways: first, it makes no mention of the landlords' finding it necessary to forgo part of the rent, and, second, it relates the agricultural distress to the development of capitalist agriculture.

In the first volume of *Capital* Marx considered the effects of the Corn Laws on Ireland. In fact it may be said that he saw the Corn Laws as having a greater effect on Ireland. The Corn Laws gave Ireland a monopoly of free importation of corn into Great Britain. This artificially favoured the cultivation of corn, so that when the Corn Laws were repealed the arable land was converted back into pasture with consequent adverse effects on the agricultural population (*Capital* I, p. 666n).

In comparing the accounts given by the two authors, several interesting points emerge. The accounts of the economic background to the introduction of the laws are substantially identical, even down to details such as the relation of the growth of the population to the development of industrial machines, a point that incidentally has implications both for the concept of the substructure of society and for the relationship between that substructure and the super-structure. Both authors agree also that the laws were ineffective in securing a high price for corn and therefore ineffective in relieving the distress of the agricultural districts. The major differences between the two, apart from the fact that Marx considers the effects on Ireland as well as those on England, are that Marx mentions the necessity for the landowners to forgo part of the rent and the replacement of the tenant farmers by a new class of agricultural capitalists. The former of these makes the problem of what advantage there was to the landowners in the Corn Laws more acute and the latter provides the basis for a solution to that problem: the growth of class of capitalist farmers might offer the landlords not only greater certainty of receiving their rents but also the possibility of increasing them even more (although this entails a similar difficulty in regard to the concept of 'class' as that examined above (pp. 46–7) in regard to the 'old' and 'new' landed proprietors and the 'old' and 'new' industrial bourgeoisie).

The Campaign for the Repeal

Engels

An initial problem that arises particularly in regard to the campaign for the repeal of the Corn Laws is whether Engels is using the term 'class' in a technical sense or merely in the imprecise way that was current in ordinary usage at the time. In his early writings the approach tends to explain legislative developments in terms of political parties and to relate the political parties to class interests, i.e. the influence of class interests on law is mediated through the political sphere. It appears that in the earliest writings he regarded the coincidence of class and parties as a specifically English phenomenon, which might suggest that at this stage he was not using 'class' in the technical sense. A good example is in the 'Letters from London' of 1843 (MECW III, pp. 379–91):

> It is well known that in England parties coincide with social ranks and classes; that the Tories are identical with the aristocracy and the bigoted, strictly orthodox section of the Church of England; that the Whigs consist of maufacturers, merchants and dissenters, of the upper middle class as a whole; that the lower middle class constitute the so-called 'radicals', and that, finally, Chartism has its strength in the working men, the proletarians. Socialism does not form a closed political party, but on the whole it derives its support from the lower middle class and the proletarians. [p. 379]

The linking together of 'social ranks and classes' suggests that 'class' was being used in a non-technical sense. The reference to the religious affiliation of the various groups also points in this direction, unless one allows the incorporation of elements that belong to the superstructure into the definition of 'class'. Even on this latter hypothesis, Engels' usage here does not correspond with that of the post-1845 works; there, religion tends to be treated as purely ideological.

Engels' earliest treatments of the campaign against the Corn laws are in the two articles in *Rheinische Zeitung* in December 1842, 'The Position of the Political Parties' and

'The Corn Laws' (MECW II, pp. 375–7 and 380–2). In the former of these articles, Engels explains that there are only three parties of any importance in England — 'the landed aristocracy, the moneyed aristocracy and radical democracy' (p. 375). Whilst he maintains the same identification of the Tories with the landed aristorcacy, his explanations of the other two groups differ somewhat from the version in the 'Letters from London'. The monied aristocracy he describes as follows:

> The kernel of the second party — the Whigs — consists of the merchants and manufacturers, the majority of whom form the so-called middle class. This middle class — which includes everyone who is a gentleman, i.e. has a decent income without being excessively wealthy — is, however, a middle class only compared with the wealthy nobility and capitalists; in relation to the workers its position is that of an aristocracy. [p. 375]

This seems to exclude the capitalists from the middle class and therefore raises the question of which party represented *their* interests. Further, the distinction between a 'decent income' and 'excessive wealth' is scarcely precise enough to provide a workable basis on which to differentiate. The difference in the treatment of 'radical democracy' is that in 'The Position of the Political Parties' it is equated with Chartism, with which the working class was becoming increasingly imbued; the lower middle class does not feature in this explanation.

The article concludes by citing the Corn Laws as the clearest indicator of the position of these parties in relation to one another. The Tories, as the party of the landed aristocracy, were totally opposed to the repeal, the Whigs favoured a compromise solution — a tariff of 8 shillings — whilst the radicals were totally opposed to any tariff (pp. 376–7). In the light of what has been said above about the effect of a high price of bread on the industrial sector of the economy, one may feel that the Whigs' support for a compromise rather than outright abolition calls for an explanation. This Engels gives earlier in his account of 'transitional shades' between the main parties; the faction led by Peel and Russell stood half way between Whiggism and

Toryism and was sure of a majority in the near future. Engels then says:

> With the further development of Chartism [this] group is bound to gain importance, since it represents the unity of Whig and Tory principles against Chartism, a unity which the latter expressly stresses. [pp. 376–7]

Since the working class was not enfranchised at this time, the weight given to Chartism implicitly alludes to extra-parliamentary activities as being relevant to the parliamentary developments.

The second of the two articles, 'The Corn Laws', makes no mention of Chartism. The emphasis in this article is on the effects of the Corn Laws on the tenant farmers. It starts by examining the Tories' opposition to the repeal, contrasting it with their lack of opposition to the Reform Bill and the Catholic Emancipation; Engels was 'firmly convinced that this time the aristocracy will remain adamant until the knife is at its throat' (p. 381). Engels then considers the impact of the Anti-Corn Law League's propaganda on the tenant farmers. Basically, it had wakened their political consciousness by making them aware of the conflict between their interests and those of the landlords, so that instead of voting Tory an increasing number of them were turning to the Whigs. The extent to which the political aspect dominated Engels' approach at this time is perhaps indicated by his conclusion that this trend would inevitably lead to a Whig majority in the House of Commons, 'particularly if the Corn Laws were repealed, for then the tenant farmer would become completely independent of the landlord' (p. 381); the implication here is that the political trend is primary rather than the specific objective of repealing the Corn Laws. The validity of this interpretation of the behaviour of the tenant farmers depends on the assumptions, which Engels expressly affirms, that the interests of landlords and tenants were directly opposed, that the Corn Laws were most unfavourable to the tenant farmers and that their repeal would make the farmers independent because leases would have to be concluded under new conditions (p. 381). Whilst the first of these assumptions is true as a generality, the second is extremely questionable and the third ignores the relative economic strength (and hence bargaining power) of landlords vis-à-vis tenants.

The account given in 'The History of the English Corn Laws' is substantially the same. Additionally, however, Engels tells how after their betrayal by the bourgeoisie the workers made it impossible to hold a successful anti-Corn Law meeting in the manufacturing districts, so that the League was driven into the agricultural districts where its propaganda at least had the effect of shaking the tenant farmers from their unquestioning dependence on the land-owners. In the conclusion of the article Engels demonstrates how the repeal of the Corn Laws would be, in effect, a supplement to the Reform Act. The Reform Act had given power to the monied middle class in principle but in reality the land-owning class still had a preponderance in Parliament; by making the tenant farmers independent of the landowners, the repeal of the Corn Laws would destroy the political power, as well as the wealth, of that class.

Marx

Marx's accounts of the campaign for the repeal of the Corn Laws consider the matter from two viewpoints. In some works, especially the economic ones, the tendency is to view the repeal in terms of the relationship between landowners and the various sorts of capitalist, i.e. in terms of the internal arrangements of the ruling class. In other places, usually where a more popular audience is aimed at, the emphasis is on the role of the proletariat.

There is a small difference between Marx's treatment of the alignments of the ruling class in the campaign for the repeal in his economic works and in his journalism for the *New York Daily Tribune*. The articles in the latter were written in 1852–3, after the repeal (and also after the passing of the Ten Hours Bill) and Marx commonly links the two together. The explanation most frequently adopted in these articles, e.g. 'Parliamentary Debates — The Clergy and the Struggle for the Ten Hour Day', 'The Chartists' and 'The Elections in England' (On Britain, pp. 153–9, 116–24 and 109–15), is that the repeal was a victory for the bourgeoisie over the landed aristocracy and the Ten Hours Bill was the aristocracy's revenge; at this more popular level Marx was not concerned to distinguish between industrial, commercial and financial bourgeoisie. In the more strictly economic texts, of which *Theories of Surplus Value* is perhaps the prime example (1861–3), he goes into the alignments within the ruling class in more specific detail. The passage we have already considered in connection with Marx's concept of 'class' (see above, p. 48) is the most detailed account: the industrial bourgeoisie wanted the Corn Laws repealed whilst 'the majority of the monied interest and some even of the commercial interest . . . were to be found amongst the allies of the landed interest'. (*Theories*, Part II, p. 123).

In some ways the 'Speech on the Question of Free Trade' of 1848 (MECW VI, pp. 450–65) falls between the two categories. It is an examination, at a more popular level, of economic questions. It looks first at the effect of the Corn Laws on wages, pointing out that wages had *fallen* more rapidly than the price of corn had risen. This is used to indicate that the movement for the repeal was far more a conflict of interest between the industrial capitalists and the landlords than between landlords and workers. He then explains the support that the working men gave to the cause of repeal in the following terms:

> The English workingmen have shown the English Free Traders that they are not the dupes of their illusions of their lies; and if, in spite of this, the workers have made common cause with the manufacturers against the landlords, it is for the purpose of destroying the last remnant of feudalism, that henceforth they may have only one enemy to to deal with. The workers have not miscalculated, for the landlords, in order to revenge themselves upon the manufacturers, have made common cause with the workers to carry the Ten Hours Bill, which

the latter had been vainly demanding for thirty years, and which was passed immediately after the repeal of the Corn Laws. [pp. 457–8]

There is a slight conflict here between the idea that the workers' objective was to 'destroy the last remnant of feudalism' and the recognition of the alliance between them and the landlords in regard to the Ten Hours Bill. The alternative explanation, that they were playing off the landlords and manufacturers against each other for whatever advantage might be gained, would fit the facts equally well, although it does assume that the workers were a significant political force even before universal suffrage.

The most important consideration of the role of the working class in the repeal of the Corn Laws is in the article 'The Chartists' (On Britain, pp. 116–124). The passage ties together economic interests and political parties in regard to the repeal in a way to which one can only do justice by extensive quotation:

> When they [the British bourgeoisie] intended to carry a Parliamentary reform they will not make a Revolution of February. On the contrary. Having obtained, in 1846, a grand victory over the landed aristocracy by the repeal of the Corn Laws, they were satisfied with following up the material advantages of this victory while they neglect to draw the necessary political and economical conclusions from it, and thus enabled the Whigs to re-instate themselves into their hereditary monopoly of government. During all the time, from 1846 to 1852, they exposed themselves to ridicule by their battle-cry: Broad principles and practical (read *small*) measures. And why all this? Because in every violent movement they are obliged to appeal to the *working class*. And if the aristocracy is their vanishing opponent the working class is their arising enemy. They prefer to compromise with the vanishing opponent rather than to strengthen the arising enemy, to whom the future belongs, by concessions of a more than apparent importance. Therefore, they strive to avoid every forcible collision with the aristocracy; but historical necessity and the Tories press them onwards. [p. 118]

The continuation of the article reveals that the 'historical necessity' referred to was that of the bourgeoisie's conquering exclusive political dominion for themselves, at which point the union of political and economic supremacy in the same hands would mean that the struggle against capital was also the struggle against the government, i.e. social revolution.

In a later article, 'A London Workers' Meeting' in *Die Presse* of February 1862 (On Britain, pp. 331–4), Marx explained the political role of the working class:

> As everyone knows, the working class, which is such a predominating constituent of a society that since time immemorial has not had a *peasant estate*, is not represented in Parliament. Still, it is not without political influence. No important innovation, no decisive measure has ever been carried out in this country without *pressure from without*. Either the opposition needed such pressure against the Government or the Government needed it against the opposition. By *pressure from without* the Englishman means great, extra-parliamentary popular demonstrations, which naturally cannot be staged without the active participation of the working class . . . The Catholic Emancipation, the Reform Bill, the repeal of the Corn Laws, the Ten Hours Bill, the war against Russia and the rejection of Palmerston's Conspiracy Bill were all the fruit of stormy extra-parliamentary demonstrations, in which the working class, sometimes artificially incited, sometimes acting spontaneously, now as *persona dramatis*, now as the chorus, played either the main part or, if the circumstances so demanded, the noisy part. [p. 331]

It is a pity that Marx did not pursue the distinction between the occasions on which the working class was acting spontaneously and those when it was artificially incited, since the latter clearly raises the question of whose interests were really being served. The theatrical metaphor also is problematic: in what sense was the working class ever more than a 'chorus' before it was given the vote? Perhaps the safest conclusion is that the metaphor is only a metaphor and cannot be interpreted as if it were a refined expression of a theoretical position. It is a plausible conjecture that the importance of the popular demonstrations derived from events abroad, particularly in France: from the French Revolution to the revolutions of 1848, the ruling class in England had vivid illustrations of the dangers inherent in any arousing of popular emotion to a high pitch.

Probably the key factor in comparing the two authors' accounts of the campaign for the repeal of the Corn Laws is the fact that the bulk of Engels' writings on the topic were written before the repeal whilst the majority of Marx's were written after. Thus naturally Engels could not relate the repeal and the passing of the Ten Hours Bill in the same way as Marx did. The second difference, i.e. as to the role of the working class in the campaign, may also relate to this difference of time. The picture Engels paints is of a working class that was not merely disinterested in the repeal but that actively opposed the holding of anti-Corn law meetings in the manufacturing districts; Marx, on the other hand, gives part of the credit for the repeal to working-class demonstrations. The lower middle class' may be the key to the resolution of this disagreement; Engels uses this term but Marx does not. If the popular demonstrations were by members of this group and if Marx assimilated this group with the working class, then both authors' accounts may stand. Throughout the treatment a difference of emphasis is noticeable: Engels places far more emphasis on the parliamentary aspects of the campaign and the political alignments involved, whilst with Marx, even where he deals with the political dimension, the emphasis is rather on the social/economic interests behind the political.

The Consequences of the Repeal

Marx

As we have seen, the bulk of Engel's writings on the Corn Laws dates from before the repeal whilst most of Marx's were written after. Apart from occasional passing references, e.g. in 'The English Ten Hours Bill' of 1850 (On Britain, pp. 96–108, p. 100), Engels' later references date from after 1880. It is appropriate, therefore, to examine Marx's treatments of the effects of the repeal first.

A distinctive feature of Marx's account of the consequences of repeal is that he considers the effects of Ireland as well as England. The matter is stated concisely in volume I of *Capital*:

> The English Corn Laws of 1815 secured Ireland the Monopoly of free importation of corn into Great Britain. They favoured artificially, therefore, the cultivation of corn. With the abolition of the Corn Laws in 1846, this monopoly was suddenly removed. Apart from all other circumstances, this event alone was sufficient to give great impulse to the turnings of Irish arable land into pasture land, to the concentration of farms, and the the eviction of small cultivators. [*Capital* I, pp. 666n]

A more extensive account of this explanation is to be found in Marx's 'Outline of a Report on the Irish Question' (16 December 1867) and in his 'Speech on the Irish Question' of the same date (Ireland, pp. 126–39 and pp. 140–2). A passage from the former dealing with the clearing of the estate of Ireland starts by showing the pooling of small leaseholds and the substitution of pasturage for crop farming as being initially the result of the deaths and emigration caused by the potato famine, but then goes on to give circumstances 'whereby this became a conscious and deliberate system':

> *Firstly, the chief factor*; Repeal of the Corn Laws was one of the direct consequences of the Irish disaster. As a result, Irish corn lost its monopoly on the English market in the ordinary years. Corn prices dropped. Rents could no longer be paid. In the meantime, the prices of meat, wool and other animal products increased steadily in the preceding 20 years. Tremendous growth of the wool industry in England. [Ireland, p. 134]

(The connecting link between the Irish potato blight of 1845–6 and the repeal of the Corn Laws may be hinted at in the article 'The Crisis in England' of 1861 (Ireland, pp. 95–6), where Marx points out that the potato was almost the only food of a considerable portion of the *English* working people; a cheapening of the price of bread would thus counteract the deficiency in the supply of potatoes (p. 95).) The 'Outline of a

Report on the Irish Question' also considers the contributory factors in the clearing of the estate in Ireland. The extension of the English Poor Law to Ireland obliged the landlords to support their own paupers, which obviously gave them a strong incentive to clear the land of such people, and the En- cumbered Estates Act of 1853, which facilitated the sale of mortgaged estates for the benefit of creditors, greatly assisted the development of capitalist agriculture since it replaced the old landlords, who thanks to the fall in the price of corn had difficulty in collecting rents with which to repay the interest on their mortgages, by capitalists who wished to run their farms on modern lines.

The effect of the repeal of the Corn Laws on England is stated in the volume of *Capital*:

> When the English corn duties were abolished in 1846, the English manufacturers believed that they had thereby turned the *land-owning* aristocracy into paupers. Instead, they became richer than ever. How did this occur? In the first place, the farmers were now compelled by contract to invest £12 per acre instead of £8. And secondly, the landlords, being strongly represented in the Lower House too, granted them- selves a large government subsidy for drainage projects and other permanent improvements on their land. Since no total displacement of the poorest soil took place, but rather, at worst, it became employed for other purposes — and mostly only temporarily — rents rose in proportion to the increased investment of capital, and the landed aristocracy conse- quently was better off than ever before. [*Capital* III, p. 725]

In the first volume of *Capital* the increase in the capital outlay in farming is referred to as a 'marvellous impulse' that the repeal of the Corn Laws gave to English agriculture (*Capital* I, p. 632) and the reference to the subsidy is confined to a footnote.

This presentation in *Capital* involves a significant change from the view Marx put forward in the decade immediately following the repeal. At that time his view was closer to the one he later ascribed to the manufacturers, namely that the repeal was a defeat for the landed aristocracy. The most detailed account of this point of view is in his article 'The Elections in England — Tories and Whigs' in the *New York Daily Tribune* of 21 August 1852 [On Britain, pp. 109–15]:

> The repeal of the Corn Laws in 1846 merely recognized an already accomplished fact, a change long since enacted in the elements of British civil society, viz., the subordination of the landed interest to the monied interest, of property to commerce, of agriculture to manufacturing industry, of the country to the city. Could this fact be doubted since the country population stands, in England, to the towns' population in the proportion of one to three? The substantial foundation of the power of the Tories was the rent of the land. The rent of land is regulated by the price of food. The price of food, then, was artificially maintained at a high rate by the Corn Laws. The repeal of the Corn Laws brought down the price of food, which in its turn brought down the rent of land, and with sinking rent broke down the real strength upon which the political power of the Tories reposed. [p. 383]

It could be said that Marx was being perhaps a little over-optimistic in this account, since even at that time he had referred to the passing of the Ten Hours Bill as the aristocracy's revenge on the manufacturers for the repeal of the Corn Laws, e.g. in the 'Speech on the Question of Free Trade' (MECW VI, pp. 450–65). If the landed aristocracy still had the power to carry the Ten Hours Bill in 1847, why were they unable to resist the repeal of the Corn Laws in 1846? The key to the answer may lie in the concept that Marx introduces later in the article on the elections of a 'compromise' between the landed aristocracy and the bourgeoisie. We have already examined this concept in the context of Marx's views of the Reform Bill (see above pp. 54–6). Here it is sufficient to observe that that concept is much more flexible than the conflict model implicit in terms such as 'victory' and 'defeat'. The government subsidy mentioned in the accounts in *Capital* becomes perfectly comprehensible as part of a compromise; the subsidy would then be a *quid pro quo* in return for the Tories' withdrawing their opposition to the repeal.

Engels

The few references to the repeal of the Corn Laws in Engels' later works hardly call for rigorous scrutiny. In 1881, in the article 'Social Classes — Necessary and Superfluous' (On Britain, pp. 382–5), the repeal is mentioned along with the reform of Parliament in 1831 as an achievement of the capitalist middle class (p. 383). A more important reference is in the article 'England in 1845 and in 1885' (On Britain, pp. 386–92). Again the repeal is linked with the Reform Act:

> The Reform Bill of 1831 had been the victory of the whole capitalist class over the landed aristocracy. The repeal of the Corn Laws was the victory of the manufacturing capitalists not only over the landed aristocracy, but over those sections of capitalists too whose interests were more or less bound-up with the landed interest: bankers, stock-jobbers, fundholders, etc. Free Trade meant the readjustment of the whole home and foreign commercial and financial policy of England in accordance with the interests of the manufacturing capitalists — the class which now represented the nation. [p. 387]

The last reference to the repeal appears in the 'Special Introduction' to the English edition of *Socialism — Utopian and Scientific* in 1892 (ME Sel W, pp. 379–98). There, the repeal is described as settling the supremacy of the bourgeoisie, especially the manufacturers, over the landed aristocracy once and for all but also as being the last victory that the bourgeoisie gained exclusively in its own interests (p. 393).

It is a little surprising that Engels should continue to use the simple conflict model of explanation at such a late stage. The increase in the wealth of the landowners that Marx mentions in *Capital* as a result of the repeal in itself raises acute problems for any explanation of the repeal as a victory over the landowners. Additionally, the refinement of the explanation to include 'bankers, stock-jobbers and fundholders' amongst those defeated by the repeal raises a further series of problems. The bankers' community of interest with the landowners may be explained by the debts the landowners had incurred as a result of the extravagant style of living they had adopted with the rise in their income in the second half of the eighteenth century, as Engels had pointed out in 'The History of the English Corn Laws' (MECW IV, pp. 656–61), but whether the 'stock-jobbers' had such a community of interest with the landowners rather than with the industrialists is far less obvious. Even to link the bankers with the landowners rather than the industrialists assumes that the industrialists were not in debt to the bankers or were not indebted to the same extent. The problem is essentially the same problem we have seen already of the relationship between the financial and the industrial bourgeoisie.

Conclusion

At this point we may summarise the points of agreement and of divergence in the two authors' accounts. The two are in complete agreement on the development of agriculture in the latter half of the eighteenth century and on the way the Napoleonic wars artificially favoured the farmers by preventing the import of grain. They also agree that the Corn Laws were introduced with the intent of preserving that position when the peace of 1815 allowed the free import of grain once again. They are equally clear that the tariff was ineffective in preventing agricultural distress. The first point of difference is in the effect on the tenant farmers: Marx saw them as being replaced by a new class of capitalist agriculturalists, which would certainly answer the question of what advantage there was to the landowners in the Corn Laws, whereas Engels thought that the effect of their situation, coupled with the propaganda of the Anti-Corn Law League, was to make them politically independent of the landowners. Of the two explanations, Marx's is perhaps more realistic. In regard to the campaign for the repeal, apart from the matter of the tenant farmers, the major difference is the one noted above p 79) on the role of the working class in the campaign: Engels held the view that the working class were not interested whilst Marx credited them with a significant part. In Marx's accounts of the repeal there is a tension between two models: sometimes the repeal is seen as a victory of the bourgeoisie over the landed aristocracy, but in other places the explanation is rather in terms of a compromise between the two groups. Of the effects of the repeal, Marx alone considers those on Ireland and, more importantly, the increase in the wealth of the landed aristocracy consequent on the increased outlay of capital in agriculture. Engels' accounts of the effects are confined to the simple view of the repeal as a defeat of the landed interest.

VI. FACTORY LEGISLATION

Once again, as with the Reform Bill and the repeal of the Corn Laws, there is a difference in the period when each of the authors was most heavily concerned with factory legislation. Again Engels came to the topic first: his most important consideration is in *The Condition of the Working Class in England,* which dates from 1845, and his next most important is the article 'The English Ten Hour Bill' of 1850. Marx's major treatments are in Chapters 10 and 15 of the first volume of *Capital*, although there are, of course, earlier references, e.g. in 'The Poverty of Philosophy' of 1847 and in the 'Speech on the Question of Free Trade' of 1848. The gap in Engels' treatments from 1850 to the article 'England in 1845 and in 1885' is however intriguing.

A much more important difference between the two authors' approaches is in the angle from which they view factory leglislation. Nowhere is Engels' predilection for the political dimension more apparent than in his treatment of the various Factory Acts; almost invariably it is Engels who examines the parliamentary history of a bill. As one would expect in *Capital*, Marx's emphasis is on the economic causes and effects of factory legislation. The difference between the two approaches is so pronounced that it is proposed to examine each of the authors separately and to draw comparisons between them in a separate concluding section.

Engels

The emphasis on the political

Engels' distinctively political approach is already evident in his first reference to factory legislation, in 'Letters from London' in 1843 (MECW III, pp. 379–91) in connection with Sir James Graham's Bill on the education of children working in factories. The Bill restricted the hours of work for such children and instituted compulsory education, which it entrusted to the Church of England. Engels says that the Bill:

> . . . has provided the parties with a fresh opportunity for testing their strength. The Whigs want to have the Bill rejected completely because it ousts dissenters from the education of the young and, by restricting the hours of children, causes difficulties for the manufacturers. Among the Chartists and Socialists, on the other hand, there is considerable agreement with the general humane tendency of the Bill, except for the provision relating to the High Church. [p. 381]

It is perhaps unwise to make too much of the choice of 'parties' rather than 'class' as categories in this explanation since, as we have seen above (p. 72), at the beginning of this very article Engels claimed that in England parties coincide with social ranks and classes, but it is worthy of note that the economic interest is given a less significant part than the religious one.

In his article 'The Condition of England. *Past and Present* by Thomas Carlyle' of 1844 (MECW III, pp. 444–68). Engels develops this explanation in terms of parties. He contrasts the Whigs, who derived their wealth from industry and therefore could see no fault in it, with the Tories, whose power had been broken by industry and who therefore provided the core of the philanthropists who sided with the factory workers against the manufacturers (p. 447). Even in *The Condition* the same preoccupation with the political arena is evident, although there is some move away from 'parties' to 'classes' as the units of explanation. Towards the end of the Introduction, Engels gives the following view:

> With every session of Parliament the working-class gains ground, the interests of the middle-class diminish in importance; and, in spite of the fact that the middle-class is the chief, in fact, the only power in Parliament, the last session of 1844 was a continuous debate upon subjects affecting the working-class, the Poor Relief Bill, the Factory Act, the Masters and Servants' Act; and Thomas Duncombe, the representative of the working-men in the House of Commons, was the great man of the session. [MECW IV, p. 322]

The Introduction concludes with an assertion that the wrath of the whole working class was so growing that before too long it must break out in a revolution that would make the French Revolution look like child's play.

The historical development, 1796–1833

In the main body of *The Condition* the first significant reference to industrial legislation is to the Health and Morals of Apprentices Act 1802. After mentioning the barbarous treatment meted out to children in the mills, Engels states that as early as 1796 public opinion began to take shape against the system, thanks to the efforts of one Dr Percival and Sir Robert Peel, the father of the Cabinet Minister and himself a cotton manufacturer. Their efforts resulted in the passing of the Act of 1802 and the removal of the most crying evils (MECW IV, p. 442).

It is perhaps again a result of Engels' orientation towards the political that he mentions the Act of 1802 and the Factory Acts of 1819, 1825 and 1831, whereas Marx dismisses them in a single sentence at the beginning of section 6 chapter 10 of volume I of *Capital*. Engels explains the Acts of 1819, 1825 and 1831 by the cooperation of Sir Robert Peel and other philanthropists with Robert Owen in calling the government's attention to the need for legislative measures to protect the health of the operatives, especially the children, (p. 459). The first two of these Acts, he says, were never enforced and the last was only enforced sporadically. The difficulty in enforcing the latter Act was that the workers were afraid to testify against their employers for fear of being dismissed; only in the large cities were the operatives militant enough to ensure that the employers found it more convenient to observe the provisions as to the working hours of children and young persons.

In *The Condition* (pp. 460–6), Engels describes the agitation for a ten hours law as having become lively among the workers as early as 1831. His account of the agitation differs somewhat from Marx's. First, Engels assigns responsibility for the spread of the agitation to the trade unions and presents the philanthropic section of the Tories under Sadler's leadership as taking up the idea from them (p. 460). Then, in keeping with his taste for political explanations, he explains the parliamentary developments that led to the Factory Act 1833 — how Sadler obtained a parliamentary committee to investigate the factory system, how this committee was composed of enemies of that system and, for party purposes, presented a report that was strongly partisan against the system, how the manufacturers demanded an official investigation to counteract the basis of the Sadler report, and how even that investigation revealed so horrible a picture of the ill-effects of the factory system on the health of the employees that the Act of 1833 was passed to restrict the hours worked by children between nine and thirteen to 48 per week at the utmost and those of young persons between fourteen and eighteen to 60 in a week or 12 in any one day, and also to provide for compulsory education for those under fourteen (pp. 461–2).

The effects of this Act were not particularly dramatic, though Engels does say that the most crying evils disappeared almost wholly, but the ones he lists as still surviving indicate a very low level of general health among the factory workers (p. 462). One of the consequences of the appointment of inspectors to enforce the Act was that, where it was possible, the labour of children was often dispensed with, though here again, as Engels points out, some employers found it more profitable to ignore the law and risk the consequences, since the fines involved were only trifling in comparison with the profits to be made, particularly when trade was brisk (pp. 462–3). After Sadler's death the agitation for a Ten Hours Bill continued under the leadership of the Tories, Lord Ashley and Oastler.

The historical development, 1843–4

The next piece of parliamentary activity in regard to the factories was the Bill that Engels had already referred to in his 'Letters from London' (above p. 86), Sir James Graham's unsuccessful attempt in 1843 to introduce a Bill restricting the working hours of children. There is a slight discrepancy between the accounts in the 'Letters to London' and *The Condition*. In the former, the Chartists and Socialist are described as agreeing with the general humane tendency of the Bill but not with the provision that entrusted the educational aspects to the Church of England. In *The Condition* Engels states that the working men were divided on the Church in question and therefore were inactive (p. 464). The result of this inactivity was that the petition got up by the manufacturers, Liberals and dissenters who opposed the Bill persuaded Graham to withdraw it *in toto*.

The following year, Graham introduced another Bill, which omitted the controversial education clauses and provided for a maximum of 6½ hours work for children. The parliamentary history of the Bill, as outlined by Engels (pp. 464–5), was somewhat tortuous. When Lord Ashley carried an amendment to the Bill, the effect of which was to limit the hours during which children might be employed to those between 6 a.m. and 6 p.m., the Ministry was not agreeable to the change and consequently it was defeated on the next vote. Peel and Graham the announced their intention of introducing a new Bill and of resigning if it was rejected. Rather than lose the Ministry, the Tories accepted the Bill, which was substantially the same as the one they had just defeated. Engels closes this portion of the work with an expression of confidence that the Ten Hours Bill would be adopted in a very short time, as in fact happened in 1847.

The Ten Hours Bill

The article 'The English Ten Hours Bill' of 1850 (On Britain, pp. 96–108) is arguably Engels' most important work on the subject of factory legislation. The emphasis on the political dimension is still noticeable throughout the piece but much more attention is paid to the economic background and effects of the Act. Whether this is to be attributed to Engels' closer acquaintance with Marx must remain a matter for conjecture but the hypothesis has a certain plausibility.

(1) *The political elements.* In this article Engels examines far more deeply the effects on the working-class political movement of their acceptance of the leadership of the philanthropic Tories, and the implications of the passing of the Ten Hours Bill for the alliance of working men and Tories. It is typical of Engels' approach that in his introductory exposition of the background to the Ten Hours Bill he should describe the earlier legislation as the products of a situation where '*the state* [my emphasis] was obliged to introduce measures to check the factory owners' utterly ruthless exploitation' (p. 97).

He continues by showing how the Ten Hours campaign gathered together, under the leadership of the philanthropists such as Lord Ashley, 'the aristocracy and all those sections of the bourgeoisie that were hostile to the factory owners' as well as the workers themselves. The heterogeneous and reactionary nature of the elements of this association necessitated the separation of the Chartists' campaign for the political rights of the workers from that for the Ten Hours Bill. According to Engels, not a single Chartist was on the Short-Time Committee or campaigned with the aristocratic and/or bourgeois advocates of the Bill. He explains the 'working-class Toryism' of the workers on that committee as being an echo of the nostalgic desire to return to the partiarchal, pre-industrial state of society (pp. 97–8).

Engels' specification of who were the reactionary elements who supported the Ten Hours Bill is interesting and anticipates the similar analysis, already quoted (p. 83), of the support for the repeal of the Corn Laws (in the later article 'England in 1845 and in 1885'). He describes the alliance thus:

> Whenever the question of the ten-hour working day became a focus of public interest, all sections of society whose interest had suffered as a result of the industrial revolution and whose livelihood was threatened by it gave their support to these elements. At such times, the bankers, stock-jobbers, shipowners and merchants, the landed aristocracy, the big landowners from the West Indies and the petty bourgeoisie rallied in ever large numbers to the support of the Ten Hours Bill campaign. [pp. 98–9]

The difficulties with this explanation are much the same as those in regard to the similar explanation of the repeal of the Corn Laws. Whilst there is no problem in accepting that the landed aristocracy had lost as a result of the rise of industry, and the bankers, too, if as was conjectured above (pp. 83–4) they derived more benefit from the indebtedness of the landowners than of the industrialists, it is difficult to see how the stock-jobbers, and even more so the shipowners and merchants, should lose from the growth of industry. These two latter groups in particular, one would have thought, would be among the principal beneficiaries of the increase in trade consequent on the increase in production. To a lesser extent the petty bourgeoisie, also, would have gained from the growth of a money economy following the spread of wage-labour.

In the case of the big landowners from the West Indies, the difficulty arises from what Engels himself says later in the same article. In describing the energy of the industrialists in the cause of Free Trade, he says that from 1842 onwards each trade crisis brought them a new victory, and continues:

> The interests of the landowners in England were sacrificed to

those of the interests of the landowners in the colonies likewise through the lifting of differential tariffs on sugar and
other produce, and those of the shipowners through the repeal
of the Navigation Laws. [p. 103]

Since the West Indies were an important sugar-growing area,
it is hard to see how the landowners there came to be opposed
to the industrialists, and whilst the abolition of the monopolist
position that British shipowners held under the Navigation
Laws gives some reason for their opposition to the industrialists, this is only a satisfactory explanation on the basis that the
disadvantage arising from the repeal outweighed the benefits
from increased trade. In the light of these difficulties, one
cannot but feel that Engels' account of the alliance supporting
the Ten Hours Bill does not adequately explain the participation of all those he describes as parties to it.

(2) *The economic background.* As we mentioned earlier, in
this article Engels considers not only the political aspects of
the campaign for the Bill but also the economic background to
the passing of the Bill and the effects of the alteration of those
circumstances. After a brief outline of the way in which the
constant improvement of machinery had led to a constant
necessity to expand the market so as to absorb surplus produce and avoid the trade crisis consequent on over-
production (p. 102), Engels goes on to show how the industrialists sought to reduce wages by reducing the cost of the
workers' necessities of life — hence the abolition of the Corn
Laws and the elimination of tariffs on produce imported from
the colonies. He then continues:

> Yet amidst this series of uninterrupted victories of the indus-
> trial bourgeoisie reactionary groups succeeded in hampering
> its advance with the fetters of the Ten Hours Bill. The Ten
> Hours Bill was passed at a time marked neither by prosperity
> nor crisis, during one of those transition periods when indus-
> try is sufficiently embarrassed by the consequences of over-
> production as to be able to put in motion only a part of its
> resources and when the factory owners themselves do not
> allow their factories to work full time. [p. 103]

He goes on to explain that it was only at such a moment that the Bill could be tolerated but that, as soon as the emptying of the markets created a new demand, the Bill was seen as a shackle on industry and, since there was insufficient support in Parliament for a repeal, other ways had to be found. The way found was to work women and young persons on the shift system so that adult workers could be kept working for up to 15 hours per day. The Justices of the Peace were divided as to whether this contravened the Act or not and the Home Secretary recommended the factory inspectors to close their eyes to such practices. Not all the inspectors were prepared to do so but when the matter was taken to a higher court, namely the Court of Exchequer, that court came down on the side of the factory owners, thus effectively repealing the Act.

Engels returns to the implications of economic factors in the conclusion of the article, when he is considering the possibility of restoring the Ten Hours Bill.

> The moment the confines of the world market become too narrow for the full deployment of all modern industry's resources, the moment this industry requires a social revolution in order that its potential may once more have free scope for action, the restriction of working hours ceases to be a reactionary measure or brake on industrial progress. On the contrary such measures emerge of their own accord. [pp. 107–8]

The resemblance between this statement and the view of Marx that factory legislation is as much a product of modern industry as cotton-yarn, self-actors and the electric telegraph (*Capital* I, p. 451) hardly needs to be pointed out.

(3) *The effects of the Act.* Engels is particularly concerned in the article with the effects on the political activity of the working class of its acceptance of the leadership of reactionary elements in the Ten Hours campaign. We have already seen how he stresses the separation of the campaign from Chartism, the political movement of the working class. In spite of this separation, in Engels' view the alliance had harmful effects on the working class as a whole. He expressly states that:

. . . this alliance contaminated the working-class movement

with a considerable influx of reactionary elements, which is
taking a long time to disappear; it gave rise to a significant
increase in the influence of reactionary elements in the
working-class movement, namely, those workers, whose
branch of production was still at the manufactory stage and
therefore threatened by industrial progress, as, for example,
the handloom weavers. [p. 99]

For this reason Engels thought that the passing of the Ten
Hours Bill in 1847 was fortunate for the workers. He mentions
the fact that the old parties in Parliament were breaking down
and had not yet been replaced by new ones, so that the
divisions on the Bill were most confused, with only the free-
trading factory owners and the protectionist landowners
voting consistently throughout. It is in this context that he
gives the explanation of the Bill that Marx used frequently:

> This Bill was seen as a cunning blow, which the aristocracy,
> some of the Peelites and some of the Whigs had dealt at the
> factory owners, so as to take their revenge for the major
> victory the latter had won by repealing the Corn Laws. [p. 100]

Even in this passage, where he uses an explanation that Marx
also puts forward, it is noticeable that Engels still tends to
think in terms of political groupings.

Apart from the obvious benefits to the workers' health in
the reduction of their working hours, Engels saw the main
advantage in the passing of the Act as being the political
advance of freeing the workers from their partnership with
reactionary elements. He did not expect this political freedom
to bear fruit immediately. We have already seen some of the
passages in which he demonstrated the rise of the industrialists in political power. It is this rise and the necessity for it to
achieve its logical fulfilment that is advanced to explain the
course of development. Having pointed out that each trade
crisis from 1842 onwards had brought a new victory for the
industrialists, Engels maintains that in order to win direct
political power for themselves the industrialists were eager to
bring new allies into Parliament, specifically that section of
the working class on whom they could rely. He does not state

which section of the working class he envisaged in this role, but the general context would seem to indicate that it was the most advanced section, i.e. those employed in the most advanced industries. He then continues:

> Despite their open hostility towards the industrialists, which has in no way been cooled, the workers are now much more inclined to support the latter in their campaign to achieve completely free trade, financial reform and an extension of the franchise, than to let themselves be rallied once more to the banners of the united forces of reaction by philanthropic mystification. They feel that their time can only come after the industrialists' energy has been completely spent and are thus responding to the right instincts in going out of their way to accelerate the process of development which will give the industrialists the power they seek and lead to their subsequent downfall. Meanwhile they do not forget that in doing so they are bringing their own, immediate enemies to power, and that they can only achieve their own liberation by overthrowing the industrialists and winning political power for themselves. The virtual annulment of the Ten Hours Bill has proved this to them once again most pointedly. The re-instatement of this Bill is futile without universal suffrage, and universal suffrage in England, two-thirds of whose population consists of industrial proletarians, implies executive power for the working class, together with all those revolutionary changes in social conditions intrinsic to that power. The Ten Hours Bill which the workers are now calling for is therefore quite different from the one which the Court of Exchequer has just abrogated. It no longer represents an isolated attempt to cripple industrial progress, it is a link in a long chain of measures aimed at radically changing the whole of the present structure of society and gradually doing away with the hitherto existing class contradictions. [p. 106]

The passage continues to explain that the effective repeal of the Ten Hours Bill served to shorten the current period of prosperity and that the end result of the continuing recurrence of trade crises would accelerate the overthrow of the industrial bourgeoisie by the industrial proletariat. Engels clearly thought that the growth of the productive forces had so outstripped the capacity of the markets to absorb the produce that in a very short time a position would be reached where crises followed one another with increasing rapidity, with only ever-briefer periods of activity in between, until the whole of society collapsed; at that point the proletarian revolution was inevitable.

(4) *Critique*. There are several difficulties in accepting this analysis and the scenario painted of the probable course of development. First, the assumption that the passing of the Act of 1847 would dissolve the partnership between the working class and the reactionary elements of society is of questionable validity, particularly in the light of the subsequent fate of the Bill; why should the working class switch from an alliance that had produced results to one with the very class responsible for undoing the progress thus achieved? Since the Ten Hours Bill had still to be fought for, the alliance that had carried it through Parliament once must surely have appeared worth maintaining. Second, the scenario of impending economic development depends on the assumption that the industrial bourgeoisie would neither voluntarily impose restrainst on production themselves nor allow such restraints to be imposed by any other class or classes. Finally, the analysis ignores the possibility that, in the event of a collapse of the economy, the classes overthrown by the rise of the industrial bourgeoise might regain power, rather than the industrial proletariat, whose importance would have been diminished, *ex hypothesi*, if the industrial system had collapsed. In such a situation, the landowners' production of food would be the crucial production in society.

Retrospective view

Engels' last important reference to factory legislation is in the article 'England in 1845 and in 1885' (On Britain, pp. 386–92). In this work, looking back on the developments of the 1840s, Engels saw that the result of the upturn in trade after the recess of 1847 and the demise of Chartism was that, politically, the working class became the tail of the Liberal party, the party of the manufacturers. The latter saw that the support of the working class was necessary for their own rise to political power and that, in return for this support, acceptance of factory legislation and of the operation of trade unions was not too great a price. This is closer to a 'compromise' model of explanation than is to be found in the earlier works.

In this work, too, he makes use of a concept of an 'aristocracy' of the working class (pp. 389, 390). This was the group that enjoyed the protection of the Factory Acts or of strong trades unions and who consequently 'succeeded in enforcing for themselves a relatively comfortable position' (p. 390). The conclusion of the article exhibits the same tendency towards political explanation that I have already noted in the earlier works:

> The truth is this: during the period of England's industrial monopoly the English working-class have to a certain extent shared in the benefits of the monopoly. These benefits were very unequally parcelled out amongst them; the privileged minority pocketed most, but even the great mass has at least a temporary share now and then. And that is the reason why since the dying-out of Owenism there has been no Socialism in England. [p. 392]

The article ends by predicting that the loss of England's monopolistic position would reduce even the privileged minority of the working class to the level of their fellow-workers abroad and that this would, in turn, lead to a resurgence of socialism in England. The interpretation of this as a political explanation depends on 'socialism' being construed as a political party such as the Lassallean Social Democrats in Germany. It must be noted, however, that the relation of these developments to economic causes is much more prominent than in some of the earlier works.

Marx

The economic significance of factory legislation

Marx considers factory legislation in two places in volume I of *Capital*. In Chapter 10, on the working day, he examines the extent to which these Acts were effective. In Chapter 15, on machinery and modern industry, he emphasises rather their effect on industry and the economy as a whole. Given the nature of the work in which these treatments appear, it is not surprising that the political dimension should be given less attention. Conversely, it may be argued that the choice of an economic work as the place to consider factory legislation, rather than, for example, an article for a newspaper or a journal, is itself indicative of a basic orientation of the author.

Marx summarises the economic effects of factory legislation at the end of section 9 of Chapter 15:

> If the general extentions of factory legislation to all trades for the purpose of protecting the working-class both in mind and body has become inevitable, on the other hand, as we have already pointed out, that extension hastens on the general conversion of numerous isolated small industries into a few combined industries carried on upon a large scale; it therefore accelerates the concentration of capital and the exclusive predominance of the factory system. It destroys both the ancient and the transitional forms, behind which the domination of capital is still in part concealed, and replaces them by the direct and open sway of capital; but thereby it also generalises the direct opposition to this sway. While in each individual workshop it enforces uniformity, regularity, order and economy, it increases by the immense spur which the limitation and regulation of the working-day give to technical improvement, the anarchy and the catastrophes of capitalist production as a whole, the intensity of labour, and the competition of machinery with the labourer. By the destruction of petty and domestic industries it destroys the last resort of the 'redundant population', and with it the sole remaining safety-valve of the whole social mechanism. By maturing the material conditions, and the combination on a social scale of the processes of production, it matures the contradictions and antagonisms of the capitalist form of production, and thereby provides, along with the elements for the formation of a new society, the forces for exploding the old one. [*Capital* I, p. 472]

Earlier in the same chapter (p. 386), Marx explains how the compulsory shortening of the working day provides an incentive for the development of machinery. Once it has become impossible to extract more surplus-value by extension of the hours of labour, capital throws its weight into the effort to increase relative surplus-value by the improvement of machinery. Furthermore, the reduction of the hours of labour facilitates the condensation of labour, as the worker can obviously work more intensely for a period of ten hours than for one of twelve (pp. 388–92). Consequently, as the factory inspectors reported, the reduction of the working day was counter-balanced by an increase in the speed of the machinery.

In section 8(e) of the chapter (pp. 442–51) he examines more fully the way in which factory legislation leads to 'the general conversion of numerous . . . small industries into a few combined industries carried on upon a large scale'. The section is headed 'Passage of modern manufacture, and domestic industry into modern mechanical industry. The hastening of this revolution by the application of the Factory Acts to those industries'. (It may be noted in passing that Marx is evidently using the word 'manufacture' in its earlier sense 'making by hand', as the etymology of the word indicates.) The following passage states the argument most succinctly:

> The compulsory regulation of the working-day as regards its length, pauses, beginning and end, the system of relays of children, the exclusion of all children under a certain age, &c, necessitate on the one hand more machinery and the substitution of steam as a motive power in the place of muscles. On the other hand, in order to make up for the loss of time an expansion occurs of the means of production used in common, of the furnaces, buildings, &c, in one word a greater concentration of the means of production and a correspondingly greater concourse of workpeople. The chief objection, repeatedly and passionately urged on behalf of each manufacture threatened with the Factory Act, is in fact this, that in order to continue business on the old scale a greater outlay of capital will be necessary. But as regards labour in the so-called domestic industries and the intermediate forms between them and Manufacture, so soon as limits are put to the working-day and to the employment of children, those industries go to the wall. Unlimited exploitation of cheap labour-power is the sole foundation of their power to compete. [pp. 446–7]

Whilst the concentration of industry may be a legitimate inference from the necessity for a greater capital outlay, the further conclusion that the destruction of the domestic industries, the 'last resort of the redundant population', somehow will create the forces necessary for exploding the old society creates difficulties. First, it ignores the possibility that the redundant population might become something analogous to the plebeians in Ancient Rome under the late republic and early empire, i.e. a mass of clients dependent on hand-outs, and second, if it is argued that such a mass is always potentially revolutionary, this conflicts with Marx's view that the industrial proletariat, not the lumpenproletariat, is the revolutionary class. It might be possible to achieve some sort of reconciliation by maintaining that those thrown out of work by the closure of the domestic industries remain in the industrial proletariat even though unemployed, but this would not fit particularly well with the concept of the 'redundant population'.

Finally, in regard to the economic consequences of factory legislation, reference must be made to *Wages, Price and Profit* of 1865 (ME Sel W, pp. 186–229). There, Marx asks what was the result of the Ten Hours Bill and gives the answer:

> A rise in the money wages of the factory operatives, despite the curtailing of the working-day, a great increase in the number of factory hands employed, a continuous fall in the price of their products, a marvellous development in the productive powers of their labour, an unheard-of progressive expansion of the markets for their commodities. [p. 192]

Whether all these consequences can legitimately be attributed to the Ten Hour Bill is questionable. The increase in the productive power of labour, as we have seen, may validly be regarded as such a consequence since the operation of the Act provided the incentive for further development of machinery, as Marx showed. The fall in the price of products is a fairly natural result of this increased productivity. What is less clear, however, is whether the expansion of markets and the increase in the labour force can also be regarded as effects of the

Act. There is no difficulty in regarding the increase in the labour force as a consequence of the expansion of the markets, but the real problem is to determine whether the expansion of the market preceded or followed the increase in production; only if the expansion of the market followed the increase in production can it be treated as a consequence of the Ten Hours Bill.

The most problematic of these suggested consequences of the Act is the rise in wages. Whilst it is obvious that an increase in the labour force entails an increased demand for labour, which one would normally expect to lead to increased wages, the difficulty arises from the fact that on the following page Marx refers to an increase in the wages of agricultural labourers in the same period; in volume III of *Capital* (p. 628) he explains the rise in agricultural wages as due to the reduction of the supply of labour consequent upon the emigration of labourers to California and Australia and the recruitment into the armed forces of others, as well as the movement into the industrial towns. The problem is, then, whether the rise in industrial wages is not equally attributable to such extrinsic factors as emigration and recruitment.

The development of legislation to 1844

Chapter 10 of the first volume of *Capital*, on 'The Working Day', is more concerned with the empirical situation onto which the Factory Acts were brought to bear, and with their effects on that situation. Throughout the chapter Marx draws heavily on the various reports of the factory inspectors and the Children's Employment Commission, from which he draws a horrifying picture of the exact situation in industry in the middle of the nineteenth century. No attempt will be made here to reproduce the detail of the empirical matters; for that there is no substitute for the original text. The treatment here will confine itself to an exposition of the development of the chapter and an examination of the theoretical conclusions and implications of it.

The first section of the chapter, 'The limits of the working-day', opens with the distinction between necessary and surplus labour and the relevance of the length of the working day for the determination of surplus-value. Marx points out that necessary labour time, i.e. that proportion of the day in which the labourer reproduces his wages, is the minimum limit to the working day, although under capitalist production the working day can never be reduced to this minimum. The maximum length of the working day is set partly by the physical limitations of labour-power, such as the need to eat and sleep, and partly by what Marx calls 'moral' limitations, e.g. the time the labourer needs to satisfy his intellectual and social wants, the number and extent of which are 'conditioned by the general state of social advancement' (*Capital* I, p. 223).

Section 2, 'The greed for surplus-labour. Manufacturer and Boyard', starts with a historical survey of the forms in which surplus-labour was extracted. After touching on slave-labour in antiquity and contemporary America, Marx gives a more extensive treatment of the corvée-labour of the Wallachian peasants under the 'Réglement organique', which he describes as a positive expression of the greed for surplus-labour. He then compares this with the English Factory Acts, 'the negative expression of the same greed' (p. 229). He explains the passing of the Act as follows:

> Apart from the working-class movement that daily grew more threatening, the limiting of factory labour was dictated by the same necessity which spread guano over the English fields. The same blind eagerness for plunder that in the one case exhausted the soil, had, in the other, torn up by the roots the living force of the nation. Periodical epidemics speak on this point as clearly as the diminishing military standard in Germany and France. [p. 229]

After quoting the provisions of the Factory Act 1850 on the working day, Marx concludes this section by illustrating from the reports of the factory inspectors the ways in which employers extended the working day in contravention of the Act by a series of petty pilferings — five minutes here, five there

— which in total amounted to over five hours per week.

Sections 3 and 4 of the chapter are mainly concerned with the empirical situation in various industries, whilst section 5 examines the historical development from the fourteenth to the seventeenth century. Section 3 'Branches of English industry without legal limits to exploitation', is mainly concerned with the detail of overwork in those industries that did not fall under the Factory Act. Section 4, 'Day and night work. The relay system', also concerns itself mainly with the empirical situation, in this case particularly the employment of persons under the age of eighteen at night. I have already considered section 5, 'The struggle for the normal working-day. Compulsory laws for the extension of the working-day from the middle of the 14th to the end of the 17th century', above in the context of pre-capitalist labour legislation (pp. 42–3).

The most important section of the chapter, from the point of view of the current examination, is section 6, 'The struggle for the normal working-day. Compulsory limitation by law of the working-time. English Factory Acts, 1833 to 1864'. The section starts by referring to the rapid growth of industry in the last third of the eighteenth century and to the five labour laws passed by Parliament between 1802 and 1833, which were totally ineffective since no provision was made for their enforcement. Little explanation is given of these Acts, except that they were purely nominal concessions won by the workpeople. Since Marx subsequently dates the repeal of the laws against trades unions at 1824 (p. 428), it would seem to follow that he was thinking of popular demonstrations as the significant tactic in the introduction of such measures. One may feel that this explanation perhaps over-emphasises the significance of the working-class movement at such an early date, or at least that it needs to be complemented by a reference to some other factor such as the ruling class's recollection of the French Revolution.

The main provisions of the Act of 1833 considered are those relating to the employment of children and young persons.

Under the age of nine no child was to be employed in a factory; between nine and thirteen years they might be employed for 8 hours but not after 5.30 p.m. or before 8.30 a.m.; and 'young persons', i.e. those between thirteen and eighteen, could be employed for 12 hours but again only during the day. In connection with this Act Marx seems to have been led astray by his indignation; in comparing the treatment of negro slaves laid down in the Emancipation Act with the protection given to children by the Factory Act, he states that the Factory Act condemned children *under thirteen* 'to 72 hours of work per week in the Factory Hell', as compared with the 45-hour limit on the work of slaves. More serious is the lack of any explanation other than an unspecific reference to 'outside pressures' of why Parliament resisted the pressure from the manufacturers to reduce the age limit of childhood from thirteen to twelve (p. 266).

The defect of the Act, reported by the factory inspectors, was that it left it open to the employer to start the work-period of children or young persons whenever he chose within the limits laid down, so that it was virtually impossible to check whether they had worked longer than the hours allowed. This defect was remedied by the Act of 1844, which provided that the hours of work of children and young persons should be reckoned from the time when any child or young person began work in the morning. This Act also placed women on the same footing as young persons as regards their hours of work and further provided that the afternoon shift must consist of different children from those employed in the morning. One retrograde provision of the Act was the reduction of the minimum age for the employment of children from nine to eight. The overall effect of the Act, however, was to subject the working day of adult males to the same limitations since in so many cases the cooperation of children, women or young persons was necessary to their work.

The Ten Hours Bill and after

In the same section Marx explains the forces involved in the campaign for the Ten Hours Bill:

> The factory hands, especially since 1838, had made the Ten Hours Bill their economic, as they had made the Charter their political, election cry. Some of the manufacturers, even, who had managed their factories in conformity with the Act of 1833, overwhelmed Parliament with memorials on the immoral competition of their false brethren whom greater impudence or more fortunate local circumstances enabled to break the law. Moreover, however much the individual manufacturer might give the rein to his old lust for gain, the spokesmen and political leaders of the manufacturing class ordered a change of front and of speech towards the work-people. They had entered upon the contest for the repeal of the Corn Laws, and needed the workers to help them to victory. They promised therefore, not only a double-sized loaf of bread, but the enactment of the Ten Hours Bill in the Free Trade millenium. Thus they still less dared to oppose a measure intended only to make the law of 1833 a reality. Threatened in their holiest interest, the rent of land, the Tories thundered with philanthropic indignation against the 'nefarious practices' of their foes. [p. 267]

In later passages (p. 632; *Capital* III, pp. 627–8), Marx describes the antagonism of the industrial bourgeoisie to this championship by the landed aristocracy of the cause of factory legislation. He refers in particular to the way they retaliated against Lord Ashley by publishing figures of the low wages and poor conditions of the agricultural labourers in his villages; this furthered the anti-Corn Law cause as it demonstrated how ineffective the Corn Laws were in advancing the interests of the actual producers of corn. The passage quoted above is a little unusual in that it is one of the few instances where Marx includes manufacturers amongst those who favoured the Ten Hours Bill.

The economic background to the passing of the Ten Hours Bill was scarcely the most favourable for the Act to have a smooth passage into operation. The years of 1846–7 had been years of crisis, with mills closing down or working short-time.

The manufacturers therefore attempted to counteract the effect of the Act by a general reduction of wages. They also started a campaign for the repeal of the Act, presenting this as what the workers really wanted. The factory inspectors were not deceived either by petitions signed by work-people or by instances of allegedly voluntary working of 12 to 15 hours; they saw that in an unfavourable labour market the workers were hardly free to refuse. In Marx's view, the June insurrection in Paris provoked, by way of reaction, a re-uniting of the various sections of the ruling class, which had been divided over the repeal of the Corn Laws and the passing of the Ten Hours Bill.

In this new situation, the manufacturers 'broke out in open revolt not only against the Ten Hours Act but against the whole of the legislation that since 1833 had aimed at restricting in some measure the "free" exploitation of labour-power' (p. 271). The first step was to reduce the number of women and young persons employed. Next, they attempted to evade the provisions of the Act as to meal-breaks by allowing the workers to have these before they came to work or after they left; Marx notes the decision of the 'crown lawyers' that meal-times must be in the interval during working hours but offers no explanation for this apparent breach of solidarity of the ruling class.

Further steps in the campaign were the exploitation of certain loopholes in the Act in regard to the employment of children in the afternoon, and a unilateral reintroduction by the manufacturers of the relay system that the Act of 1844 had outlawed. The Home Secretary, in response to pressure from the manufacturers, recommended the factory inspectors not to lay informations in such cases unless they had reason to believe that young persons had actually been worked for longer than the statutory hours; in Scotland the Factory Inspector acceded to this suggestion and the relay system reappeared, whereas in England the factory inspectors took the view that the Home Secretary had no power to suspend the law, and continued to prosecute. Here again no explanation is offered for this behaviour of the factory inspectors against the interests of their class. The efforts of the factory inspectors, however, were stultified by the response of the magistrates to informations laid concerning breaches of the Act. The lay magistrates were usually more sympathetic to the mill-owner than to their employees and, in some cases, despite an express statutory provision forbidding mill-owners to act as magistrates in cases concerning the Factory Act, the bench consisted of or included magistrates who were themselves mill-owners. Thus the relay system re-appeared in England too.

Wh n the Court of Exchequer upheld the masters' evasion of the Act, the workers in Lancashire and Yorkshire organised meetings of protest. The situation was unsatisfactory too from the point of view of the employers because of the unevenness in the enforcement of the Act, depending on the character of the local bench of magistrates. The solution was reached in the Act of 1850, which Marx describes as a 'compromise between masters and men'. Under this Act, the working hours of women and young persons during the week were extended from 10 to 10½ with 1½ hours for meal-breaks, the meal-times to be the same for all and the work to be between the hours of 6 a.m. and 6 p.m. The final stage of the development was the closing, by the Act of 1853, of the loophole by which the masters were able to employ children both before women and young persons were allowed to work and after.

In connection with the Acts of 1850 and 1853 there is an apparent gap in Marx's explanation. He points out the attack by the manufacturers on factory legislation during the period of solidarity of the ruling class after the June Revolution in Paris, but he offers no explanation of how this solidarity disappeared or how the Act of 1853 came to be passed at all, except perhaps indirectly in his earlier references to pressure from the work-people and the desire of some manufacturers for consistency in the enforcement of the Acts. Two objections may be made to this: first, it appears to attach a far greater weight to the pressure from the working people than many would regard as warranted in the light of the actual political situation of the time, and, second, no evidence is offered that the unevenness in the enforcement of the Acts disappeared with the passing of the Act of 1850. (In fact, it is improbable that such evidence could be found since the unevenness derived from the mode of selecting magistrates, a matter on which the Act of 1850 had nothing to say. Therefore, any pressure from the manufacturers for the Act of 1853 would simply have been pressure for the repetition of a remedy that had already proved ineffective.)

Marx concludes this section by referring to the 'wonderful improvement' in 'those branches of industry which form the most characteristic creation of the modern mode of production'. He attributes the 'physical and moral regeneration' of the factory workers between 1833 and 1860 to the Factory Acts and sketches briefly their extension to a variety of other industries in the period after 1860.

The last section of Chapter 10, 'The struggle for the normal working day. Reaction of the English Factory Acts on other countries', outlines the development of comparable legislation in France, Belgium and the United States of America. The section also contains some passages of great theoretical importance on the relation of law to society; they will be examined in that context.

Comparison of Marx's and Engels' Views

The first point that stands out in comparing the approaches of Marx and Engels is the one already mentioned, namely Engels' emphasis on the political aspect. His treatment of the Acts of 1819, 1825 and 1831 in terms of the political personalities responsible for their introduction contrasts with Marx's passing reference to them; Marx was not particularly interested in Acts that had no effect on the industry. The same contrast emerges from the treatment of Sir James Graham's unsuccessful Bill of 1843; Engels goes into detail of its parliamentary history whilst Marx ignores it completely. It is typical of this difference that Engels refers to 'the Chartists' where Marx simply says 'the working-class' or 'the working-class movement' and that it should be Engels who considered the adverse effects on the working-class movement of its acceptance of the leadership of 'reactionary elements'.

A second area in which there are differences between the two authors is in regard to the class alignments involved in the agitation for the various Acts. As with the Reform Bill and the campaign for the repeal of the Corn Laws, Engels ascribes a part to the 'petty bourgeoisie' or 'lower middle class', a group that Marx never mentions. Marx's treatment of the class alignment fits quite closely into the picture he gave of the Ten Hours Bill as the revenge of the landed aristocracy on the industrial bourgeoisie for the repeal of the Corn Laws, which is to view the Act in terms of the internal differences within the ruling class; his references to the working class supply the extra dimension of the external relationships of the ruling class to the proletariat. It is a little surprising that Engels' account of the alliance that supported the cause of factory legislation is more detailed than Marx's, but it is perhaps significant that the articles in which he includes the commercial and financial bourgeoisie on the side of the landowners are the later ones, which were written when his collaboration with Marx had had time to mature.

The third area of difference is in the economic aspect of the legislation. The most important difference here is simply that Engels has nothing that even approaches Marx's analysis of the impact of factory legislation on the economy. A relatively minor difference is in the accounts of the economic background that enabled the Act of 1847 to be passed: for Marx the years of 1846–7 were years of crisis, whereas Engels sees them as a sort of in-between period of neither crisis nor prosperity. The difference does not affect the explanation however, since both are agreed that it was not a time in which the full productive capacity could be set to work and that once it became possible again to produce at full capacity the manufacturers' opposition to the Ten Hours Bill became active.

CHAPTER 3

Law and Class Interests: France

I. INTRODUCTION AND BACKGROUND

In this chapter I shall concentrate on the explanations Marx and Engels gave of the events in France between 1848 and 1852. The classic texts on these events are both by Marx — 'The Class Struggles in France' of 1850 (MECW X, pp. 45–145) 'The Eighteenth Brumaire of Louis Bonaparte' of 1852 (PSE, pp. 143–249) (henceforth to be referred to as the 'Class Struggles' and '18th Brumaire'). Engels, on the other hand, had comparatively little to say about the revolutions; the articles he wrote for the *Neue Rheinische Zeitung* in June and July 1848 (MECW VII, pp. 124–7, 130–3, 139–43, 157–64) were far more concerned with the military aspects of the revolution than with the political implications or economic causes. Interestingly, in the period leading up to the February revolution it is to Engels that we owe the accounts of political developments in France.

Apart from an early piece of journalism for *The Northern Star*, in which he mentions a strike at Lyons, the strength of republicanism in Paris and the war in Morocco (MECW III, pp. 527–9), Engels' first examination of the political situation in France was in an item for the same journal in September 1846, now reprinted under the title 'Government and Opposition in France' (MECW VI, pp. 61–3). There, Engels starts by showing how the then government was dominated by the

110

financial interest:

> Three-fifths, at least, of the Deputies are thorough friends of
> the Ministry; or, in other words, either great capitalists, stock-
> jobbers and railway speculators of the Paris Exchange, ban-
> kers, large manufacturers, etc., or their obedient servants.
> The present legislature is, more than any preceding one, the
> fulfilment of the words of Laffitte, the day after the revolution
> of July: Henceforth we, the bankers, shall govern France. [p.
> 61]

The article continues explaining this subordination to the
financial interest and then examines the opposition. The
opposition centred on Paris. The middle-class voters there
belonged to the party of Thiers and Barrot, which was not
completely opposed to electoral reform. Engels describes the
position of the disfranchised groups thus:

> The majority of non-voting tradesmen, shopkeepers, etc., are
> of a more radical cast, and demand an electoral reform, which
> would give them the vote; a number of them are also partisans
> of the *National* or *Réforme*, and join themselves to the demo-
> cratic party, which embraces the great bulk of the working
> classes, and is itself divided into different sections, the most
> numerous of which, at least in Paris, is formed by the Com-
> munists. [p. 62]

The article concludes by noting the choice of Rothschild
rather than Louis-Philippe as the target for attack in a pam-
phlet written by a working man.

Engels follows the developments in a series of articles in
The Northern Star in 1847 and 1848 and in the *Deutsche-
Brüsseler-Zeitung* in 1848. The first of these, 'The Decline and
Approaching Fall of Guizot' (MECW VI, pp. 213–19), is
mainly an account of the scandals and corruption that sur-
rounded the Guizot ministry. Towards the end of the article,
however, he develops a contrast between the position of the
manufacturers in England vis-à-vis the aristocracy and the
fund-holders and bankers who supported them and that of
manufacturers in France vis-à-vis the financial interest (there
being no landed aristocracy in France). He says:

There is no important struggle possible in France between the fund-holders, bankers, shippers, and manufacturers, because, of all the fractions of the middle classes, the fund-holders and bankers (who, at the same time, are the principal share-holders in the railway, mining, and other companies) are decidedly the strongest fraction, and have, with a few interruptions only, ever since 1830, held the reins of government. The manufacturers, kept down by foreign competition in the foreign market, and threatened in their own, have no chance in growing to such a degree of power, that they successfully might struggle against the bankers and fund-holders. [p. 218]

He concludes from this that the government of the bourgeoisie is incapable of achieving progress and can only go backwards. The existing electorate would always elect a government such as that of Guizot and that would necessarily entail the sort of scandals described; the alternative of electoral reform, however, would admit the smaller tradesmen to the suffrage and this would be the end of the monarchy.

The subsequent articles follow the development of the reform movement closely. The movement apears to have started in the middle of 1847 when all shades of the opposition got together to organise a demonstration in favour of the electoral reform. It is apparent from Engels' account of it in November 1847 in 'The Reform Movement in France' (MECW VI, pp. 375–82) that an alliance of such heterogeneous elements would scarcely be stable and a large part of this article is, in fact, taken up with descriptions of the disagreements between the royalist elements and the democratic ones as to whether to drink a toast to the King at the various dinners that were held as a major activity of the campaign. The article continues by listing the points that the Liberals and Radicals had in common — the vote for the learned professions, enlargement of the smallest electoral districts and changes in the manner of conducting elections — and goes on to examine the more radical proposals for lowering the voting qualifications. The most radical was that proposed by the *National*, the paper of the republican small tradesmen. This was to extend the franchise to all members of the National Guard, which would enfranchise the whole class of small tradesmen and shop-keepers. In Engels' view, if this were granted the conflict of interests between them and the financial interest would compel them to join up with the working class and grant universal suffrage, a proposal that the *National* endorsed. The article concludes by examining the concurrent development of the working-class movement, which was preparing for the revolution, the coming of which was beyond doubt.

The instability in the reform movement soon became apparent. The most obvious signs of it were to be found in the split between the *Réforme* and the *National*, which Engels describes in his articles of December 1847 'Split in the Camp' and 'The *Réforme* and the *National*' (MECW VI, pp. 385–7, 406–8). The substance of the split was that the *National* was moving to the right, to support the dynastic opposition, and the *Réforme* was either staying in its old, democratic stance or moving to the left, towards communism. Engels refers to the split between the two papers in the article of January 1848, 'The "Satisfied" Majority' (MECW VI, pp. 438–44) in a passage that conveniently describes the various elements of which the opposition was made up:

> In the meantime the Reform banquets and the polemic between the *National* and the *Réforme* have continued. The allied oppositions, that is, the left centre (M. Thiers' party), the left (M. Odilon Barrot's party) and the 'sensible Radicals' (the *National*), had the banquets of Castres, Montpellier, Neubourg, and others; the ultra-Democrats (the *Réforme*), had the banquet of Chalon. [p. 439]

As described in 'The Split in the Camp' the incident that appears to have been the occasion for the rift to come to the surface occurred at the banquet at Lille. At that banquet Odilon Barrot refused to speak to the toast, 'Parliamentary Reform', unless this was qualified in a manner that endorsed the July monarchy, which obviously would have excluded the republicans from drinking the toast. When the qualification was rejected, Barrot walked out. The split between the two papers arose because in its accounts of the incident the *National* censured Barrot's opponents rather than Barrot.

The final move in the dispute between the two papers is reported in the article 'Extraordinary Revelations' (MECW IV, pp. 469–72 at p. 472), written in mid-January 1848: the papers agreed to submit the dispute to a jury selected by both parties. Whether the jury ever met is unclear; events appear to have overtaken the dispute.

Although Engels had referred to the situation in France as revolutionary, the actual outbreak in February appears to have taken him a little by surprise. In the article 'The Reform Movement in France' he had spoken of the workers' conviction that there would be a revolution. In 'The Movements of 1847' (MECW VI, pp. 520–9), a survey of the advance of the bourgeoisie throughout Europe and America written in the latter half of January 1848, he described the situation in France as 'more revolutionary than elsewhere' (p. 526), but the context makes it clear that he was thinking of the situation between different elements of the bourgeoisie. Consequently, when the revolution did break out in February Engels seemed unprepared for the participation in it of the workers. In the article 'The Revolution in Paris' (MECW VI, pp. 556–8) he describes the events of 22 and 23 February and concludes the first part of the article:

> The bourgeoisie has made its revolution, it has toppled Guizot and with him the exclusive rule of the Stock Exchange grandees. Now, however, in the second act of the struggle, it is no longer one section of the bourgeoisie confronting another, now the proletariat confronts the bourgeoisie. [p. 558]

The final passage, which appears to have been added after the rest of the article was drafted, brings the acount up to date with the latest developments. It starts:

> News has just arrived that the people have won and proclaimed the Republic. We confess that we had not dared hope for this brilliant success by the Paris proletariat. [p. 558]

The addendum continues by referring to the inclusion in the Provisional Government of three democrats of the *Réforme* and a worker besides two men from the *National*. The inclusion of the four democrats seems to have raised Engels' expectations, since he goes on to predict the end of the rule of the bourgeoisie. He might, perhaps, have been warned by the inclusion of the men from the *National* and moderate republicans that the bourgeoisie was by no means finished.

After the February revolution the attention of both Marx and Engels seems to have been taken up with events in Germany, since their next items about France are in the *Neue Rheinische Zeitung* of 25 and 26 June giving the first news of the fresh outbreak of fighting in Paris (MECW VII, pp. 121 and 123). These are closely followed by a series of articles by Engels — 'Details about the 23rd June', 'The 23rd June' 'The 24th of June', 'The 25th of June' (MECW VII, pp. 124–7, 130–3, 134–8, 139–43) — which are mainly concerned with the military aspect of the street fighting. A brief item by Marx under the heading 'News from Paris' (MECW VII, p. 128) informs us of the resignation of Ledru-Rollin and Lamartine, of the military dictatorship of Cavaignac and of Marrast's role on the civil side. The item welcomes the revolution with enthusiasm as the revolution of the proletariat against the bourgeoisie and expresses confidence that the 'victory of the people is more certain than ever'. By 28 June the revolution had been suppressed. In his article 'The June Revolution' (MECW VII, pp. 144–9) Marx contrasts the February revolution, in which the interests of the bourgeoisie and the proletariat coincided, with the June revolution, in which those interests were in direct opposition:

> None of the numerous revolutions of the French bourgeoise since 1789 assailed the existing *order*, for they retained the class rule, the slavery of the workers, the *bourgeois order*, even though the political form of this rule and this slavery changed frequently. The June uprising did assail this *order*. Woe to the June uprising! [pp. 147–8]

By the beginning of July 1848 the *Neue Rheinische Zeitung* was describing the events as a victory for the party of the *National* under Marrast and predicting the decline of that party in favour of the combination of the Orleanists under Thiers with the dynastic opposition; the article in question, 'Marrast and Thiers' (MECW VII, pp. 168–9), is unsigned, but the content, particularly the concern with events in the National Assembly, might suggest that the author was more probably Engels.

For the next few months the authors' attention again was taken up with events elsewhere in Europe, particularly in Germany. The article in August entitled 'Proudhon's Speech against Thiers' (MECW VII, pp. 321–4) is simply an almost scornful critique of Proudhon's economics, and Marx's articles 'The *Réforme* on the June Insurrection' and 'The Paris *Réforme* on the Situation in France' (MECW VII, pp. 478–9, 493–5), written in October and early November respectively, are more concerned with criticism of that paper than with the current political developments. The former of these articles does mention 'the obvious resurrection of the Thiers party' (p. 478) as one of the things it took to bring the *Réforme* to its senses. The latter article, in addition to presenting the *Réforme* as a paper of the republicans who cling to the traditions of 1789 rather than as a 'democratic' journal, also advances an important explanation of the relationship between the bourgeoisie and the monarchy:

> The despotism of the bourgeoisie, far from having been broken during February revolution, was completed by it. The Crown, the last feudal halo, which concealed the rule of the bourgeoisie, was cast aside. The rule of capital emerged undisguised. Bourgeoisie and proletariat fought against a common enemy during the February revolution. As soon as the common enemy was eliminated, the two hostile classes held the field of battle alone and the decisive struggle between them was bound to begin. People may ask, why did the bourgeoisie fall back into royalism, if the February revolution brought bourgeois rule to its completion? The explanation is quite simple. The bourgeoisie would have liked to return to the period when it ruled without being responsible for its rule; when a puppet authority standing between the bourgeoisie and the people had to act for it and serve it as a cloak. A period when it had, as it were, a crowned scapegoat, which the proletariat hit whenever it aimed at the bourgeoisie, and against which the bourgeoisie could join forces whenever that scapegoat became troublesome and attempted to establish itself as an authority in its own right. The bourgeoisie could

use the King as a kind of lightning-conductor protecting it from the people, and the people as a lightning-conductor protecting it from the King. [p. 494].

The difficulty with this explanation is that it implies that the February revolution was inspired by some attempt of Louis Philippe to establish himself as an authority in his own right, which does not easily combine with the earlier explanations of the February revolution as a rising against the financial aristocracy by the other sections of the bourgeoisie with the support of the proletariat.

The next events in France on the political scene were the adoption of a new Constitution of 4 November and the presidential elections of 10 December. The first of these attracted no attention from Marx or Engels at the time. On the second we have an article written by Engels before the election, 'The French Working Class and the Presidential Elections' (MECW VIII, pp. 123–8), and Marx's observations written at the end of the month in his article 'The Revolutionary Movement' (MECW VIII, pp. 213–15). As its title suggests, Engels' article is more concerned with the prospects of the more democratic or socialist candidates, who might be expected to gain the support of the working people. He starts by examining the socialist-democratic party, which he observes,

> even before February, consisted of two different factions; first, of the spokesmen, deputies, writers, lawyers, etc., with their not inconsiderable train of petty bourgeois who formed the party of the *Réforme* proper; secondly, of the mass of Paris workers, who were not at all unconditional followers of the former, but, on the contrary, were very distrustful allies, and adhered more closely to them or moved farther away from them, according to whether the *Réforme* people acted with more resolution or more vacillation. [p. 124]

The article continues by showing how the two wings drifted apart after February when Ledru-Rollin, the leader of the *Réforme* party, accepted an invitation to join the Executive Commission but how the connection was resumed after June when the democratic-socialist petty bourgeoisie went into opposition on the rise of the pure republicans. Engels then considers the prospects of the three presidential candidates, Cavaignac, Louis Napoleon and Ledru-Rollin. He dimisses the first two out of hand:

> For the workers Cavaignac was out of the question. The man who shot them down in June with grape-shot and incendiary rockets could only count on their hatred. Louis Bonaparte? They could only vote for him out of irony, to raise him by the ballot today and overthrow him again by force of arms tomorrow, and with him the honourable, 'pure' bourgeois republic. [p. 125]

The article continues by explaining how Ledru-Rollin lost the confidence of the workers by a speech he made on 25 November in which he took the side of the victors of June, and examining the support the workers gave to Raspail. At this point it is unclear whether the election had already been held; some of the expressions seem to indicate that the voting had already taken place, but no mention is made of the result of the election. Marx's view of the election is contained in a brief passage in 'The Revolutionary Movement':

> But the defeat of the French workers in June was the defeat of the June victors themselves. Ledru-Rollin and the other men of the Mountain were ousted by the party of the *National*, the party of the bourgeois republicans; the party of the *National* was ousted by Thiers–Barrot, the dynastic opposition; these in turn would have had to make way for the legitimists if the cycle of the three restorations had not come to an end, and if Louis Napoleon were something more than an empty ballot-box by means of which the French peasants announced their entry into the revolutionary social movement, and the French workers their condemnation of all leaders of the preceding periods — Thiers–Barrot, Lamartine and Cavaignac–Marrast. [pp. 213–14]

Whether either of these accounts is adequate is questionable if the voting figures given in the *New Cambridge Modern History* (Vol. X, p. 404) are accurate — Raspail 40,000 votes, Ledru-Rollin 400,000, Cavaignac 2½ million and Louis Napoleon 5½ million. Marx's recognition of the peasantry's support for Napoleon is important, but where did Cavaignac get his 2½ million supporters?

II. From the Presidential Election To 2 December 1851

In 1849 the attention of Marx and Engels was taken up to a great extent by events elsewhere in Europe, particularly in Hungary. In fact, the only items specifically on France are two pieces on 'The Situation in Paris' (MECW VIII, pp. 281–5) published in the *Neue Rheinische Zeitung* and its special supplement of 31 January and an article on 'The Millard' (MECW IX, pp. 79–83) published in mid-March. Of these, the second item on the situation in France is mainly a quotation from the first coupled with the claim that the reports from Paris printed below vindicate the interpretation. This situation that inspired the first of the articles arose out of the failure of the ministry to resign on being defeated in the Assembly; the *National* thought that the ministry should resign or that the President should dismiss them. The author of the piece in the *Neue Rheinische Zeitung* thought that the only alternatives were a royalist coup d'état or a 'red republic' (pp. 282–3). The article on 'The Milliard' concerns itself with the agitation for the repayment of the milliard of compensation, which had been granted in 1825 to those who had emigrated after the Revolution. Of more significance than that agitation is the light the article casts on the support the French peasantry gave to Louis Napoleon; the 45 centime tax that the Provisional Government had imposed on the peasants in March 1848 had alienated them from the February revolution.

The remainder of the political developments in 1849, 1850 and 1851 are described in 'The Class Struggles in France' and 'The Eighteenth Brumaire of Louis Bonaparte', which differ from the items considered so far in that they are retrospective rather than contemporary accounts of those events. For present purposes it will suffice to give the main outlines of the developments; Marx's analysis will be examined in section IV (see pp. 128–40 below).

The period from December 1848 to May 1849 was the period of the Constituent Assembly. Initially the Assembly appeared to have had some degree of success in opposing the President; in December they rejected a proposal to retain the salt tax and in January the ministry was defeated on a proposal to ban the clubs. However, the failure to defeat Rateau's motion that the Constituent Assembly dissolve already indicated the weakness of that body even though, or perhaps particularly because, that failure was facilitated by the occupation of the Assembly building by troops. The Bill on clubs was passed in March 1849. When the French army attacked Rome in May the ministry was defeated and an attempt was made to impeach the President on the grounds that this use of French forces was unconstitutional. These events coincided with the election campaign for the Legislative National Assembly.

The Legislative National Assembly convened on 28 May 1849. On 11 June Ledru-Rollin reintroduced his Bill for the impeachment. The Bill was defeated on 12 June and when the petty bourgeois of the Montagne took to the streets in protest the following day they were easily put to rout by Changarnier. The rest of June saw the disbandment of the petty bourgeois sections of the National Guard and the introduction of a new Press Law and a law on associations. The Paris by-elections of July strengthened the Party of Order. In mid-August the Assembly prorogued for two months, during which time the issues of revision of the Constitution was first raised, only to be rejected by the councils of the departments.

When the Assembly reconvened in October the breach between it and the President rapidly came to the fore again. Bonaparte made a shrewd move in linking together in one motion a proposal for the recall of the banished royal families and one for an amnesty for the June insurgents; the rejection of the motion by the Assembly cannot but have strengthened the President's support among the electorate. The dismissal of the Barrot ministry in November 1849 and the inclusion of the financier Fould as Minister of Finance in the new one indicates perhaps that the President was aiming for the support of the financial aristocracy and was prepared to sacrifice the peasants. The abolition of income tax may have been a concession to the former and the restoration, in November, of the wine tax certainly was a sacrifice of the latter. In January and February of 1850 the alienation of the peasantry elicited new laws on education, on school-masters and on the provincial mayors.

The elections of March 1850 marked an important turning-point. The results of the elections showed a decided swing to the Left as Engels describes in the fourth of his 'Letters from France' (MECW X, pp. 27–9). This prompted the majority to commit what was to prove a fatal blunder: they abolished universal suffrage. After this Bill was passed at the end of May there was no way in which the Assembly could appeal to the people against the President. During the summer recess of the Assembly the question of revision of the Constitution was again canvassed and this time the councils of the departments favoured some form of revision. At the same time, Bonaparte was attempting to win over the army and the seeds of his struggle with Changarnier were sown. When the Assembly reconvened in November it failed to take any decisive initiative against the executive. In January 1851 the President dismissed Changarnier and the Assembly still failed to take any really decisive action such as requisitioning armed forces of their own, thereby abandoning yet another means of defence against Bonaparte.

In the first part of 1851 the President established his supremacy over the Assembly. When the Assembly passed a vote of no confidence on 18 January in the ministers he had appointed on 12 January, Napoleon accepted the ministers' resignations, set up a transitional ministry and played off the parliamentary factions against each other until finally, in April, he was able to restore the ministry that had been rejected in January. Effectively, the Assembly was vanquished.

The last year of the Assembly's duration began on 28 May. From that point on the main question was whether or not to revise the Constitution. The summer recess came at a most inconvenient time from the point of view of the Assembly; to have no forum of discussion operative whilst the issue was being pursued could only assist Bonaparte. In August the councils of the department came out in favour of revision. In October, just before the Assembly reconvened, the President proposed the restoration of universal suffrage, which was a shrewd move on his part. When the Assembly met they rejected the restoration of universal suffrage, thereby putting themselves in the wrong vis-à-vis the electorate, and, worse still, they failed to carry a Quaestors Bill that would have given them the power to requisition troops. The way was open for Bonaparte; the coup d'état took place on 2 December.

III. THE ECONOMIC BACKGROUND

Marx and Engels give a detailed account of the economic background to these events in a Review published in 1850 in the *Neue Rheinische Zeitung. Politisch-ekonomische Revue* nos 2, 4 and the double issue 5–6 (MECW X, pp. 257–70, 338–41, 490–532). Two excerpts from the last of these also constitute the bulk of the fourth part of 'The Class Struggles in France'. In the course of the Review the authors survey the economic situation in the major countries of Europe and in America, but, at least as far as Europe is concerned, the central position is occupied by England. In one of the passages quoted in the 'Class Struggles' the reasons for this are given:

> Just as the period of crisis occurs later on the Continent than in England, so does that of prosperity. The original process always takes place in England; it is the demiurge of the bourgeois cosmos . . . This export to England, however, in turn depends on the position of England, particularly with regard to the overseas market. Then England exports more to the overseas lands incomparably more than the entire Continent,

so that the quantity of Continental exports to these lands is always dependent on England's overseas exports at the time. While, therefore, the crisis first produce revolutions on the Continent, the foundation for these is, nevertheless, always laid in England. [MECW X, p. 509 and p. 134]

Because of this primacy of the English economic development, a proper understanding of the events in France requires as a basis an understanding of this economic background.

The double issue of May–October traces the economic development from as far back as 1837. Apparently, the years 1837–42 were a period of almost uninterrupted depression. The next three years were a time of prosperity, which inevitably gave rise to speculation, with railways as the main speculative outlet (pp. 490–1). In the next two years agricultural failure was the significant factor. The potato blight that affected Great Britain and the Continent as well as Ireland in both those years combined with a poor grain harvest to send the price of corn continuously upwards until a peak was reached in May 1847. This was aggravated by speculation, which had been in need of an outlet since the collapse of the railway boom in the early part of the 1846 (pp. 492–3). When corn prices were at their peak, in April and May of 1847, the credit and money markets were also disrupted and numerous large-scale bankruptcies occurred on the Corn Exchange when the discount rate was raised. The raising of the discount rate appears to have been a response to a balance of trade deficit: the increased imports of corn and cotton at prices inflated by the speculation, which itself was partially responsible for the increase, and the investment in railway projects overseas created a drain on bullion that was not countered by any increase in exports since some of the markets for cotton were glutted as early as 1845. The crisis spread from the corn trade to other trades and even into the banking sphere until the Bank Act was suspended in October 1847 (pp. 493–6).

The exact timing of the next upsurge is a little unclear. The Review states:

In the first four months of 1847 the general condition of trade and industry still appeared satisfactory, with the exception however of iron production and the cotton industry. [p. 493]

The decline of iron production is an understandable consequence of the collapse of the railway boom, and the weakness of the cotton industry follows from the rise in prices resulting from the increased price of raw cotton and the glutting of markets, as the Review notes, but if two such central industries were depressed it is hard to see how the general condition of trade could be satisfactory. It might perhaps be safer to date the upturn from somewhere in 1848. This would agree with the point the Review itself makes that the February revolution was *beneficial* to the British economy:

> Already between March and May [of 1848] Britain derived direct advantage from the revolution, which brought here large amounts of continental capital. From this moment on the crisis must be regarded as over; in every branch of business an improvement came about, and the new industrial cycle began with a marked tendency towards prosperity. [p. 497]

The Review continues by illustrating the upsurge by reference to the increase in the manufacture of cotton — from £475 million in 1847 to £713 million in 1848.

The years 1848, 1849 and 1850 were years of prosperity in Great Britain. The harvests in these years were also good both in Britain and on the Continent. All branches of trade except the iron industry, which, presumably, was still suffering from the collapse of the railway boom, also prospered, none more so than the cotton industry. The consumption of the main colonial products also increased constantly in spite of the fact that the low price of corn did not permit any increase in the consumption of these items in the agricultural areas. The discovery of gold in California, the development of Australia and the opening up to trade of the Dutch East Indies not only created new markets but also generated a demand for increased production of steamships (pp. 497–500, 504–6).

The prosperity contained within itself the seeds of its own destruction. The collapse of the railway boom and the succession of good harvests eliminated these potential outlets for speculative capital, the attempt to speculate in raw materials and colonial produce was terminated by an increase in the supply of these commodities and the political unrest on the Continent made government bonds too uncertain. Consequently a greater proportion of speculative capital was diverted into the productive sector, thereby increasing the risk of over-production and glutting of the markets. The Review predicts the collapse of the current period of prosperity:

> If the new cycle of industrial development which began in 1848 follows the same course as that of 1843–7, the crisis would break out in 1852. As a symptom of the fact that the over-speculation which is produced by over-production, and which precedes every crisis, can no longer be far away, we would mention here that for two years the Bank of England's rate of discount has stood no higher than 3 per cent. [p. 502]

After explaining how the increased amount of capital on the loan market and the freer availability of credit enables the Government to reduce the interest rate on its consolidated debts and the landowners to renew their mortgages on favourable terms, it goes on:

> Thus, at a time when the income of all the other classes is rising, the capitalists of the loan market see their own diminished by a third or more. The longer this state of affairs lasts, the more they are compelled to look around for a more profitable investment for their capital. Over-production gives rise to numerous new projects, and the success of a few of them suffices to propel a whole series of capital investments in the same direction, until the bubble gradually becomes universal. [p. 502]

This section concludes by examining the interaction with agriculture and comes to the conclusion that the next industrial crisis will coincide with a crisis in agriculture that will set the manufacturers and the mass of industrial workers against the landowners and the agricultural workers (p. 503).

The other potential cause of a collapse, failure of the cotton crop, is considered by the Review immediately after the authors' examination of the implications of the great industrial exhibition that was to be held in 1851. After asserting that this, the greatest festival of the bourgeoisie, was being held at a time when the bourgeoisie's collapse was at hand, the Review turns to the prospects of the cotton harvest:

> Just as the potato blight in 1845 and 1846, since the beginning of this year the deficiency of the cotton harvest is spreading universal terror amongst the bourgeoisie. This terror has been further considerably intensified since it has become clear that the cotton harvest of 1851 will certainly not prove to be much more abundant than that of 1850 either. The deficiency, which would have been insignificant in former times, is of major proportions in view of the present size of the cotton industry has already had a most restrictive effect on its activity . . . If but a single moderately poor cotton harvest and the prospect of a second one could provoke grave alarm amid the jubilation of prosperity, a few years in succession of outright failure in cotton will inevitably hurl the whole of civilised society temporarily back into barbarism. [pp. 500–1]

At the beginning of 1852 Marx re-examined the commercial developments in 1851 in 'The 18th Brumaire'; the development was much as the Review had predicted but the passage will not be examined till after we have considered the way Marx and Engels saw the Continental development as dependent on the British one, since the passage in question continually relates the French crisis to the English one of which it was a consequence.

At this point we can begin to consider the way in which the development in England affected the Continent, according to Marx and Engels. In the first part of the Review, published in issue no. 2 of the *Neue Rheinische Zeitung. Politische-ekonomische Revue* for 1850, the authors mention in passing that the trade upswing of 1849 'incidentally extended to a great part of continental industry' (p. 264). In the next part, after noting that the crisis that was just breaking (March/April 1850) in England was the first to coincide with an agricultural crisis, they point out:

> This double crisis in England is being hastened and extended, and made more inflammable by the simultaneously impending convulsions on the Continent, and the continental revolutions will assume an incomparably more pronounced socialist

character through the recoil of the English crisis on the world Market. [p. 340]

An Addendum added a month later starts by noting that the usual spring-time upturn in trade had occurred at last and that French industry especially had profited from it and concludes with a reaffirmation of the conviction that the coincidence of trade crisis and revolution was becoming more and more certain (pp. 340–1).

The more important passages are in the double issue of the Review. They are the passages that Engels included in the 1895 edition of the 'Class Struggles' as the concluding part. The upswing that started in 1849 gained momentum in 1850. Tariff reforms in Spain and Mexico improved French export performance in both markets, capital growth was already giving rise to speculation and by August payment in specie, which had been suspended in March 1848, was reintroduced. On the agricultural front, however, things were less rosy: the good harvests of the last few years had forced the price of corn down even lower than in England, so that the 25 million peasants, who already suffered under a crippling burden of debt and taxation, were even worse off than usual. The passage continues with the explanation, quoted above (p. 122), of how England is the demiurge of the bourgeois cosmos and says that a real revolution is only possible when the modern productive forces come into collision with the bourgeois forms of production. It concludes: '*A new revolution is possible only in consequence of a new crisis. It is, however, just as certain as this crisis*' (p. 510). The second of the excerpts included in the 'Class Struggles' (pp. 516–25) is of less importance, being more concerned with the course of political events in 1850; some aspects of the passage are relevant to the examination of Marx's analysis of the groupings involved in the events and will be considered in that context.

The later course of events is described in the passage already mentioned at the end of the '18th Brumaire' (PSE, pp. 143–249, esp. pp. 225–7). Marx starts by pointing out that France had undergone a minor trade crisis, which he illustrates. His account of the interdependence of the French and English crises arises by way of his refutation of the argument of the French bourgeoisie that political uncertainty was the cause of the stagnation in trade. He argued that the industrial crisis in France was the off-shoot of the commerical one in England. After demonstrating the parallels between the two, he cites the uncertainties about the cotton harvest in 1850 and 1851, the inadequacy of the silk harvest and overproduction in the woollen industry as reason for the stagnation. He goes on:

> During such interruptions in the course of trade commercial bankruptcies break out in England, while in France industry itself is reduced to immobility, partly because it is forced to retreat by the competition of the English in all the markets, which becomes intolerable at precisely such moments, partly because, producing luxury goods, it is a preferential target of attack in every business stagnation. Thus apart from the general crisis, France undergoes her own national trade crises, which are nevertheless determined and conditioned far more by the general state of the world market than by the French local influence. [p. 227]

IV. THE ANALYSIS — CLASSES AND FRACTIONS

As the introduction sketched above may have indicated, in the 'Class Struggles' and the '18th Brumaire' the references to law usually occur in contexts where the particular piece of leglislation was an instrument to achieve some political end. Since in these works the political groupings feature more prominently in the explanation, the reaction of the law to the interests of any particular class is at best indirect. There is a further difficulty in that the explanations in these works frequently have recourse to 'fractions' of class, which raises the basic question of whether the concept of 'a class' is sufficiently refined to have any value in the explanation of any specific empirical instance of legislation.

The major problems in this area concern the bourgeoisie and its various fractions, their relationships with each other and the political parties that Marx claimed to represent their interests. There are also similar problems concerning the division of the peasants and the petty bourgeoisie into 'revolutionary' and 'conservative' elements. Finally, there are difficulties as to the criteria that differentiate the 'lumpen-proletariat' from the 'industrial proletariat'.

Marx's analyses of the events in France of the years 1848 to 1852 entail the subdivision of the bourgeoisie on various levels that interrelate but do not exactly coincide with each other. First, there are the fractions based on economic interests. Second, there are non-economic, political/ideological group-ings and, third, there is a distinction between the bourgeoise in general and its parliamentary representatives, although this distinction only emerges at the end of the '18th Brumaire'.

The Bourgeois Republicans

Since the political groupings are more readily identifiable they form the most convenient point of entry into the examination of Marx's analysis of the bourgeoisie. Politically, the main division of the bourgeoisie was that between the Party of Order and the bourgeois republicans. In both works Marx expressly states that the latter were not an economically based fraction of the bourgeoisie:

> The bourgeois republicans of the *National* did not represent any large economically based fraction of their class. As opposed to the two bourgeois fractions, which only under-stood their *particular* rule, their only significance and histori-cal claim lay in having asserted, under the monarchy, the *general* rule of the bourgeois class . . . ['Class Struggles', MECW X, p. 95]

In the '18th Brumaire' Marx supplements this with a positive statement of what did unite the bourgeois republicans:

> This was not a fraction of the bourgeoisie bound together by great common interests and demarcated from the rest by conditions of production peculiar to it; it was a coterie of

republican-minded members of the bourgeoisie, writers, lawyers, officers and officials. Its influence rested on the personal
antipathies of the country towards Louis Philippe, on
memories of the old republic, on the republican faith of a
number of enthusiasts, and, above all, on *French nationalism*,
for it constantly kept alive hatred of the Vienna treaties and
the alliance with England. [PSE, p. 157]

It is noteworthy that in this passage all the factors mentioned
as sources of the influence of the group are ideological rather
than material, so that already in the treatment of this group is
raised the necessity for a more complex theory of the relationship between economic base and the various elements of the
superstructure than the simple uni-directional one in which
the base is the active force and the superstructure is merely the
passive reflector of that influence.

The passage also raises the question of what Marx meant by
the 'bourgeoisie'. The inclusion of 'writers, lawyers, officers
and officials' in the class necessitates a revision of the criteria
by which the class is defined, since the first two of these groups
earn their living by their own labour and the two latter groups
are paid by the state, but none of them derive their living
directly from the exploitation of the wage-labour of the proletariat. It is submitted that any such revision would have to
include within the criteria reference to elements of the superstructure; any revision that simply retained the economic one,
e.g. by including the 'indirect' exploitation of wage-labour,
would be wide enough to include members of the proletariat
who derive benefit from the exploitation of labour in the
production of raw materials.

The Party of Order

Legitimists and Orleanists

The other political grouping of the bourgeoisie, the Party of
Order, was both politically and economically a coalition of
different interests. The political subdivision of this party was
simply between the Legitimists, i.e. those who wanted the
restoration of the Bourbon monarchy, and the Orleanists,

who wanted the restoration of the royal house of Orleans. It is in the relation of these political sub-groups to economic (and other) interests that the difficulties occur.

The accounts of the interests represented by the Party of Order differ from one another in varying degrees. The first account in the 'Class Struggles' explains the secret of the existence of the Party of Order as being the coalition of the Orleanists and Legitimists in one party and continues:

> The bourgeois class was divided into two great fractions which had alternately maintained a monopoly of power — *big landed property* under the *Restoration*, the *financial aristocracy* and the *industrial bourgeoisie* under the *July monarchy*. Bourbon was the royal name for the dominance of the interests of one fraction; Orleans was the royal name for the dominance of the interests of the other. The *nameless realm of the republic* was the only form of rule under which both fractions were able to maintain their common class interest with equal power and without giving up their mutual rivalry. [MECW X, p. 95]

Later, in the third of the articles that make up the 'Class Struggles', in explaining how the Party of Order labelled various demands as socialist that elsewhere were regarded as eminently bourgeois, Marx gives a slightly different account of the fractions of which the Party of Order was composed:

> Abolition of the protective tariffs — socialism! For it strikes at the monopoly of the *industrial* fraction of the party of Order. Regulation of the state budget — socialism! For it strikes at the monopoly of the *financial* fraction of the party of Order. Free admission for foreign meat and corn — socialism! For it strikes at the monopoly of the third fraction of the party of Order, *large landed property* . . . Voltaireanism — socialism! For it strikes at a fourth fraction of the party of Order — the Catholic fraction. [MECW X, p. 125]

The inclusion of the 'Catholic fraction' clearly entails a departure from the explanation of the fractions in terms of economic interests.

Two other passages also call for some extension of the concept of the 'bourgeoisie', although the main lines of the account of the differences between Legitimists and Orleanists are not affected. Both occur in the '18th Brumaire':

> This bourgeois mass was however royalist. One section of it, the great land-owners, had ruled during the Restoration and was therefore Legitimist. The other, the aristocracy of finance and the big industrialists, had ruled under the July monarchy and was therefore Orleanists. The high dignitaries of the army the university, the church, the bar, the academy and the press, were to be found on both sides both in varying proportions. Here in the bourgeois republic, which bore neither the name 'Bourbon' nor the name 'Orleans', but the name 'Capital', they had found the form of state in which they could rule *jointly*. [PSE, p. 165]

> Under the Bourbons, *big landed property* had ruled, with its priests and lackeys; under the July monarchy, it had been high finance, large scale industry, large scale trade, i.e. *capital*, with its retinue of advocates, professors and fine speech-makers. The legitimate monarchy was simply the political expression of the immemorial domination of the lords of the soil, just as the July monarchy was only the political expression of the usurped rule of the bourgeois parvenus. It was therefore not so-called principles which kept these fractions divided but rather their material conditions of existence, two distinct sorts of property; it was the old opposition between town and country, the old rivalry between capital and landed property. [p. 173]

The second of these passages continues to examine the influence of ideological factors on the adherence to one or other of the royal houses; this will be considered later. For the present, however, the issue in hand is the extension of the concept of the 'bourgeoisie'. Both passages indicate the necessity to extend the concept so as to include a periphery of people who do not necessarily derive their living from the exploitation of wage-labour, e.g. lawyers, academics, churchmen and officers.

The second passage also raises the issue we have already seen (p. 48), of whether the industrial and commerical bourgeoisie are one fraction or two. It may also be noted that the classification of the financial aristocracy and the industrial bourgeoisie as one fraction rather than two raises a similar problem; by the time he wrote the third volume of *Capital*

Marx clearly appreciated that the interests of these two groups were by no means identical (see the last two paragraphs of Chapter 23).

It is perhaps useful at this point to recapitulate the composition of the bourgeoisie as it emerges from the passages considered thus far before examining the coherence of the explanations based on these units. The texts disclose four economically based fractions of the bourgeoisie — big landed property, the financial aristocracy, the industrial bourgeoisie and the commercial bourgeoisie — but in addition to these there are also the Catholic fraction and the bourgeois republicans and the periphery of lawyers, writers, churchmen, officers, officials and academics, whose membership of the bourgeoisie must be based on some criterion other than the economic one.

The bourgeoisification of landed property

The main problem in regard to the adequacy of these explanations derives from the recognition that, in practice, the economic interests were not mutually exclusive but rather overlapped in varying degrees. Thus, in explaining the rivalry between the Legitimists and the Orleanists, Marx says:

> This had no other meaning than that each *two great interests* into which the bourgeoisie is divided — landed property and capital — was endeavouring to restore its own supremacy and the subordination of the other interest. We refer to the two interests of the bourgeoisie because big landed property in fact has been completely bourgeoisified by the development of modern society, despite its feudal coquetry and racial pride. [PSE, p. 174]

The first question that this concept of the 'bourgeoisification' of landed property raises is what were the behavioural correlates that Marx envisages as distinguishing 'bourgeois' landed property from 'non-bourgeois'. The question is a difficult one since Marx clearly considered that landed property might be 'bourgeois' whilst at the same time retaining the attitudes of feudalism.

Second, there is the question of whether the concept of 'bourgeoisification' explains too much; it provides an explanation of why the landed proprietors belonged to the bourgeois class rather than a separate one, but only by demolishing the basis of the distinction between the two fractions. This impression is strengthened by the following passage from the 'Class Struggles' where Marx is explaining how the bourgeois coalition could tolerate the rule of the financial aristocracy, which had been consolidated under the republic:

> First of all, the financial aristocracy itself forms a decisive and substantial party of the royalist coalition, whose common governmental power is called a republic. Are not the spokesmen and authoritative figures of the Orleanists the old allies and accomplices of the financial aristocracy? Does it not itself represent the golden phalanx of Orleanism? As far as the Legitimists are concerned, even at the time of Louis Philippe they had taken a practical part in all the speculative orgies on the Bourse, in mines and in railways. The combination of large landed property and high finance is in general a *normal fact*, as evidenced by England, and even Austria. [MECW X, p. 115]

Similarly, earlier in the 'Class Struggles' Marx states:

> Under Louis Philippe it was not the French bourgeoisie as a whole which ruled but only one fraction of it — bankers, stock-market barons, railway barons, owners of coal and iron mines and forests, a section of landed proprietors who had joined their ranks — the so-called *financial aristocracy*. . . The actual *industrial bourgeoisie* formed part of the official opposition; that is, it was represented in parliament only as a minority. [MECW X, p. 48]

If the combination of large landed property and high finance is a normal fact, then the reason for the financial aristocracy's adherence to the house of Orleans rather than that of Bourbon must be sought in some sphere other than the economic. Equally, the recognition that a section of the landed proprietors had joined the financial aristocracy contradicts the opposition of these two interests on which the economic explanation of the support for the two royal houses is predicated. The inclusion of a section of landed proprietors in the financial aristocracy also raises the question of whether economically based 'fractions' of a class are any more adequate units of explanation than classes as a whole, or whether some smaller unit still is required to explain the actual behaviour in question. The difficulty with this, however, is that the logical result of such a process is that the units ultimately arrived at are distinguished purely by political criteria not economic ones.

The financial aristocracy and the industrial bourgeoisie

The exact status of the industrial bourgeoisie and their relationship to the financial aristocracy and the Orleanists is put in question by a passage in the '18th Brumaire' where Marx gives a slightly different account of the alignment of the fractions:

> The *parliamentary republic* was more than the neutral territory where the two fractions of the French bourgeoisie, Legitimists and Orleanists, big landed property and industry, could live side by side with equal rights. It was the inescapable condition of their *joint* rule, the only form of state in which both the claims of these particular fractions and the claims of all other classes of society were subjected to the general interest of the bourgeois class. As royalists, they fell back into their old antagonism, into the struggle between landed property and money for supremacy, and their kings and dynasties formed the highest expression of this antagonism, its personification. [PSE, p. 215]

Here, in contrast with the 'Class Struggles', Marx treats the industrial interest as identical with the financial one.

The dialectical solution

It may be suggested that the difficulty arising out of the different views presented of the relationship between landed property and high finance or that between finance and industry can be solved by recourse to a dialectical understanding. The first difficulty with this is that Marx himself neither described the relationship as dialectical nor gave any indication in the text that he was aware of the conflict between the two accounts he had given, so that the proposed dialectical relationship is rather a commentator's interpretation of Marx than a straightforward account of Marx's thought.

The second difficulty is that a dialectical relationship does not solve the difficulty but merely shifts the question. If it is possible to posit a dialectical relationship between 'the old antagonism between landed property and capital' and the 'combination of large landed property and high finance' as a 'normal fact', it is equally possible to posit a similar dialectical relationships between the industrial bourgeoisie and the financial aristocracy (MECW X, p. 48). Such being the case, the question that now arises is: 'Given substantially identical dialectical relationships between the landed interest and the financial aristocracy and between the industrial bourgeosie and the financial aristocracy, why was it the conflict side of the relationship that governed the political action of the landed proprietors but the community side of the relationship that governed the political action of the industrialists?'

The final difficulty is that the consistent application of dialectical reasoning in such cases would undermine even so central a concept as the 'class struggle'. That there is a conflict of interests between the bourgeoisie and the proletariat is common-place throughout Marx's writings. That there is also a community of interests emerges from his explanation of the failure of the proletariat to resist the abolition of universal suffrage (MECW X, p. 137), from which it appears that the proletariat shared some of the benefits of commercial prosperity. If the conflict of interests provides the thesis and the community of interests constitutes the antithesis, dialectical reasoning would require a synthesis that transcends both; a mere return to one or other side of the antithesis does not achieve this. This problem of the absence of a synthesis applies equally to the attempt to solve the difficulties of conflicting explanations of the relationships between other classes or fractions.

Ideological factors and material interests

In the '18th Brumaire' Marx advanced the beginnings of a theoretical explanation of the relationship between ideological factors and material interests in explaining political behaviour. The importance of the passage justifies extensive quotation:

> It was therefore not so-called principle which kept these fractions divided, but rather their material conditions of existence, two distinct sorts of property; it was the old opposition between town and country, the old rivalry between capital and landed property. Who could deny that at the same time old memories, personal enmities, articles of faith and principles bound them to one or other royal house? A whole superstructure of different and specifically formed feelings, illusions, modes of thought and views of life arises on the basis of the different forms of property, of the social conditions of existence. The whole class creates and forms these out of its material foundations and the corresponding social relations. The single individual, who derives these feelings, etc. through tradition and upbringing, may well imagine that they form the real determinants and starting-point of his activity. The Orleanist and Legitimist fractions each tried to make out to their opponents and themselves that they were divided by their adherence to the two royal houses; facts later proved that it was rather the division between their interests which forbade the unification of the royal houses. A distinction is made in private life between what a man thinks and says of himself and what he really is and does. In historical struggles one must make a still sharper distinction between the phrases and fantasies of the parties and their real organisation and real interests, between their conception of themselves and what they really are. [PSE, pp. 173–4]

The passage continues with the restatement of the opposition between Orleanist and Legitimists as the opposition between capital and landed property already quoted above (p. 132).

There are two main difficulties with this explanation of the operation of ideological factors. First, as we have just seen, the division between the material interests was not in fact so rigid but rather there was an overlapping between them so that the material interests do not provide a basis for the division of political interests. Second, the assertion that 'the *whole* class' creates the form of thought out of its material foundations (a) contradicts the distinction between the various *fractions* of the class, and (b) is not supported by any evidence or even demonstration of the process by which the material foundations are translated into 'modes of thought and views of life'. It is submitted, therefore, that the attempt to explain political actions by reference to economic interests ultimately is inadequate and that the result is that the only units of explanation left are ideological/superstructural ones. (Similar problems beset the distinction between conservative and revolutionary sections of the petty bourgeoisie, (MECW X, pp. 96–7) and of the peasants (PSE, p. 240), and the characteristics that make the lumpenproletariat into a 'mass quite distinct from the industrial proletariat' (MECW X, p. 62) are not immediately obvious.)

The Bourgeoisie outside Parliament

The most serious difficulty in regard to this type of explanation, however, arises out of the distinction that Marx makes towards the end of the '18th Brumaire' between the parliamentary representatives of the bourgeoisie and the bourgeoisie outside Parliament. In making such a distinction, it may be argued, Marx undermined the whole basis of his previous analysis, as such a distinction necessarily entails the recognition that the actions of the parliamentary representatives cannot be explained immediately in terms of the interests of the economic fraction to which they belong but, at best, in terms of the participating actors' view of those interests. Once the explanation is sought in terms of the actors' motives, however, it is difficult to restrict the focus purely to economic motives and not to take into account others, e.g. ideological, which in any given instance may be of greater effect than the economic motive. Marx's own recognition of a 'Catholic' fraction of the bourgeoisie and of a group of 'bourgeois republicans' already implies such an approach.

The introduction of the distinction between the parliamentary and the extra-parliamentary members of the bourgeoisie marks the start of a volte-face in Marx's explanation:

> Not only was the parliamentary party of Order split into its two great fractions and each of these fractions divided within itself, but the party of Order within the parliament had also fallen out with the party of Order *outside* parliament. The spokesmen and writers of the bourgeoisie, its platform and its press, to put it briefly the ideologists of the bourgeoisie, had become alienated from the bourgeoisie itself. [PSE, p. 221]

He then continues to demonstrate how the various fractions of the bourgeoisie supported Louis Bonaparte, the financial aristocracy in particular having their interests well looked after since Fould's entry into the ministry. He then states:

> The financial aristocracy thus condemed the party of Order's parliamentary struggle aginst the executive as a *disturbance of order*, and celebrated every victory of the President over its own supposed representatives as a *victory of order*. By the 'financial aristocracy' must be understood not merely the big loan promoters and speculators in public funds, whose interests, it is immediately apparent, coincide with the interests of the state power. The whole of the modern money market, the whole of the banking business, is most intimately interwoven with public credit. A part of their business capital is necessarily put out at interest in short-term public funds. [p. 222]

In the following pages Marx explains that the industrial and commercial bourgeoisie also viewed the parliamentary bickering between the executive and the parliamentary Party of Order as adverse to their interests (pp. 222–4). It is submitted that the admission of such a gulf between the interests of the bourgeoisie as seen by the parliamentary Party of Order and those same interests as seen by the bourgeoisie outside Parliament invalidates the whole of the previous explanation, based as it is on the premise that the parliamentary party represented *the* interests of the bourgeoisie. In fact it may be argued that the introduction of this distinction removes the material interests from the explanation completely, in favour of the ideological explanation in terms of the participant actors' views of those interests.

V. SPECIFIC PIECES OF LEGISLATION

The Constitution

Of the various specific examples of legislation that these two works consider, the most basic is the Constitution, first because, analytically, the Constitution is prior to any specific piece of law-making and, second, because, in these particular works, the discussion of particular laws is often in terms of their relationship to or conflict with the provisions of the Constitution. The difficulty that arises from this property of the Constitution is that, at that basic level, it is not easy, if it is possible at all, to avoid being drawn from the legal sphere into the political. It is because of this close relationship between the legal and the political at this level that the consistency and validity of the political analysis become relevant.

In both the 'Class Struggles' and the '18th Brumaire' Marx presents the Constitution as the work of the bourgeois republicans. Having led the June struggle in which the proletarians were defeated (MECW X, p. 71), the bourgeois republicans came into political power, which lasted until the election of 10 December. Marx summarises the results of this period as 'the drafting of a republican constitution and the state of siege in Paris' (PSE, p. 158). In both works Marx takes the line that the new constitution was merely a combination of a change of nomenclature and the recognition of existing facts:

> The re-christening of the Christian calendar as a republican one, or of St. Bartholomew as St. Robespierre, no more changed wind and weather than this constitution changed, or was intended to change, bourgeois society. Where it went beyond a *change of costume*, it documented *existing* facts. Thus it solemnly registered as fact the existence of the republic, the existence of universal suffrage, the existence of a single sovereign National Assembly in place of two constitutionally limited Chambers. It registered and regulated the fact of Cavaignac's dictatorship by replacing the stationary, irresponsible, hereditary monarchy with an ambulatory, res-

ponsible, elective monarchy, with quadrennial presidency. To the same degree, therefore, it elevated to the status of a constitutional law the extraordinary power which the National Assembly had providently invested in its chairman in the interests of its own safety after the terror of 15 May and 25 June. The rest of the Constitution was a work of terminology. The royalist labels were torn off the machinery of the old monarchy and republican labels were stuck on. [MECW X, p. 77]

The parallel passage in the '18th Brumaire' (PSE, pp. 158–9) is slightly less detailed and contains no significant differences, but is followed by a discussion of constitutional rights (pp. 159–60) and an extensive analysis of the political weakness of the Constitution (pp. 160–2). The latter of these two points is of less concern in connection with Marx's idea of law since it is the political consideration of the balance of power between the Legislative Assembly and the President; Marx thought that by giving actual power to the executive whilst attempting to reserve moral power to the legislature, i.e. by providing that the legislature could remove the President under the Constitution, whilst the President could only remove the legislature unconstitutionally, the Constitution invited its own overthrow. This reaffirms the analysis he had made in his earlier article 'The Constitution of the French Republic' of May/June 1851 (MECW X, pp. 567–80). In the conclusion of that article, sub-titled 'The Game of Napoleon', he points out that, since Napoleon lacked the majority necessary to revise the Constitution, his only alternative was to defy it (pp. 579–80). At the end of the article he summarises the situation prophetically:

The game of Napoleon is, first, to play off the people against the middle-class. Then to play off the middle-class against the people and to use the army against them both. [p. 580]

As the introduction may have indicated, this is precisely the course of action Napoleon followed.

In his consideration of 'constitutional rights' Marx is much concerned with the relationship between these rights and derogations from the generality in which the Constitution expresses them. Thus he says in the 18th Brumaire:

> The inevitable general staff of the liberties of 1848, personal freedom, freedom of the press, speech, assembly, education, religion, etc., received a constitutional uniform which made it impossible to establish any cases where they might have been infringed. Each of these liberties is proclaimed to be the *unconditional* right of the French citizen, but there is always the marginal note that it is unlimited only in so far as it is not restricted by the '*equal rights of others* and the *public safety*', or 'laws' which are supposed to mediate precisely this harmony of the individual liberties with each other and with the public safety. [PSE, p. 159]

He then cites the constitutional freedom of education and inviolability of the home, both of which expressly refer to modifications fixed 'by law', as illustrating the way in which the Constitution needed to be supplemented by organic laws that had not yet been made.

When these organic laws were made, Marx says, they were introduced by the friends of Order so that in the end the various liberties were regulated in such a way that they could be enjoyed by the bourgeoisie free of the competing claims of other classes. The net result of this was that the name of freedom and its constitutional existence were preserved whilst its actual physical existence was abolished. The same viewpoint is expressed in the article 'The Constitution of the French Republic' (MECW X, pp. 567–80) in an even more forceful way. There Marx claims that the reservations of power to limit constitutional rights by organic laws shows 'that the middle-class can be democratic in *words*, but will not be so in deeds' (p. 568). There is difficulty with this approach to the relationship between constitutional rights and their legal limitation in that, although in the particular case the organic laws probably were such as to favour the bourgeoisie, there seems to be implicit in the argument reference to an ideal situation in which the various freedoms are unlimited. Such an ideal is only tenable on the basis of a view of human nature such as that people are 'basically' good and that it is only the arrangements of society that make people indulge in anti-social behaviour. If one admits, however, that in each individual there is a greater or lesser conflict between egoism and altruism, then the logic of the situation of such individuals living in community requires some normative framework to regulate the conflicts that will arise when an individual allows his egoistic impulses to override his altruistic ones to the detriment of other members of the society; hence, on this view of human nature, rights without legal limitation are not viable.

The Electoral Law

The abolition of universal suffrage in 1850 provides a good illustration of what has been said above about the interrelation of constitutional law and politics; the form was the legal one of the passing of a new electoral law but the substance was political, a redistribution of the means to power. Whilst he relates the parliamentary history of the new electoral law, Marx gives little explanation of the reasons for it except to present it as a reaction of the Party of Order, who were the majority in the Legislative Assembly, to the by-elections of March and April 1850 in which mainly social democratic candidates were returned.

It is not clear whether the initiative for the introduction of the Bill came from the executive or the legislature since Marx says in the 'Class Struggles':

> The government took great care not to take responsibility for the presentation of this bill. It made an apparent concession to the majority by delegating the preparation of the bill to the high dignitaries of this majority, the seventeen burgraves. Thus the abolition of universal suffrage was not proposed to the Assembly by the government; the majority of the Assembly itself made the proposal. [MECW X, p. 136]

This seems to imply that the initiative in fact came from the government but was eagerly taken up by the majority in the Assembly. It does not explain why the government should have proposed such a measure and since it was precisely the votes of the peasants, the petty bourgeoisie and the proletariat that had bought Louis Bonaparte into office (MECW X, pp. 80–1) it is difficult to see what advantage there could have been for him in the revision of the electoral law.

In the '18th Brumaire' the explanation demonstrates abundantly the advantages in this law for the bourgeoisie, but still gives no reason why the Bill should have been proposed by the government:

> The law of 31 May 1850 was the bourgeoisie's coup d'etat. All its previous victories over the revolution had only a provisional character. They were put in question as soon as the existing National Assembly withdrew from the stage. They depended on the chance result of a new general election, and the history of elections since 1848 proved irrefutably that the moral domination of the bourgeoisie over the masses declined in direct proportion to the development of its physical domination. On 10 March universal suffrage declared directly against the rule of the bourgeoisie, and the bourgeoisie replied by outlawing it. The law of 31 May was therefore a necessity of the class struggle. Moreover, the Constitution required a minimum of two million votes to make the election of a President of the Republic valid. If none of the presidential candidates received this minimum, the National Assembly was to choose the President from among the three candidates who received the most votes. At the time when the Constituent Assembly made this law, ten million electors were registered on the voting lists. In the Constitutent Assembly's sense, then, a fifth of the voting strength was sufficient to make the election of the President valid. The law of 31 May struck at least three million electors from the voting list, reducing the number of people entitled to vote to seven million, but it nevertheless retained the legal minimum of two million for the election of the President. It therefore raised the legal minimum from a fifth to nearly a third of the possible votes, i.e. it did everything to smuggle the election of the President out of the hands of the people and into the hands of the National Assembly. Thus the party of Order seemed to have its rule doubly secure by the electoral law of 31 May; it placed both the election of the National Assembly and the election of the President of the republic in the hands of the stationary part of society. [PSE, pp. 194–5]

Whilst the reasons given in this explanation account adequately for the Assembly's passing of the electoral law, Marx also notes that the unintended consequence of the law was to strengthen Bonaparte's hand in his struggle with the Assembly. By demanding the repeal of the law of 31 May he was able to present himself as the champion of the rights of the whole nation and the Assembly as 'the usurping parliament of a class' (p. 230). The Party of Order was thus isolated from any support it might have had in resisting Bonaparte's encroachments. This still leaves unexplained, however, why the government participated in the passing of the law in the first place.

There is a suggestion of a possible explanation of this in the 'Class Struggles'. After explaining that the Party of Order regarded it as a victory over Bonaparte that the government had left the formulation of the law to the Commission of Seventeen and also since the law reduced the electorate and thereby reduced Bonaparte's power base, Marx continues:

> Bonaparte, for his part, treated the electoral law as a concession to the Assembly, with which he claimed to have brought harmony between the legislative and executive powers. By way of payment the base adventurer demanded an increase in his civil list of three million francs. Could the National Assembly enter into a conflict with the executive at a moment when it had divested the great majority of the French people of its rights? [MECW X, p. 139]

The demand of an increase in the civil list as a *quid pro quo* is eminently plausible, but for this to be a completely satisfactory explanation one would have to assume that the initiative for the law came from the Assembly; to reconcile it with a governmental initiative, one would have to suppose that the increase in the civil list was Bonaparte's objective and that the electoral law was the bait with which he lured the Assembly.

Engels considered the electoral law in the sixth and seventh of his 'Letters from France' of 1850 (MECW X, pp. 33 and 34–7). The first of these was written before the Bill was passed. It assumed as a matter of course that the Bill would pass but wondered what sort of reaction it might provoke; Engels clearly though that if it failed to provoke the people the Ordermongers would be encouraged to make more attacks on the Constitution and the Republic. The seventh letter, written at the end of June 1850, attempts to analyse why the people of Paris made the serious mistake of *not* revolting. His explanation was that the working people were not satisfied with the various systems of socialism and were disillusioned with their leaders, so that whilst the people were still looking for a system suited to their needs, they were inactive (p. 35). The continuation of the article makes it appear that the initiative for the electoral reform must have come from the Assembly since Engels specifically describes the 3 million francs increase of the President's salary as 'the price for his adhesion to the Electoral Law' (p. 35).

The Press Law

The press law is considered by Engels in the fourth and eighth of his 'Letters from France' (MECW X, pp. 27–9 and 38–40), and by Marx in the 'Class Struggles' (MECW X, pp. 137–8). The fourth of the 'Letters from France' was written in March 1850 and simply mentions the laws that re-established the newspaper stamp and doubled the caution money along with one on electoral meetings as having been laid on the table of the Assembly; in the context they are simply cited as illustrations of attacks on the people by the 'Ordermongers' (MECW X, pp. 28–9).

A much more detailed account of the measures is given in the eighth letter, written in July when the Assembly was considering the Bill. Engels gives this account of its content:

> Thus the 'law of hatred' has been enacted. The caution money has been raised. The stamp is re-established on newspapers. An extra stamp is put upon the 'roman-feuilleton', that part of a newspaper which is dedicated to the publication of novels . . . All works published in weekly numbers or monthly parts of less than a certain size, are subjected to the stamp in the same manner as newspapers. And lastly, every paragraph appearing in a newspaper must be provided with the signature of the author. [p. 38]

He then examines the effect of the law (p. 39). The first point he notes is that it fell just as heavily on the counter-revolutionary press as on the socialist and republican papers since the requirement that every article must be signed revealed that the authors of the columns in the 'respectable' papers were nothing but hack journalists. The second consequence was the increased cost of newspapers and journals as a result of the higher stamp duties. This would put such items above the reach of many working-men and most country people. This was of less consequence in the countryside since the burden of tax and debts had always been a more important source of disaffection amid the peasantry than anything they read in the press. In the towns the working-men could not be completely excluded from seeing the newspapers and to some extent they could make up for the loss of them by increased activity in secret debating clubs. The third consequence Engels foresaw as a result of the law was the ruin of the publishing and bookselling trades, which he thought would probably contribute to the breaking up of the Party of Order both in and out of the Assembly.

Marx's examination of the press law, in the 'Class Struggles' (MECW X, pp. 137–8), covers much the same points but in slightly less detail. His main emphasis is on the press law as a complement to the electoral law. He goes further than Engels in that he claims the law killed off the revolutionary press — the same point he makes about the law in his passing reference to it in the '18th Brumaire' (PSE, p. 193). Marx does not examine the effects of the law on the country people nor the way the working-men in the towns could compensate for the loss of the papers by forming debating clubs. In the 'Class Struggles' the remainder of his treatment is given over to showing how the removal of anonymity discredited the press of the Party of Order, (MECW X, p. 138). Marx's account brings out particularly tellingly the distinction between intended and unintended consequences of legislation: the raising of the caution money killed off the revolutionary press, which presumably was what was intended by the measure, and the removal of anonymity discredited the majority press, which, again presumably, was the last thing the Party of Order desired.

The Education Law

Another piece of legislation whose effect Marx considers was the 'education law'. Unfortunately he does not specify the exact content of this law, but it appears to have been a measure that favoured the religious interests in the field of education. In the 'Class Struggles' the reference to the education law occurs in the context of a whole number of measures such as the redivision of France into new military districts, a law that subjected school-teachers to the power of the prefect and another that facilitated the dismissal of mayors. Marx describes all these measures as 'Desperate attempts to re-conquer the departments and their peasantry for the party of order' (MECW X, p. 123). He immediately points out, how-ever, that they were not successful in regard to this but were actually counter-productive:

> . . . the laws and measures quoted here made the attack and resistance *general*, the talking-point in every cottage; they inoculated every village with the revolution; *they made the revolution a local matter for the peasants*. [MECW X, p. 123]

By the time he came to write the fourth article of the 'Class Struggles' Marx had revised his opinion of the revolutionary potential of the peasantry. In fact he states that the history of the previous three years proved that 'this class is absolutely incapable of any revolutionary initiative' (MECW X, p. 134). This is echoed in the treatment of the education law in the '18th Brumaire', where he says that it is understandable how three years of rule by the gendarme, *consecrated by the rule of the priests*, 'were bound to demoralise the immature peasant masses' (PSE, p. 188).

The education law raises a difficulty for Marx's theory of the alliance of bourgeois fractions inasmuch as the Legitimate monarchy favoured the Catholic interest whereas the Orleans monarchy tended to favour the free-thinking sections. The education law therefore appeared to be a victory for the Legitimists. Marx faces the difficulty and answers it:

> The *education law* shows us an alliance of the young Catholics and old Voltaireans. Could the rule of the united bourgeoisie be anything else but the despotic coalition of the pro-Jesuit Restoration with its free-thinking pretensions? Had not the weapons which the one bourgeois fraction had distributed among the people for use against the other in their struggle for supremacy to be torn from the people again now that it confronted their united dictatorship? [MECW X, p. 124]

Engels had explained the education law in much the same way in the second of his 'Letters from France' (MECW X, pp. 21–3 at pp. 22–3). Although, like Marx, he sees the law as aimed primarily at the peasantry, Engels thought it was also aimed at the alliance of working-men in the towns.

In the '18th Brumaire' Marx advances substantially the same explanation with the inclusion of a reference to the repressive functions of religion as a further reason why the Voltaireans were prepared to support the measure (PSE, p. 188). This is, of course, very much in keeping with Marx's view of religion but, like that view, it is open to the criticism that it overestimates the influence that religion actually has on the majority of a population even when formal recognition is given to it. The explanation also appears to allude to a 'Catholic' fraction of the bourgeoisie and, as we have seen above (p. 131), this entails a departure from explanation in terms of economic interests.

VI. THE RESULTS OF THE COUP D'ÉTAT

The final treatment of the law that calls for attention in these two works occurs towards the end of the '18th Brumaire' where Marx is describing the results of Bonaparte's coup d'état. The first tangible result of 2 December was, he says, the victory of Bonaparte over the Assembly, of the executive over the legislature, of force without words over the force of words. He then continues in a somewhat obscure way:

> In the Assembly the nation raised its general will to the level of law, i.e. it made the law of the ruling class its general will. It then renounced all will of its own in face of the executive and subjected itself to the superior command of an alien will, to authority. The opposition between executive and legislature expresses the opposition between a nation's heteronomy and its autonomy. France therefore seems to have escaped the despotism of a class only to fall back beneath the despotism of an individual, and indeed beneath the authority of an individual without authority. [PSE, p. 236]

The first sentence here appears to start with a straightforward application of Rousseau's theory of the 'volonté générale' to the particular historical situation but the continuation, equating the general will with the law of the ruling class, has an almost sarcastic ring to it. The use of the Kantian distinction between the autonomy and the heteronomy of the will in the context of the opposition between the legislature and the executive is not entirely free from difficulty since to treat the legislature as representing the autonomy of the nation's will appears to entail the acceptance of the ideological presentation of such assemblies put forward by bourgeois democrats and to ignore the class theory of such institutions entirely.

Finally, in presenting the coup d'état as the victory of the despotism of an individual, Marx leaves himself open to the very criticism he himself makes of Victor Hugo's 'Napoleon le petit', namely that:

> He sees in it only the single individual's act of violence. He does not notice that he makes this individual great instead of little by ascribing to him a personal power of initiative which would be without precedent in world history. [PSE, p. 144]

Indeed this criticism may be made of the greater part of the '18th Brumaire' up to part way through the sixth article (PSE, p. 221), where he introduces the split between the parliamentary Party of Order and the Party of Order outside parliament; only at that point does there appear any coherent relation of the actions of Bonaparte to the interests of a class.

VII. CONCLUSION

To conclude this examination of the 'Class Struggle' and the '18th Brumaire' we may summarise the conclusions reached. First, the recourse to 'fractions' of classes in the explanation indicates that the 'class' itself is not a sufficiently precise concept to be of value in explaining particular events. Second, the introduction of a 'Catholic' fraction of the bourgeoisie and of the 'bourgeois republicans', both fractions not based on economic interest, puts in question the feasibility of explaining politics purely in economic terms. Third, even with the economically based fractions, the inconsistencies in the accounts of their interrelationships and the way they relate to political units, e.g. the discrepancy between the explanation of the difference between Legitimists and Orleanists as the conflict between landed property and capital and the assertion that landed property and high finance normally go hand in hand, raise the question of whether there is any valid explanation in economic terms or whether it is only the political explanation that holds good. Fourth, the admission of a split between the interests of the bourgeoisie in parliament and those of the bourgeoisie outside invalidates the whole attempt to explain parliamentary events in terms of the interests of the bourgeoisie as a whole.

These objections are basic to the whole approach in these works. Consequently they affect, to a greater or lesser extent, the various instances of explanation of specific laws. Thus, in regard to both the Constitution and the electoral law, the question must be asked whether these laws served the interests of the bourgeoisie inside parliament or those outside or both. With the education law the problem is to what extent this was for the benefit of the bourgeoisie as a whole as distinct from the Catholic fraction; it would be equally possible to explain the measure as the price paid for the support of the Catholic fraction. Again, there is the question of whether it was a Catholic fraction of the bourgeoisie rather than some other wider grouping of Catholics in whose interest this measure was passed, which would raise further objections to the explanation in terms of economic units. The general conclusion reached here then is that the relationships between political and economic units proposed in these two works are not sufficiently consistent to support an economic explanation of the events described and that therefore all that is left is a political explanation of political events (including legislation as a political event).

CHAPTER 4

Crime and Criminal Justice

I. ENGELS

Statistical Regularities

A subject to which Engels gave a certain amount of attention in his early works and on which Marx had little to say is that of crime. Engels first referred to it in 1844 in his 'Outline of a Critique of Political Economy' (MECW III, pp. 418–43). The passage occurs towards the end of the work as an aside from the main theme of the ill-effects of private property and the competition it begets:

> Competiton governs the numerical advance of mankind; it likewise governs its moral advance. Anyone who has any knowledge of the statistics of crime must have been struck by the peculiar regularity with which certain causes produce certain crimes. The extension of the factory system is followed everywhere by an increase in crime. The number of arrests, of criminal cases — indeed, the number of murders, burglaries, petty thefts, etc., for a large town or district — can be predicted year by year with unfailing precision, as has been done often enough in England. This regularity proves that crime, too, is governed by competition, that society creates a *demand* for crime which is met by a corresponding supply. [p. 442]

The fascination with statistical regularities is also evident in *The Condition of the Working Class in England* where the interpretation is even more markedly deterministic:

> The contempt for the existing social order is most conspicuous in its extreme form — that of offences against the law. If the influences demoralising to the working-man act more powerfully, more concentratedly than usual, he becomes an offen-

153

der as certainly as water abandons the fluid for the vaporous state at 80 degrees, Reaumur. Under the brutal and brutalising treatment of the bourgeoisie, the working-man becomes precisely as much a thing without volition as water, and is subject to the laws of Nature with precisely the same necessity; at a certain point all freedom ceases. [p. 425]

Even though the assertion that under certain conditions the individual loses his free will and becomes subject blindly to the laws of nature is of a kind that is scarcely amenable to scientific refutation, the latter of these two formulations of the relationship between individual actions and their appearance on the social level is preferable to the former, which treats the statistical regularity as a cause of the phenomena it records. The mistake of failing to recognise the distinction between the statistical regularity and the emprical residue is the same one that Durkheim, following Quetelet, also made, in regard to the statistics on suicide. A further difficulty with the former statement is that there is a slight inconsistency between the idea of a progressive increase in the amount of crime and that of predictability of the amount; to reconcile them it would be necessary to assume predictability also of the growth of population, to name but one factor.

The second of the two passages cited continues by quoting statistics on the increase in crime that show a seven-fold increase between the years 1805 and 1842. The weakness of Engels' use of these statistics is that he does not correlate them either to the extent of law enforcement or to the size of the population. Similarly, the figure he quotes on the following page comparing offences against property to the total population and offences against the person to the total population, in England, France and the Netherlands, are of little value in the absence of relevant information as to the definition of the categories or as to law enforcement in the different countries, to say nothing of any technical problems relating to the collection of the data.

The 'Social War'

Two other passages reveal a slightly different approach, relating crime to what Engels called 'the social war of all against all'. In the 1845 'Speeches in Elberfeld' (MECW IV, pp. 245–64), he contrasts the amount of crime in the existing state of society with what could be expected in the future, communist society:

> In order to protect itself against crime, against direct acts of violence, society requires an extensive, complicated system of administrative and judical bodies which requires an immense labour force. In communist society this would likewise be vastly simplified, and precisely because — strange though it may sound — precisely because the administrative body in this society would have to manage not merely individual aspects of social life, but the whole of social life, in all its aspects. We eliminate the contradiction between the individual man and all others, we counterpose social peace to social war, we put the axe to the root of crime — and thereby render the greatest, by far the greatest, part of the present activity of the administrative and judicial bodies superfluous. Even now crimes of passion are becoming fewer and fewer in comparison with calculated crimes, crimes of interest — crimes against *persons* are declining, crimes against property are on the increase. [p. 248]

He continues by pointing out that if in the present state of society there is a noticeable decrease in crimes of passion, then even more in communist society will the need for criminal justice be reduced and, since in communist society everyone would receive what he needs in the way of material goods, crimes against property would cease.

The second place in which Engels relates crime to the 'social war' is in the chapter of *The Condition* entitled 'Labour Movements' (MECW IV, pp. 501–29). There Engels presents crime in the context of the emotional situation of the working-men in bourgeois society (p. 502). In this, without using the actual word, he approaches quite close to the concept of 'alienation'. He says that the 'working-man is made to feel at every moment that the bourgeoisie treats him as a chattel' (p. 501), and that 'no single field for the exercise of his manhood is left him save his opposition to the whole conditions of his life' (p. 502). In these two observations alone there is exhibited a grasp of a significant aspect of the phenomenon of alienation.

He continues to explain that the revolt of the workers began soon after the first industrial development and passed through several stages. Crime was the earliest for of this rebellion. Engels mentions two specific sorts of crime in this context: first, the poverty of their situation encouraged working-men to steal, and, second, the workers' opposition to the introduction of machinery initially took the form of destroying the machines. Engels distinguishes between these two forms of crime on the ground that theft was an individual act and was never the 'universal expression of the public opinion of the working-men', whereas the destruction of machinery was the first expression of the opposition of the working-men as a class to the bourgeoisie. Although it is questionable whether the riots that led to the destruction of machines ever involved the entirety of the workers in the area affected, the social nature of such riots is an adequate ground to support the distinction Engels makes. He concludes this treatment by pointing out that the lack of success that accompanied these methods necessitated the adoption of a new form of opposition, which was provided by the growth of trades unions.

The most general criticism that can be made of Engels's treatment of crime is that it fails to take account of the distinction between behaviour that contravenes the norms of the criminal law and behaviour contrary to the criminal law that is made the subject of attention by the agencies of law enforcement; the latter is a sub-class of the former and consequently narrower in range. Thus, although he quotes statistics that indicate a massive preponderance of working-class amongst 'criminals' (p. 425), he never asks whether this is because the working-class commits more crimes or because it is caught more often or because other classes are more successful in securing acquittals. Each of these possibilities would call for a different explanation and would raise a series of further questions, e.g. in regard to the second question the obvious further question would be whether the working-class criminal was caught because a greater concentration of law enforcement agencies in areas where such crimes were committed reduced his chances of escaping undetected or whether other factors such as lack of planning increased the possibilities of detection. A second criticism of the explanation is that it over-emphasises the social factors to the complete exclusion of the individual ones.

The Judicial Process

Engel's earlier articles in *Vorwärts* in 1844 on 'The Condition of England. The English Constitution' (MECW III, pp. 489–513), had included several passages in which he examined the law of England as it operated in actual practice, particularly the criminal law. In some of these passages Engels came much closer to a class theory of law than in the passages we have just examined. The point comes across strongest in the last two of these articles (pp. 506–13).

In the first of these, Engels consider the right of habeas corpus/bail and the right to trial by one's peers. The right to bail, he says, is more a privilege of the rich than a right of all since the poor cannot afford to raise bail and therefore are detained in custody pending trial. In examining the right to trial by one's peers, Engels starts by treating it in terms of the difference in practice between the operation of the right in the case of the poor man and its operation for the rich: the property qualification for jury service ensures that the rich man is tried by his peers, the poor man by his enemies.

Engels goes on to develop the theme from the mere generality of the dichotomy between rich and poor to a more specific identification of these groups. He cites recent trials of chartists where the juries were made up of 'landlords and tenant farmers, who are mostly Tories, and by manufacturers and merchants, who are mostly Whigs' and the trial of O'Connell by a jury exclusively composed of Protestants and Tories without a single Catholic or Repealer. This is not quite a class explanation since there is at least equal emphasis on the political and in fact Engels continues by stating:

> Trial by jury is in essence a political and not a legal institution; but because all law is essentially political in origin, the *reality* of legal practice is revealed in it, and the English trial by jury, because it is most highly developed, is the consummation of juridical mendacity and immorality. [p. 506]

The most obvious points of note in this statement is the assertion that all law is essentially political in origin. Perhaps more than any other passage does this reveal beyond doubt that at this early stage of his development Engels had not reached a truly sociological viewpoint. It also tends to suggest that in the early works ambiguous terms should be interpreted in a political rather than a sociological sense.

Quite what Engels meant by claiming that the reality of legal practice is revealed because law is political in origin is not clear. One possible explanation in the context is that the practice of the law discloses a political effect, but the disclosure derives from the practice not the origin of law and consequently this interpretation does not account for the causal relationship that Engels asserts. The difficulty stems from the word 'reality': it is not at all clear what he meant to convey by this term.

In the continuation of the article, Engels contrast the theoretical impartiality of the jury and of the judge with the actual practice. The contrast he makes to some extent anticipates the conclusions reached in this century by the American Legal Realists. (By applying a behaviouristic psychological approach to the study of legal decision-making the Legal Realists reached a conclusion described a 'rule scepticism', i.e. the view that judges make their decisions first and then find reasons to support them in the rules, rather than deciding purely by applying the rules to the facts; some of the school took the method further and applied it to the decisions of juries or judges in finding the facts of the case — 'fact scepticism'.) Engels himself, obviously, did not reach these extreme conclusions, but the very fact that he treated the impartiality of the judge as a 'fiction' indicates the similarity of approach, as does the use of the actual practice of the courts as a criterion of the validity of the theoretical description of the courts.

The scepticism as to the activities of juries is more clearly stated in the following article (pp. 508–9). The main target of his criticism is the rule requiring unanimity in the verdict of the jury; he points out that this leads to recourse to various expedients that technically constitute a violation of the juror's oath, such as drawing straws to settle a deadlock. A further aspect of the criminal trial of the time that Engels seems to have regarded as coming under the general description of 'juridical mendacity' was the formalism by which a defendant could escape because of a purely technical error in the indictment. Engels shows poor judgement here inasmuch as that very formalism was an effective way of mitigating the severity of the law, which, as he himself points out (p. 509), restricted the death penalty to seven offences in only 1837. His point is valid, however, to the extent that such mitigation was by its very nature unsystematic and placed a premium on the services of a barrister, which as Engels observes the poor could not afford.

At the end of the articles he concludes that the whole of the English Constitution and of constitutional public opinion is nothing but a big lie that is constantly supported and concealed by a number of small lies (p. 512). He did not think that this could endure much longer; public opinion was developing in a democratic direction and the democracy that would develop would be the antithesis of middle-class property. This would, however, be only a transitory stage on the way to the rise of socialism. These views are, of course, very much in keeping with his whole outlook in these early years. They do not, however, provide any serious contribution to the understanding of the course of legal development.

II. MARX

Theories of Crime

Marx's views on crime and punishment constitute an area in which it is difficult to maintain that there was an 'epistemological break' between the early works and those of the author's maturity. If anything, the reverse is probably the case: the distinction between 'crime' and 'breach of regulations' made in the 'Debates on the Law on Thefts of Wood' (see above p. 13), carrying as it does the implication that some things are criminal by their very nature, arguably is implicit in the famous passage from Part I of the *Theories of Surplus Value* (see below p. 161), and the Kantian/Hegelian theory of punishment described in *The Holy Family*, written in 1844, is again used in the article on 'Capital Punishment', written in 1853.

The following passage from the 'Debates on the Law on Thefts of Wood' makes the distinction between 'crime' and 'offence' (or 'breach of regulations') most clearly:

> . . . it is at least the legislator's absolute duty not to convert into a *crime* what circumstances alone have caused to be an *offence*. He must exercise the utmost leniency in correcting as a social *irregularity* what it would be the height of injustice for him to punish as an anti-social crime. Otherwise he will be combating the social instinct while supposing he is combating its anti-social form. In short, if popular customary rights are suppressed, the attempt to exercise them can only be treated as the simple *contravention of a police regulation*, but never punished as a crime. Punishment by police penalties is an expedient to be used against an act which circumstances characterise as a superficial irregularity not constituting any violation of the eternal rule of law. [MECW I, p. 35]

Perhaps the key to the view of crime implicit here is to be found in the concept of the 'social instinct' and in its expression in behaviour. The argument appears to be that any regular pattern of behaviour (other than at the purely individual level) is an expression of the social instinct and therefore cannot be a 'crime', since the essence of 'crime' is its *anti-social* nature. The weakness of the argument is that it leaves no place for the recognition of socially conditioned patterns of deviance. It might be argued that such a view could only have been advanced by Marx at this early stage in his development, since implicitly it contains a unitary view of society that is fundamentally contradictory to the class view of society that he was soon to develop. The expression, 'the eternal rule of law', is so heavily redolent of Natural Law thinking that it suffices to note that integral to any such theory is a belief in the existence of some sort of law other than, and superior to, the merely man-made rules of positive law.

The reappearance of such ideas of crime in Part I of the *Theories of Surplus Value* occurs in a difficult passage in the 'Addenda'. The passage appears under the heading 'Apologist Conception of the Productivity of All Professions' (Part I, pp. 387–8) and this gives a hint of the difficulty in interpreting the passage — Marx was using the example of crime to rebut the view that all professions are productive. A further problem is that, given Marx's penchant for sarcasm, it is not always easy to decide with any degree of certainty whether a particular statement was intended to be construed literally or ironically. The main drift of the argument is that if one can call philosophers, poets and clergymen 'productive' because they 'produce' ideas, poems and sermons respectively, then it can equally be said that criminals 'produce'. Marx then illustrates how criminals 'produce' the police, judges, hangmen, etc. and goes on, after a digression on how criminals 'produce' art and drama such as Sophocles' *Oedipus*, to ascribe the technological developments of crime prevention to the productive capacity of criminals. The value of the argument in terms of economic theory is not in issue here; the point at which the view of crime under discussion arguably reappears is close to the beginning of the Addendum, when Marx says: 'The criminal produces not only crimes but also criminal law, and with this also the professor who gives lectures on criminal law' (p. 387). This could be interpreted as reaffirming the priority of 'crime' over 'criminal law', which would again entail the necessity for some norm to act as the criterion by reference to which behaviour was classified as criminal. Whilst the text will bear this construction, it can equally well be interpreted simply as an allusion to the common practice by which the criminal law is amended so as to close off loop-holes that the ingenuity of criminals has discovered in the existing law.

Theories of Punishment

Marx's first examination of theories of punishment appears in one of the chapters he wrote for *The Holy Family* (MECW IV, pp. 3–211, at pp. 176–91). The book is rather obscure because of the indirectness of its approach. The principal object of the work was to criticise the philosophical trend that Marx and Engels referred to a 'critical criticism', i.e. Bruno Bauer and his group. Part of this exercise consisted in criticising Eugene Sue's novel *Les Mystères de Paris*. It is only through Marx's reaction to Sue's views on punishment that his own view emerge and, since Sue's views are implicit in the behaviour of his hero rather than expressed straightforwardly as they would have been in a non-fictional work, the approach is even more circuitous.

The first theory of punishment referred to in the book is that of Bentham. The passage in question is rather a passing reference to Bentham's *Punishments and Rewards* than an examination of the views he actually propounded, but it may serve as a useful illustration of the indirectness of the approach. In the novel the hero, Rudolph, punishes a criminal of extraordinary strength by blinding him. There is a two-fold purpose in this punishment: first, since the crime consisted of an abuse of his strength, the punishment consists of paralysing that strength, and second, by cutting the criminal off from the outer world, Rudolph forces him to look into himself and thus he will be led to repentance. Marx's reaction to this is that Rudolph/Sue:

. . . wants to link *vengeance* on the criminal with *penance* and *consciousness of sin* in the criminal, corporal punishment with spiritual punishment, sensuous torture with the non-sensuous torture of remorse. Profane punishment must at the same time be a means of Christian moral education.

This penal theory, which links *jurisprudence* with *theology*, this 'revealed mystery of the mystery', is no other than the penal theory of the *Catholic* Church, as already expounded at length by *Bentham* in his work *Punishments and Rewards*. In that book Bentham also proved the moral futility of the punishments of today. He calls legal penalties 'legal parodies'. [p. 178]

Apart from revealing that Marx was acquainted with the work of Bentham, the passage is of no great weight, and how Marx came to link Bentham and Catholic theology together must remain something of a 'mystery'.

The account of Hegel's theory of punishment arises out of Marx's view of the theory that punishment must make the criminal the judge of his own crime. In Marx's opinion this latter view was nothing more than Hegel's penal theory:

According to Hegel, the criminal in his punishment passes sentence on himself. *Gans* developed this theory at greater length. In Hegel this is the *speculative disguise* of the old *jus talionis*, which *Kant* expounded as the only *juridical* penal theory. For Hegel, self-judgement of the criminal remains a mere *'Idea'*, a mere speculative interpretation of the *current empirical punishments for criminals*. He thus leaves the mode of application to the respective stage of development of the state, i.e. he leaves punishment as it is. Precisely in that he shows himself more critical than this Critical echo. A penal theory which at the same time sees in the criminal the *man* can do so only in *abstraction*, in imagination, precisely became *punishment, coercion*, is contrary to *human* conduct. [p. 196]

There is, perhaps, a trace of the influence of Feuerbach here, particularly in the idea that coercion is contrary to 'human' conduct. The continuation of the passage amplifies the view that the criminal can only be treated as a man as a mental exercise, by showing that it would be impossible to do so in practice since the practice would entail subjective judgements by the appropriate officials in each case. Marx then continues:

> Plato long ago realised that the *law* must be one-sided and *take no account* of the individual. On the other hand, under *human* conditions punishment will *really* be nothing but the sentence passed by the culprit on himself. [p. 179]

Here again the implicit contrast between the existing conditions and 'human conditions' is distinctly reminiscent of other Feuerbachian works such as the 1844 manuscript on 'Alienated Labour'.

In the article on 'Capital Punishment' (On Britain, pp. 149–52), written at the beginning of 1853, Marx makes much the same critique of Hegel's theory but no longer looks to a 'human' condition of society in which things will be different. In this article he refers to the Kantian theory of punishment in its more rigid formulation by Hegel as the only theory of punishment that recognises human dignity in the abstract. He then quotes the following passage from Hegel's *Philosophy of Right*:

> Punishment is the *right* of the criminal. It is an act of his own will. The violation of right has been proclaimed by the criminal as his own right. His crime is the negation of right. Punishment is the negation of this negation, and consequently an affirmation of right, solicited and forced upon the criminal by himself. [pp. 150–1]

Marx's commentary starts by noting the apparent attractiveness in this theory in that it treats the criminal as a free and self-determined being rather than as a mere object, but he then goes on to point out that on closer examination this reveals it to be the typical German idealist practice of giving a transcendental sanction to the rules of the existing society. Before reiterating the point he had made in *The Holy Family* about the old 'jus talionis', he expresses himself in a way that is suggestive of a deterministic mode of thinking:

> It is not a delusion to substitute for the individual with his real motives, with multifarious social circumstances pressing upon him, the abstraction of 'free will' — among the many qualities of man for man himself. [p. 151]

This could be interpreted in two ways, either as an assertion that 'free will' is an abstraction, i.e. an observers' category imposed on the actual manifestations of behaviour, or as an objection to the attribution to a single causal factor (free will) of behaviour that in reality is due to a multiplicity of operative agencies. After repeating the view that Hegel's theory is merely the old 'an eye for and eye' in metaphysical disguise, Marx expresses his own opinion:

> Plainly speaking, and dispensing with all paraphrases, punishment is nothing but a means of society to defend itself against the infraction of its vital conditions, whatever may be their character. Now, what state of society is that, which knows of no better instrument for its own defense than the hangman, and which proclaims through the 'leading journal of the world' its own brutality as eternal law? [p. 151]

The difference between this and the comparable passage in *The Holy Family*, though obvious, is worth pointing out: the later passage no longer accepts any idea of the criminal passing sentence on himself, under any condition of society; the later passage sees punishment as being essentially and exclusively geared to the preservation of the existing order, of whatever kind that order may be.

Criminal Statistics

There are two quite distinct strands in Marx's reference to criminal statistics. On the one hand, in the article on 'Capital Punishment', he expressly quotes Quetelet and his treatment is taken rather by the predictability of the amounts and kinds of crime (pp. 151–2). On the other hand, in 'Population, Crime and Pauperism' (Ireland, pp. 92–4), written in 1859, the emphasis is more on crime as the product of law-enforcing agencies, in a way that approaches the view now familiar as 'labelling' theory.

In 'Capital Punishment', immediately after the last passage quoted above, Marx quotes from Quetelet's *L'homme et ses facultés*, and cites the author's prediction of the amounts and kinds of crime in France in 1830 based on the statistics of crime in France in 1829. He then continues:

That it is not so much the particular political institutions of a country as the fundamental conditions of modern bourgeois society in general which produce an average amount of crime in a given national fraction of society, may be seen from the following table, communicated by Quetelet, for the years 1822–4. [The table follows] Now, if crimes observed on a great scale thus show, in their amount and their classification, the regularity of physical phenomena . . . is there not a necessity for deeply reflecting upon an alteration of the system that breeds these crimes, instead of glorifying the hangman who executes a lot of criminals to make room only for the supply ot new ones'? [On Britain, pp. 151–2]

Here, the, Marx quite clearly has rejected the Kantian/ Hegelian view that sees crime as an expression of the 'will' of the individual and has adopted the view that crime is the off-shoot of the conditions of society. Whether the use of expressions such as society 'producing' crime and the 'system breeds' crimes should be interpreted in a deterministic manner or simply in the loose sense of everyday usage is unclear. Certainly, Quetelet's formulation did suggest that he thought of social regularities as subject to 'laws' in exactly the same way as regularities in physical phenomena. Finally, in contrast with Engels' treatment of regularities in criminal statistics, it should be noted that Marx avoids the fallacy of attributing to the regularities themselves any causal relationship with the phenomena they record (apart, of course, from the obvious one that the phenomena cause the statistics).

In 'Population, Crime and Pauperism' (Ireland, pp. 92–4), Marx was again concerned with criminal statistics. The starting point of his discussion is the apparent decrease in crime in the years from 1855 to 1858. Marx explains the phenomenon as due solely to the Juvenile Offenders' Act and the Criminal Justice Act 1855. (The former enabled juvenile offenders between twelve and sixteen to be sent to corrective schools rather than prison. Marx describes the latter as authorising 'the Police Magistrates to pass sentences for short periods with the consent of the prisoners'. Technically, the reform was more likely to have been the authorisation of summary trial, i.e. by magistrates, for indictable offences, i.e. those triable by juries, provided the accused agreed; this reveals that the statistics Marx was using were those for indictable offences, not for 'crime' in general). The article then continues:

> Violations of the law are generally the offspring of economical agencies beyond the control of the legislator, but, as the working of the Juvenile Offenders' Act testifies, it depends to some degree on official society to stamp certain violations of its rule as crimes or as transgressions only. This difference of nomenclature, so far from being indifferent, decides on the fate of thousands of men, and the moral tone of society. Law itself may not only punish crime, but improvise it, and the law of professional lawyers is very apt to work in this direction. [pp. 92–3]

The distinction between 'crimes' and mere 'transgressions' is difficult. It might be that here Marx was still retaining his earlier distinction between 'crimes' and mere 'breaches of regulations', in which case it could be argued that even at this late stage of his development we have a vestigial trace of Natural law thinking. If, on the other hand, the distinction is synonymous with the distinction between indictable and summary offences, there is a conflict between what Marx has already stated of the results of the Criminal Justice Act and what he says immediately afterwards using the distinction between 'crimes' and 'transgressons'; since, under the Act, people could be sent to prison both by jury courts, i.e. for 'crimes', and by magistrates, i.e. for 'transgressions', how does the distinction between 'crimes' and 'transgressions' decide on 'the fate of thousands'? Similarly, it is difficult to see how the distinction affects the 'moral tone of society'. A final point of note in the passage is the relative absence of the class dimension; one might have expected that having seen the role of 'official society' in labelling certain acts as crimes, Marx would have gone on to demonstrate that 'official society' is the instrument of the ruling/owning class in protecting its interests and/or suppressing rival classes. (The point is of no great consequence; it may have been simply that Marx took it as too obvious to mention.)

CHAPTER 5

Regulation of Economic Institutions

Marx deals with three types of law that have a more direct effect on the economy. First, there are the attempts made at various times to regulate industry by law. Second, the regulation of rights of property is one of the most important areas for the operation of law. Third, Marx refers extensively to legal regulations affecting the financial and monetary side of the economy.

I. LEGAL REGULATION OF INDUSTRY

In Marx's time the legal regulation of industry was confined rather to the manner in which the enterprise was carried on, e.g. to such matters as safety regulations and limitations on the employment of women, children and young persons. Attempts to control the scale of industry or to promote the growth or development of an industry by law appear to be a phenomenon of the earlier and the later stages of industrial development.

An interesting aspect of Marx's treatment of early legislation relating to industry is that the examples he gives are all of laws that restrict industry. In *The Poverty of Philosophy* of 1847 (MECW VI, pp. 105–212), after citing instances of the Dutch burning spices and destroying clove trees so as to restrict the supply, he asserts that this was general in the Middle Ages:

During the whole of the Middle Ages this same principle was acted upon, in limiting by laws the number of journeymen a single master could employ and the number of implements he could use. [p. 116]

Similarly, in the *Grundrisse* (1857–8) Marx cites two statutes of Edward VI, one of which limited the number of looms and apprentices that could be employed by clothiers and weavers residing outside the cities and the other prohibited the use of machinery (p. 784). The first of these statutes seem to have been aimed at protecting the industry of the towns and cities and preventing the growth of industry in the villages. The second appears to have been a purely negative measure designed to protect the *status quo* and prevent any development in the direction of industrialisation, although the vested interests of the guilds were perhaps also influential in the promotion of such a measure.

In the first volume of *Capital* (Chapter 15, section 5) further instances of legislation against machinery are given from the various parts of Europe in the seventeenth century. With these instances Marx also quotes contemporary sources describing popular disturbances by way of reaction against the introduction of machinery. This offers a possible alternative explanation of the legislation, viz. that it was aimed at preventing the introduction of machinery since this led to breaches of the peace. Even under this explanation the legislation would still be essentially conservative since the popular agitation to which it acceded was itself conservative. If this is the case then there are difficulties in the way of reconciling this legislation with the class theory of law, unless perhaps it could be argued that the popular agitation coincided with or was instigated by or used to advance the interests of either the ruling class or some rising class that opposed them.

II. LEGAL REGULATION OF PROPERTY

Landed Property

A most important passage on the use of law to regulate property in land (and, in fact, on the relationship between law and economy in general) is to be found in the *Grundrisse*:

> Laws may perpetuate an instrument of production, e.g. land, in certain families. These laws achieve economic significance only when large-scale landed property is in harmony with the society's production as e.g. in England. In France, small-scale agriculture survived despite the great landed estates, hence the latter were smashed by the revolution. But can laws perpetuate the small-scale allotment? Despite these laws, ownership is again becoming concentrated. The influence of laws in stabilising relations of distribution, and hence their effect on production, requires to be determined in each specific instance. [p. 98]

This passage will require closer consideration in the section where the issue of economic determinism is considered (see below pp. 193–5), since it contains both a recognition of the influence of laws on the economy and, at the same time, a suggestion of a doubt as to whether law can be effective in the face of a contrary movement of the economy.

An early example of Marx's treatment of legislation affecting rights incidental to landed property is his article of July 1848 on 'The Bill for the Abolition of Feudal Burdens' (PR 1848, pp. 137–42). There Marx compares the Bill and the German revolution of 1848 with the treatment accorded to feudal dues by the French Revolution of 1789. He contrasts the German Minister's readiness to abolish the feudal dues with his reluctance to interfere with the contracts by which the peasants had redeemed some of the dues:

> Of course the minister is attacking property — that is undeniable — but it is feudal, not modern bourgeois property he is attacking. Bourgeois property, which raises itself on the ruins

of feudal property, is *strengthened* by this attack on feudal property. The only reason for Herr Gierke's refusal to revise the redemption contracts is that those contracts have changed feudal property relations into *bourgeois* property relations, and that he cannot therefore revise them without at the same time formally injuring bourgeois property. [p. 142]

The Irish tenants' rights agitation also provided several opportunities for Marx to reflect on the use of law in the regulation of landed property, particularly in the context of the relationship between landlord and tenant. The grievance that inspired the agitation was one that arose out of the general law of landlord and tenant, through the harshness of it was felt much more acutely in Ireland. Under that law, at the end of the lease the property reverted to the landlord and the tenant received no compensation for any improvements he may have made and might even have to pay an increased rent on the renewal of the lease since the property was now more valuable. Marx explains the economics of this, in dealing with ground-rent, in Chapter 37 of the third volume of *Capital* (pp. 625–6). The attempts to secure legislative redress of this grievance are referred to in the articles on 'The Indian Question — Irish Tenant Right' and 'The War Question — Doings of Parliament' written in July and August 1853 (Ireland, pp. 59–65 and pp. 67–9). In the latter article Marx relates the opposition of the House of Lords to three Irish Bills, two of which provided for compensation for the tenant. He observes:

> The House of Lords could, of course, not object to parliamentary interference between landlord and tenant, as it has laden the statute book from the time of Edward VI to the present day, with acts of legislation on landlord and tenant, and as its very existence is founded on laws meddling with landed property, as for instance the *Law of Entail*. [p. 67]

This article continues by showing how strongly the House of Lords felt the infringement of the landlords' interests, so much so that the Bills were in fact shelved. Similarly, in the 'Outline of a Report on the Irish Question of 1867 (Ireland, pp. 126–39), Marx demonstrates how the Encumbered Estates Act 1853 operated to the benefit of capitalists at the expense of landlords by facilitating the sale of mortgaged estates (p. 134). In all these instances, the treatment of the laws assumes as a matter of course and without seeing any theoretical problem that the economy can be affected by legislation.

Abstract Treatments of Property

The more abstract treatments of property usually contain an allusion to the distortion resulting from the attempt to treat of property outside the context of the social relations of production. In his letter to Annenkov of 28 December 1846 (ME Sel Cor, pp. 29–39). Marx says:

> Finally, the last category in Mr. Proudhon's system is *property* In the real world, on the other hand, division of labour and all Mr. Proudhon's other categories are social relations forming in their entirety what is today known as *property*; outside these relations bourgeois property is nothing but a metaphysical or legal illusion. [pp. 33–4]

Exactly the same ideas appear in the opening paragraphs of Chapter 2, Section 4, of *The Poverty of Philosophy* (MECW VI, p. 197), again in the context of a criticism of Proudhon.

A much more important treatment occurs in the *Grundrisse* in the section of the introduction devoted to 'The method of political economy' (pp. 100–9). The passage of particular interest here follows after an extensive criticism of the way 'Hegel fell into the illustion of conceiving the real as the product of thought concentrating itself' (p. 101). This arises by way of a contrast Marx is making between the method he sees as scientifically correct, namely to proceed from simple relations and build up to the level of the state, the world market, etc., and other methods.

Arising out of this discussion is the question whether 'these simpler categories also have an independent historical or natural existence predating the more concrete one?'. He answers:

> That depends. Hegel, for example, correctly begins the *Philo-*

sophy of Right with possession, this being the subject's simplest juridical relation. But there is no possession preceding
the family or master–servant relations. However, it would be
correct to say that there are families or clan-groups which still
merely *possess*, but have no property . . . One can imagine an
individual savage as possessing something. But in that case
possession is not a juridical relation. It is incorrect that possession develops historically into the family. Possession rather,
always presupposes this 'more concrete juridical category'.
[*Grundrisse*, p] 102.

The first problem with this passage is the concept of 'possession without property'. If this is a reference to the fact that
there are or have been societies that have not developed the
concept of 'ownership', then it is true but the formulation
adopted is misleading. Marx rightly notes that the juridical
relation 'possession' is not identical with the physical fact of
possession — the latter is a relationship between an person
and a thing, whereas the former is a relation between persons
in regard to a thing — but ignores the functional identity of the
juridical relations of 'possession' and 'ownership'. Both function as claims to exclude others from the use of the thing in
question. Therefore, insofar as both fulfil this function, it is
illogical to restrict the description 'property' to subject-matter
to which a person relates as 'owner'.

The second difficulty with the passage lies in the attempt to
relate 'possession' to 'the family' and to establish a priority
between them. Behind Marx's presentation there appears to
be a contrast between two views of the development of such
relations as 'possession'. One view, which he elsewhere described as a 'Robinsonade', starts from the single individual
and builds up to more complex units. The other view would
regard such a procedure as fundamentally unrealistic since no
development takes place as long as the individual remains
isolated and the arrival of other individuals presupposes the
existence of some sort of family unit. If this is the meaning,
then the thesis is true but trivial: true, because juridical relations depend on the existence of people and hence of family
units, and trivial because that sort of logical priority is too far
divorced from any empirical manifestation of the relations of

'family' or 'possession'.

Later in the same passage Marx generalises his ideas on the relationship between simpler and more concrete categories, in the following way:

> . . . it may be said that the simpler category can express the dominant relations of a less developed whole, or else those subordinate relations of a more developed whole which already had a historic existence before this whole developed in the direction expressed by a more concrete category. [p. 102]

The category 'possession' fits this description perfectly. In simpler stages of social and legal development 'possession' is the dominant legal category, as Ehrlich demonstrated.* When the category of 'ownership has developed, the relation of 'possession' remains as a subordinate category.

Pre-Capitalist Forms

Marx

Later in the *Grundrisse*, at the end of the fourth and the beginning of the fifth notebook, there is an extensive treatment of early forms of property, which Hobsbawm edited for separate publication under the title *Pre-Capitalist Economic Formations*. The section is headed 'Forms which precede capitalist production. (Concerning the process which precedes the formation of the capital relation or of original accumulation)'. As may be surmised from the inclusion of the concept of 'original accumulation', the treatment of 'property' in these pages is economic rather than legal. Since this work is concerned only with the legal aspects, the section in question will only be examined for the development it discloses on the ideas advanced in *The German Ideology* (see above, pp. 29–30).

The first major difference from the treatment in *The German Ideology* is that private property is no longer seen as arising out of the disintegration of the community. Probably the most important reason for this is that Marx's views of

Fundamental Principles of the Sociology of Law Cambridge, Mass.: Harvard University Press, 1936.

primitive society had undergone development. Where in the earlier work there was a single model of early society, in the *Grundrisse* Marx distinguishes between the Oriental/Asiatic, the Roman and the Germanic types of communities.

In the Asiatic form of community, the unit of proprietorship is neither the individual nor the empirical communities. Instead, as Marx says: '. . . the *comprehensive unity* standing above all these little communities appears as the *higher proprietor* or as the *sole proprietor*; the real communities hence only as *hereditary* possessors' (pp. 472–3). The instances that Marx apparently had in mind were those of oriental despotic regimes, but he does also mention developments of the form in Slavonic communities, in Mexico, among the Celts and in a few clans in India.

The Roman form presupposes as its base the town rather than the countryside. War is the basic activity of this type of community. The grouping of households into the town is a defensive arrangement. The commune is organised in a military way to defend its territory (and also to acquire new territory) and the individual derives his right of private proprietorship of land from his membership of the commune, the military organisation. This creates a reciprocal relationship between citizenship and proprietorship so that 'the private proprietor of land is such only as a Roman, but as a Roman he is a private proprietor of land' (p. 476). Thus Marx describes the relationship in antiquity between state property in land and private property in land in the following way, of which Rome was the prime example:

> The form of state property in land and that of private property in land [are] antithetical, so that the latter is mediated by the former, or the former itself exists in this double form. The private proprietor of land hence at the same time urban citizen. [p. 484]

This relates to the military organisation of the community in that military service (or eligibility for it) is, in such a society, a basic element of citizenship.

The Germanic form approaches more closely to the pure

form of private property. Here the community itself exists in and through the coming together of its members, e.g. in tribal assemblies for war or religious activities. Since the community of language and kinship is prior to the individuals there may still be communal property, e.g. communal hunting and grazing lands, but because the real presence of the commune only exists in the assembly such property is the common property of the individuals rather than the property of the union of them.

In this section, as in the Introduction, Marx rigorously rejects any attempt to derive 'property' from the isolated individual. One example will suffice:

> The relation to the earth as property is always mediated through the occupation of the land and soil, peacefully or violently, by the tribe, the commune, in some more or less naturally arisen or already historically developed form. The individual can never appear here in the dot-like isolation in which he appears as mere free worker. [p. 485]

Thus the economic aim of property in these societies is the reproduction of the individual within the particular relation to the commune that is the basis of the particular society; the particular relation varies, as we have seen, between the Asiatic, the Roman and the Germanic forms.

A second important change in this later presentation of primitive society is that Marx expressly considers the nomadic, pastoral type of society. He recognises the primacy of movable property in such societies:

> Property is, it is true, originally *mobile*, for mankind first seizes hold of the ready-made fruits of the earth, among whom belong e.g. the animals, and for him especially the ones that can be tamed. Nevertheless even this situation — hunting, fishing, herding, gathering fruits from trees, etc. — always presupposes appropriation of the earth, whether for a fixed residence, or for roaming, or for animal pasture, etc. [p. 492]

(In regard to the translation one may wonder whether 'movable' would be a better translation than 'mobile' since this is the more usual term to express in English the technical distinction made in Continental jurisdictions between 'movable' and immovable' property). In the passage quoted there is a slight conflict with what Marx has said on the previous page, namely that what is in fact appropriated and reproduced in such societies is not the earth but the herd. It is a pity that Marx did not investigate this problem further.

Engels

In Engels' writings there is an interval of about thirty years between the writing of *The German Ideology* and the re-appearance of the ideas on law, property, etc. in any extensive treatment. In 1882 in 'The Mark' and again in 1884 in *The Origin of the Family, Private Property and the State* he re-examined the development of private property. As with the writings of Marx, there is a problem in regard to the concept of property and also as with Marx's subsequent works no attempt will be made to expound to full range of the idea; instead, the treatment here will aim primarily at demonstrating to what extent the later works built on the ideas of *The German ideology* and to what extent those ideas were modified or abandoned.

In 'The Mark' (PW, pp. 135–53) Engels considers the old German mark community. In this form of community the basic principle was that the land belonged to the community; although in some circumstances land might be allocated to individuals for tillage, pastures, forests and hunting grounds remained in common ownership. This differs slightly from *The German Ideology* where common ownership was seen as vested in the tribe. The difference is not significant, however, since in the earlier work the authors appear to have been considering the nomadic pastoral stage whereas the mark is a product of a later, sedentary stage and also since Engels shows the relation of the mark to the tribe via the hundred and the shire.

In *The Origin* (ME Sel W pp. 455–593) Engels attempts a much wider-ranging theory. Starting from Lewis Morgan's work *Ancient Society** and Marx's notebooks on it, he presents a monistic theory of the development of society, using

*London: Macmillan, 1877.

materials on the Iroquois Indians, ancient Greece, ancient Rome and tribal Germany, with occasional references to the ancient Celts — Irish, Welsh and Scots — and to tribes in India. Though the validity of such an approach is problematic, I shall not look into that problem; rather I shall compare the treatment made on those presuppositions with that in *The German Ideology*.

The object of *The Origin* was to relate the development of the three institutions of the title to the schema that Morgan proposed for the development of society. Morgan's schema envisaged three stages of human development — savagery, barbarism and civilisation — each of which has a lower, a middle and an upper stage distinguished mainly by criteria of the technological/economic development. It will not be possible here to exclude completely Engels' ideas on the development of the family and the state since they are presented as following the same course of development as property, whereby changes in one have an effect on the others, although primacy is usually accorded to the economic. The thesis Engels advances in regard to property is that communal ownership, by the tribe or by the gens, preceded the development of private property. As Engels presents it, the usual course of development was for the tribe to be divided into two gentes, which with the increase of population subdivided into further gentes, the original two now becoming phratries; the gens consisted of several household communities, each of which comprised several generations.

> He locates the gentile organisation in the overall development thus: Growing out of the middle stage and developing further in the upper stage of savagery, the gens reached its prime, as far as our sources enable us to judge, in the lower stage of barbarism. [p. 576]

According to the schema, the middle stage of savagery was that in which fire came into use, e.g. for cooking, fish became part of the diet and stone axes were used. In the upper stage, the bow and arrow were used, timber was used for building and villages were formed. The lower stage of barbarism was marked by the invention of pottery, the domestication and breeding of animals and the cultivation of plants.

Engels traces the gentile organisation among the Iroquois, the Greeks of Homeric times, the Irish, the Welsh, the Scots, the ancient Germans and the Romans in the time of the kings. At least as far as those of these societies that had reached the stage described as 'lower barbarism' were concerned, the picture presented is of common ownership of land, although he admits private ownership in ancient Greece 'as far back as written history goes' (p. 538). A further common pattern is discerned, at least in the Celtic and Germanic examples, in the division of arable land into strips, which were then allocated to household communities with periodical reallocation, whilst moorland and pastures were for common use.

A major difficulty in regard to *The Origin* is that it is not clear what definition of 'law' Engels had in mind. On the one hand, he refers to rights of inheritance (pp. 494–5, 520, 532, 574, 556), and regulations concerning marital property and divorce (pp. 530, 556). He also expressly refers to the 'laws' of the Twelve Tables in ancient Rome (p. 547) and to the ancient Celtic and Welsh 'laws' (p. 555), and describes the ancient German tribal assembly as a 'court of justice' amongst its other functions. On the other hand, he regards Bachofen's use of the term 'mother right' to describe the system of recognising inheritance through the maternal line as a misnomer, 'for at this social stage there is as yet no such thing as right in the legal sense' (p. 484). Similarly, he says:

> In the realm of the internal, there was as yet no distinction between rights and duties; the question of whether participation in public affairs, blood revenge or atonement for injuries was a right or a duty would have appeared as absurd to him as the question of whether eating, sleeping or hunting was a right or a duty. [p. 576]

The question is, then, what were the criteria to which implicit reference is made in asserting that at a given stage there was no such thing as 'right in the legal sense'. The reference to the actors' views of the matter is not conclusive even if the view attributed was actually held by them, since this simply demonstrates the inadequacy of their conceptualisation of their actions, and the references to the various codifications of 'laws' raise doubt as to whether the view asserted was in fact held by the actors. The difficulty may, of course, be solved by postulation: if one postulates a definition of law in which courts and a specialised division of labour to include lawyers are requisites for the application of the word 'law', then the difficulty disappears. However such a solution merely transfers the problem since it then arises as a problem of justifying the selection of such definitional criteria; do regulations concerning divorce, inheritance, etc. take on such significantly new forms simply because a new way of enforcing them has been developed?

The final difficulty in regard to the treatment of property in *The Origin* concerns movable property and the relationship between the development of private property in movables and private ownership of land. The following passage poses the question neatly:

> But to whom did this new wealth (sc cattle) belong? Originally, undoubtedly to the gens. But private property in herds must have developed at a very early stage. It is hard to say whether Father Abraham appeared to the author of the so-called First Book of Moses as the owner of his herds and flocks in his own right as head of a family community or by virtue of his status as actual hereditary chief of a gens. One thing, however, is certain and that is that we must not regard him as a property owner in the modern sense of the term. Equally certain is it that on the threshold of authenticated history we find that everywhere herds are already the separate property of the family chiefs, in exactly the same way as were the artistic products of barbarism, metal utensils, articles of luxury and, finally, human cattle — the slaves. [p. 493]

It does look very much as if in this passage Engels allows his initial thesis to dictate the interpretation of the evidence. Hence the assertion that 'undoubtedly' the herds originally were the property of the gens even though the authenticated historical examples were of separate ownership of herds. Again, the assertion that the artistic products, metal utensils and articles of luxury belonged to the *family chiefs* rather than to individual persons seems to derive more from the *a priori* view of property relations in such early stages than from any specific evidence. Lastly, the denial that owning the herds made the chief a property owner in the modern sense is either a truism deriving from the definition of 'property owner in the modern sense' or it is a refusal to modify the theory in the light of facts that fail to fit.

Comparison

The later presentations of pre-capitalist economic forms both by Marx in the *Grundrisse* and by Engels in *The Origin* differ from the version given in *The German Ideology*. The earlier account appears to have been based to a greater extent on the model of ancient Rome: the description of 'several tribes living together in one city' and tribal property as 'state property' and the explicit reference to 'dominium ex iure Quiritum' all point to this conclusion. The later works show up the deficiency of the earlier. In *The Origin* Engels presents the Roman state as a development of the closing stages of the kingdom further developed after the expulsion of the last king (pp. 553–4), thus giving due weight to the importance of this change. In the *Grundrisse* Marx develops his account of the interrelationships between citizenship, military service and tenure of land.

Neither the early work nor the later re-examinations are particularly at ease with the problem of property in nomadic pastoral societies. As we have seen, Engels comes dangerously close to forcing the facts to fit the theory in regard to Abraham's ownership of cattle and whilst Marx recognises some sort of priority of movable property he immediately attempts to relate this to the apropriation of the earth. The point should not be over-emphasised, however, since neither of the authors was primarily interested in pre-history or anthropology (although *The Origin* is moving rather in that direction). Additionally, much of the weakness can be attributed to the inadequacy of the materials at their disposal;

even in 1885 anthropology was still relatively in its infancy.

As to comparison of Engels' treatment of property in *The Origin* with that of Marx in the *Grundrisse*, it will suffice here to list the most obvious differences. The first difference is a relatively minor one: Engels' treatment of the Roman form is geared to the late kingdom and the earliest stages of the republic, whereas Marx's account seems to relate more to a slightly later stage in the republic. The second difference is in the author's view of the basic unit of proprietorship: for Marx it was the family whereas Engels preferred the gens. The third difference is the most important since it concerns the basic methodology: Engels' approach is monistic and developmental whilst Marx not only avoids expressing such a monistic view but also uses a typology whose tendency is not particularly compatible with a developmental approach either.

III. MONETARY AND FINANCIAL REGULATIONS

As one might expect, the main references to monetary and financial legislation are to be found in those text that examine purely economic questions, e.g. the *Grundrisse*, the *Contribution to the Critique of Political Economy* and *Capital*. For the same reason one does not expect to find extensive coverage of these questions amongst Engels' writings.

The treatment of these questions in the *Grundrisse* may be dealt with in a fairly summary fashion since the items Marx considers there are given more substantial treatment in either the *Contribution to the Critique of Political Economy* or in *Capital*. There is, for example, a reference to the introduction into Scotland of the Bank Act 1844 in the context of a discussion of the views of certain economic theorists (*Grundrisse*, p. 133), and later (p. 783) he mentions in note form various statutory provisions as to what was to be treated as legal tender, e.g. a statute of Maryland that made tobacco legal tender at the rate of a penny per pound. In neither of these instances is there any concern othern than with the purely economic discussion in connection with which the references were made.

A fuller treatment of the use of legislation in regard to monetary questions is in the chapter of the *Contribution to the Critique of Political Economy* on money (pp. 72–5). There, in addition to noting the necessity to use law to establish units of measure as money (since such units, although purely conventional, must be universal to fulfil the function of money within the area of the given currency), Marx also refers to the abolition by law of silver as a standard of money, as well as to the Maryland statute and Sir Robert Peel's Bank Act, which were referred to in the *Grundrisse*. In the continuation of this passage Marx notes the limits of the effectiveness of law in the monetary sphere:

> The history of the monetary system in England from the reign of Edward III up to the time George II consists of a continuous series of disturbances caused by conflict between the legally established ratio between the values of gold and silver and the actual fluctuations in their value. Sometimes the value of gold was too high, sometimes that of silver. The metal whose value was estimated at too low a rate was withdrawn from circulation, melted down and exported. The value-ratio of the two metals was then once again changed by law; but soon the new nominal value in its turn clashed with the actual value-ratio. [*Contribution*, p. 75]

He concludes the section by stating that all historical experience shows that wherever there are two commodities that are legally valid measures of value in practice only one of them maintains that position (p. 76).

The later reference to the specification by law of the metal content of coins shows a similar approach (p. 113). A contrast is presented between the legal regulation of the metal content of coins and the necessity in any country with an advanced circulation for coins to circulate as symbols of value regardless of any accidental diminution of their metal due to normal wear and tear.

The treatment of the Bank Act of 1844 in Chapter 24 of the third volume of *Capital* typifies Marx's treatment of such economic legislation. The title of the chapter indicates the approach that is to be followed — 'The Currency Principle and the English Bank Legislation of 1844'. The chapter opens with a brief restatement of what was said in the *Contribution to the Critique of Political Economy* in answer to Ricardo's theory that fluctuations in the price of commodities are attributable to fluctuations in the value/supply of money. Marx quotes statistics to show that fluctuations in the bullion reserve affected the market rate of discount but bore no correlation to the price of commodities (*Capital III*, pp. 550–1). He explains the Bank Act as an attempt to put Ricardo's currency principle into practice, i.e. to make the issue of bank-notes conform to the laws of metallic currency by being regulated by the import or export of precious metal. (The import of gold from abroad, according to this theory, proves that currency is in under-supply and thus the value of money is too high and the price of commodities too low; hence bank-notes must be put into circulation in proportion to the newly imported gold. Conversely, with the export of gold, notes must be withdrawn from circulation (pp. 548–9). In the previous chapter Marx had pointed out that the Bank Act 'compels the Bank of England to contract its note circulation at the very time when the whole world cries out for notes' (p. 527), i.e. in times of a crisis of credit when no one would accept payment by bill of exchange but demanded payment in legal tender. Thus the suspension of the operation of the Act in 1847 had the immediate effect of drawing back into circulation the notes that were being hoarded, and thus terminated the panic.

Later in Chapter 24, after referring to the evidence before the Bank Act Enquiry as to the effect of the Act on the rate of discount, Marx takes up the question of the object of restricting the silver content of the Bank of England's bullion reserve to one-fifth of the total reserve. He gives the following answer:

The purpose was to make money dear; aside from the Currency Theory, the separation of the bank into two departments and the requirement for Scottish and Irish banks to hold gold in reserve for backing notes issued beyond a certain amount had the same purpose. This brought about a decentralisation of the national metal reserve, which decreased its capability of correcting unfavourable exchange rates. All the following stipulations aim to raise the interest rate: that the Bank of England shall not issue notes exceeding 14 million except against gold reserve; that the banking department shall be administered as an ordinary bank, forcing the interest rate down when money is plentiful and driving it up when money is scarce; limiting the silver reserve, the principle means of rectifying the rates of exchange with the continent and Asia; the regulations concerning the Scottish and Irish banks, which never require gold for export but must now keep it under the pretence of ensuring an actually illusory convertibility of their notes. The fact is that the Act of 1844 caused a run on the Scottish banks for gold in 1857 for the first time. [*Capital* III, pp. 558–9]

After this description of the purposes and effects of the Act, he continues by quoting the evidence of a private banker to the effect that the Act had provided a rich harvest to bankers and money-capitalists of all kinds (p. 560). This tends to confirm what he had said at the end of the previous chapter about the credit system giving fabulous power to a class of parasites, the bankers and money-lenders to despoil the industrial capitalists and even to interfere in actual production (pp. 544–5). The main purpose of Marx's account of the Act, however, is to demonstrate the invalidity of the currency theory; any references to the practical consequences of the Act derive from this object.

CHAPTER 6

Law and Society

In some ways the problem of the exact nature of the relationship between law and society may be said to be central to the whole understanding of the thought of Marx and Engels on Law. In fact, it might be argued that the relationship between the economic base and the various superstructures built upon it is the central problem in regard to Marx's thought, the problem to which sooner or later any discussion will lead back; the relationship of law to society is simply a specific example of this central problem. Having examined a fairly wide range of instances of the authors' treatment of particular examples of law(s), we are now in a position to consider this central problem. Since Marx was the dominant member of the partnership, to the extent that Engels modified his own views to accord with those of Marx, his views will be presented first. A further reason for this approach is that Engels' views underwent a further change after the death of Marx, which could be explained either as a re-emergence of certain aspects of Engels' own early views or, alternatively, as his response to the exigencies of the praxis involved in his relationship with the German Social Democrats.

MARX

General

We have already seen (pp. 13–20) that in his earlier writings Marx favoured a somewhat uni-directional view of the relationship between law and society: the 'legal nature of things' cannot be regulated by law but rather law must be regulated by the legal nature of things. The question to be considered now is whether his views remained the same in his later writings or, is they changed, in what way they did so.

An important statement occurs in his speech in his own defence at the 'Trial of the Rhineland District Committee of Democrats' in 1849 (PR 1848, pp. 245–64):

> However, society does not depend on the law. That is a legal fiction. The law depends rather on society, it must be an expression of society's communal interests and needs, arising from the material mode of production, and not the arbitrary expression of the will of the single individual. I have here in my hands the Code Napoleon, but it is not the Code which created modern bourgeois society. Instead, it is bourgeois society, as it originated in the eighteenth century and underwent further development in the nineteenth century, which finds its merely legal expression in the Code. As soon as the Code ceases to correspond to social relations, it is no more than a bundle of paper. Social relations cannot make old laws the foundation of the new development of society; nor could these old laws have created the old social circumstances. These laws emerged from these old circumstances, and they must perish with them. They must necessarily alter in line with changes in the condition of life. The defence of old laws against the new needs and claims of social development is fundamentally nothing but a hypocritical defence of outdated particular interests against the contemporary interests of the whole. This *attempt to maintain the legal foundation* involves treating particular interests as *dominant* when they are in fact *no longer dominant*; it involves the imposition on a society of laws which are themselves condemned by that society's condition of life, its mode of appropriation, its trade and its material production; it involves the prolongation of the activities of legislators who only serve particular interests; it involves the misuse of state power in order to forcibly subordinate the interests of the majority to the interests of the minority. [pp. 250–1; Marx's emphasis]

Before drawing any conclusions from the statements quoted here, one must take careful note of the occasion and context in which the speech was made. It would be an extremely questionable procedure to treat the statements on the rela-

tionship between law and society as definitive of Marx's theoretical position on the issues without bearing in mind that in
the specific context his concern was to belittle the law under
which he was charged; it clearly was very much in his own
interest to persuade the jury that such laws lost their validity
when circumstances changed. However, even granted these
limitations, the overall impression that emerges from the
passage is very much one of a uni-directional relationship in
which society is the active participant and law is merely passive.

The argument Marx advances here as to the necessity for
the old to give way to the new in law appears to conflict with
his earlier defence of the customary rights of the poor, in the
articles in 1842 on the 'Debates on the Law of Thefts of Wood'
(see above pp. 13–20). The reasoning in the later work could
be applied so as to argue that since the development of society
had turned the forests into bourgeois property there was no
longer room for such feudal limitations as the right of the poor
to take wood. Clearly this is not an argument that Marx would
ever have advanced, but it does perhaps illustrate the danger
noted above of extending the line of thought to areas other
than the specific ones that were in issue in the trial in which the
speech was made.

A more complex picture of the relationship between law
and society is given in the article of 1853 'The Indian Question
— Irish Tenant Right' (Ireland, pp. 59–65):

> Legislature, magistracy and armed force, are all of them but
> the off-spring of improper conditions of society, preventing
> those arrangements among men which would make useless
> the compulsory intervention of a third supreme power . . .
> England has subverted the conditions of Irish society. At first
> it confiscated the land, then it suppressed the industry by
> 'Parliamentary enactments', and lastly, it broke the active
> energy by armed force. And thus England created those
> abominable 'conditions of society' which enable a small *caste*
> of rapacious lordlings to dictate to the Irish people the terms
> on which they shall be allowed to hold the land and to live on
> it. Too weak yet for revolutionising those 'social conditions',

the people appeal to Parliament, demanding at least their mitigation and regulation. [p. 61]

This passage contains an interesting combination of the recognition both of the dependence of legal institutions on other aspects of society and of the possibility of altering those aspects of society by law. The implications of the first sentence are intriguing. The suggestion that some arrangements among men would 'make useless the compulsory intervention of a third supreme power' contains by implication a whole view of human nature. The view implied is the same as that necessary to make the 'withering away of Law and the State' a credible possibility, namely that everyone is by nature a social being and that it is only the arrangements of society that induce anti-social behaviour. This view, like any view of what people are 'basically' like (i.e. abstracting from the empirical human situation), is of course a value judgement.

A further point worthy of note in the passage is the relatively slight significance Marx attaches to the use of force both in regard to England's alteration of the conditions of Irish society and in regard to the Irish attempts to ameliorate their condition. The implication that amelioration was possible by appeals to Parliament at a time when the people were too weak to obtain them by force does not fit easily with the more extreme formulations of the class nature of Parliament.

In the chapter of volume I of *Capital* dealing with machinery and modern industry Marx twice uses expressions that treat law as a *product* of *society* (rather than of any particular class). Since both of these instances occur in the prefatory remarks with which he opens the particular section, again it is inadvisable to accord them the status of fully developed theoretical utterances, which their appearance in *Capital* would otherwise warrant. Section 3(c) of the chapter begins with the sentence:

The immoderate lengthening of the working-day, produced by machinery in the hands of capital, leads to a reaction on the part of society, the very sources of whose life are menaced; and, thence, to a normal working-day whose length is fixed by law. [*Capital* I, p. 385]

Section 9, on the Factory Acts, opens:

> Factory legislation, that first conscious and methodical reaction of society against the spontaneously developed form of the process of production, is, as we have seen, just as much the necessary product of modern industry as cotton yarn, self-actors, and the electric telegraph. [p. 451]

Whatever the limits that the introductory position puts on the interpretation of these remarks, the departure from the class model of explanation is thought-provoking. The second of the two statements provides a further puzzle, namely that of reconciling the idea of legislation as a 'conscious reaction' of society with the idea of it as a 'necessary product' of modern industry. In fact, in the very evidence Marx himself gives of the reaction of the industrialists to any suggestion of factory legislation there is abundant demonstration that the conscious awareness of the need for such laws was by no means the necessary product of modern industry.

Economic Determinism

A more specialised form of the question of the relationship between law and society is the question of economic determinism. Before one can state whether Marx was or was not an economic determinist it is important to make clear what one means by the expression 'economic determinsim'. At least three approaches can be specified that could be described as determinist. The first would be the view that the relationship between the economic base and the superstructure of society is uni-directional, the base being the active element and the superstructure passive, i.e. the denial that the superstructure can/does influence the base. A second view might be that economic factors are the sole influential ones in regard to any changes, e.g. in law; this would be essentially a denial of the importance of other factors such as ideological ones. The third view is closely related to the second; it is the denial of the relative autonomy of the superstructure. This view, perhaps, summarises the other two in that it entails both the claim that changes in the base must be followed by changes in the super-stucture and the denial that the action of other factors independent of economic ones is also significant. These three views are rather differences of emphasis than distinctly different positions.

Two obvious difficulties arise in trying to determine whether Marx was an economic determinist in any of these senses. First, as he never expressed himself in the direct form e.g. by denying the possibility of the base being influenced by the superstructure, it is a question of what inference as to his view should be drawn from the strong statements about the influence of the base on the superstructure in the absence of any balancing statement about the reciprocal action of the superstructure. Second, where he does refer to the influence of other factors in regard to legislation, e.g. political considerations in regard to the promotion of three Irish bills in 'From Parliament' written in 1855 (Ireland, p. 77), there is still the problem of whether he regarded these factors as independent or whether he would have insisted that, in the final analysis, these political considerations could be reduced to economic ones. In the light of these difficulties it is improbable that an definitive conclusion will ever be reached; all that can be done is to examine the texts and to try and do justice to the whole range of the statements contained in them.

Earlier writings

We have already seen (above p. 13–22) that Marx's early works tended to adopt a highly theoretical mode of expression which suggested a uni-directional view of the relationship between society and law. A particularly clear example is the conclusion of the article of 1842 'Communal Reform and the *Kölnische Zeitung*' (MECW I, pp. 266–73):

> Even apart from general grounds, the *law* can only be the ideal, self-conscious image of reality, the *theoretical* expres-

sion, made independent of the practical vital forces. In the *Rhine Province* town and countryside are not separated in reality. Therefore the law cannot decree this separation without decreeing its own nullity. [p. 273]

Two points call for attention in this passage: first, in describing the law as the theoretical expression of the practical vital forces *made independent*, Marx lays a foundation that could be developed into a theoretical recognition of the autonomy of the various elements of the superstructure, and second, which is more important here, the last sentence clearly denies the possibility of one kind of change in the base being brought about by law.

The question that then arises is whether, at this stage of his development, Marx would have allowed the possibility of other changes in the base being so effected.

The first major work in which Marx considers the relationship between law and society is *The Poverty of Philosophy* written in 1847 (MECW VI, pp. 105–212). There are several passages in the work that have a bearing on the problem:

Truly, one must be destitute of all historical knowledge not to know that it is the sovereigns who in all ages have been subject to economic conditions, but they have never dictated laws to them. Legislation, whether political or civil, never does more than proclaim, express in words, the will of economic relations. [p. 147]

To make 'every commodity acceptable in exchange, if not in practice then at least by right', on the basis of the role of gold and silver is then, to misunderstand this role. Gold and silver are acceptable by right only because they are acceptable in practice; and they are acceptable in practice because the present organisation of production needs a universal medium of exchange. Right is only the official recognition of fact. [p. 150]

In England combination is authorised by an Act of Parliament, and it is the economic system which has forced Parliament to grant this legal authorisation. In 1825, when, under the Minister Huskison, Parliament had to modify the law in order to bring it more and more into line with the conditions resulting from free competition, it had of necessity to abolish all laws forbidding combinations of workers. The more

modern industry and competition develop, the more elements
there are which call forth and strengthen combination, and as
soon as combination becomes an economic fact, daily gaining
in solidity, it is bound before long to become a legal fact. [p.
209]

Of these passages the first two differ from the conclusion of
the article on 'Communal Reform and the *Kölnische Zeitung*'
(above pp. 191–2) only in that they assert that law never *does*
change the economic realities whereas the earlier formulation
goes to the extreme of denying that law *can* can change those
realities. The last of the three equally maintains the priority of
economic change over legal change and even suggests, by the
use of the word 'bound', that there is some necessity in the
change in law. The modification 'before long' does leave open
the possibility, however, of an implicit recognition of the
relative autonomy of law, but the evidence is too slight for any
firm conclusion to be built on this passage alone.

Substantial the same view of the relationship between law
and society is stated in the passage quoted above (p. 187) from
the 'Trial of the Rhineland District Committee of Democrats': social relations make the laws, not vice versa, and the
laws must alter when social conditions change. Similarly, in
the 'Class Struggles' the description of the new French Constitution as a mere change of nomenclature and documentation
of existing facts (see above p. 140) tends towards the same
approach.

Writings after 1855

(1) *The Grundrisse*. Marx's writings of the late 1850s reveal
a certain ambivalence. On the one hand, some passages in the
Grundrisse indicate a move towards a recognition of a reciprocal effect of the law on the economy, although elsewhere in
that work the more uni-directional approach is used. On the
other hand, however, the preface to *Contribution to the Critique of Political Economy* written scarcely two years later
contains one of the most deterministic passages in the whole
of Marx's work.

The relevant passages in the *Grundrisse* all occur in the section entitled 'Introduction'. The first one arises in the context of a discussion of bourgeois economics and particularly the use made in bourgeois economics of the protection by law of property. On this point Marx notes:

> Protection of acquisitions etc. When these trivialities are reduced to their real content, they tell more than their preachers know. Namely that every form of production creates its own legal relations, form of government, etc. In bringing things which are organically related into accidental relation, into a merely reflective connection, they display their crudity and lack of conceptual understanding. [p. 88]

The presentation of the relationship between legal relations and the relations of production as an *organic* one gives a new dimension to earlier statements about this relationship, and the disdain expressed for those who reduce this to a mere accidental relation indicates that this view was not a casual statement on Marx's part but belonged to the core of his thinking. Unfortunately, however, the concept of an 'organic relation' is not self-explanatory; the question therefore arises of what Marx meant by it.

The second of the passages is the one quoted already (above p. 170), in which Marx recognises the possible use of law to maintain property in certain families, for example. After referring to the survival in France of small-scale agriculture, Marx continues:

> But can laws perpetuate the small-scale allotment? Despite these laws, ownership is again becoming concentrated. The influence of laws in stabilising relations of distribution, and hence their effect on production, requires to be determined in each specific instance. [p. 98]

In spite of the interrogative form used in the first sentence, the overall impression created by the first two sentences is of exactly the same view as in the passages from *The Poverty of Philosophy* quoted above. In the last sentence the description of the influence of laws as 'stabilising' the relations of distribution also tends to minimise that influence inasmuch as it suggests an image of the relations of distribution as being influenced by various forces with law intervening to reduce the violence of the disturbances; in such a picture the primary forces are obviously the ones on which law is brought to bear, i.e. the forces emanating from society, rather than the law itself.

The last passage, unfortunately, is expressed in extremely terse noteform. It occurs in a list under the general direction 'Notabene in regard to points to be mentioned here and not to be forgotten':

(6) *The uneven development of material production relative to e.g. artistic development.* In general, the concept of progress not to be conveived in the usual abstractness. Modern art, etc. This disproportion not as important or so difficult to grasp as within practical-social relations themselves. E.g. the relation of education. Relation of the *United States* to Europe. But the really difficult point to discuss here is how relations of production develop unevenly as legal relations. Thus e.g. the relation of Roman private law (this less the case with criminal and public law) to modern production. [p. 109]

The passage is most tantalising. The recognition of this unevenness might lead to the development of a theoretical recognition of the relative autonomy of the superstructure, but in the absence of a more articulated treatment of the point we are left with mere conjectures as to where such development would have led Marx. The last phrase indicates that Marx was thinking of the problem of relating Roman law, which had recently been introduced into Germany, with contemporary economic conditions that were substantially different from those that provided the background against which that law originally developed. The meaning of the parenthetical remark about criminal and public law is not clear: it could mean either that there was less of a problem in the relation of (contemporary German) criminal and public law to modern industry or that there was less problem in the relation of Roman criminal and public law to modern industry.

(2) *The 'Contribution to the Critique of Political Economy'* The fact that in the *Grundrisse* Marx was making tentative

movements towards a more complex view of the relationship between law and society makes it even more surprising that, less than two years later, in the preface to the *Contribution to the Critique of Political Economy* he should express himself in the most deterministic fashion. The passage is all the more important in that here Marx was expressly addressing himself to a conscious examination of his own intellectual development, unlike the other passages where the treatment of the relationship between law and society was usually incidental to some other purpose. The importance of the passage justifies extensive quotation.

> My inquiry led me to the conclusion that neither legal relations nor political forms could be comprehended whether by themselves or on the basis of a so-called general development of the human mind, but that on the contrary they originate in the material conditions of life, the totality of which Hegel, following the example of English and French thinkers of the eighteenth century, embraces within the term 'civil society'; that the anatomy of this civil society, however, has to be sought in political economy . . . The general conclusion at which I arrived and which, once reached, became the guiding principle of my studies can be summarised as follows. In the social production of their existence, men inevitably enter into definite relations, which are independent of their will, namely relations of production appropriate to a given stage in the development of their material forces of production. The totality of these relations of production constitutes the economic structure of society, the real foundation, on which arises a legal and political superstructure and to which correspond definite forms of social consciousness. The mode of production of material life conditions the general process of social, political, and intellectual life. It is not the consciousness of men that determines their existence but their social existence that determines their consciousness . . . The changes in the economic foundation lead sooner or later to the transformation of the whole immense superstructure. In studying such transformations it is always necessary to distinguish between material transformation of the economic conditions of production, which can be determined with the precision of natural science, and the legal, political, religious, artistic or philosophic — in short, ideological forms in which men

become conscious of this conflict and fight it out. [*Contribution*, pp. 20–1]

The tenor of the passage is unmistakeable: the material forces of production are primary and any change in the superstructure merely reflects a previous change in the base. The only mitigation of the outrightly determinist mode of expression lies in the recognition that the changes in the superstructure follow 'sooner or later' on the changes in the base. This formula perhaps relects Marx's observation in the *Grundrisse* (see above p. 195) of the uneven development of the forces of production as legal relations. It would certainly be possible to use the phrase as justification for modifying Marx's presentation by the introduction of a more articulated theory of the relative autonomy of the superstructure. The difficulty with such a procedure is that it hardly agrees with the organic relation between law and economy that Marx took as basic in the *Grundrisse* (see above p. 194). More generally, it would involve a reinterpretation of the other texts in a sense for which their wording provides no support.

As we have already seen (p. 183), in the main body of this work in dealing with the establishment by law of a value-ratio between gold and silver, Marx was clearly of the view that law was impotent in the face of the forces of the actual money market. This tends rather to argue against the reinterpretation of the Preface in a way that favours a more complex relationship between law and society.

(3) *Capital*. In *Capital*, as we saw in examining Marx's view of the relationship between law and society (see above pp. 189–90), the view of law as a *product* of modern industry is clearly stated. In that context the reference was to factory legislation not law in general. For the theoretical statement of the relationship of law in general to the material relations of production one must refer to volume I, Chapter 25. There Marx quotes from Sir F. M. Eden's history of the labouring classes in England: 'There are others who, though they "neither toil nor spin", can yet command the produce of industry, but who owe their exemption from labour solely to civili-

sation and . . . They are peculiarly the creatures of civil institutions'; at this point Marx appends the following footnote:

> Eden should have asked, whose creatures then are 'the civil institutions'? From his standpoint of juridical illustion, he does not regard the law as a product of the material relations of production, but conversely the relations of production as the products of law. Linguet overthrew Montesquieu's illusory 'Esprit des lois' with one word: 'L'esprit des lois, c'est la propriété.' [p. 577. n2]

Inasmuch as the statement is directed against one that erred in the opposite direction, it would not be safe to attach too much weight to it on its own, but in the context of the rest of the statements we have seen it may fairly be regarded as evidence of the general trend of Marx's thought.

Finally, in volume III of *Capital*, Chapter 21, there is a difficult passage in which Marx deals with the relationship of justice to the relations of production:

> The justice of the transactions between agents of production rests on the fact that these arise as natural consequences out of the production relationships. The juristic forms in which these economic transactions appear as wilful acts of the parties concerned, as expressions of their common will and as contracts that may be enforced by law against some individual party, cannot, being mere forms determine this content. They merely express it. This content is just whenever it corresponds, is appropriate to the mode of production. It is unjust whenever it contradicts that mode. Slavery on the basis of capitalist production is unjust; likewise fraud in the quality of commodities. [pp. 339–40]

The first point of note here is that it underestimates the importance of legal forms. The history of English law reveals not a few instances where substantive rights have been altered by means of changes in procedure; in fact this phenomenon is not uncommon in many legal systems at certain stages of their development.

The second point is that the concept of justice expressed here is a very strange one, which has remarkably conservative overtones. With this concept of justice, for example, it would be impossible to criticise existing wage-rates as falling short of

a 'just wage', since the existing going rate for the job corresponds to the mode of production. If one attempts to avoid
such a conclusion by modifying the meaning of the term
'corresponds', it can only be done by implicit reference to
some extraneous standard of values and this strains the meaning of Marx's statement since he appears to be expressly
limiting the criterion of justice to the empirical correlation
between the content of the transaction and the mode of
production. If Marx did not intend this but rather was con-
templating some extrinsic standard of what was 'appropriate'
to the mode of production, then the sentence says nothing
since we are not told what this extrinsic standard was.

Conclusion

Having considered the texts, we are now in a position to
compare these writings with the concepts of economic
determinism mentioned earlier. The theoretical treatments
will be considered separately from the empirical ones and a
contrast will be made between the two.

The first of the ideas of economic determinism suggested
was the uni-directional view of the relationship between the
economic base and the superstructure of society, the denial
that the superstructure can/does influence the base. Statements denying the *possibility* of such influence are rare: the
conclusion of the article 'Communal Reform and the
Kölnisch Zeitung' (above pp. 191-2) and the passage from 'The
Trial of the Rhineland District Committee of Democrats'
(above p. 187) are the most obvious examples of this kind,
although the doubt expressed in the *Grundrisse* as to whether
laws could perpetuate the small-scale allotment (above p.
194) tends in the same direction. The passages from *The
Poverty of Philosophy* (above pp. 192-3) are the most explicit
statements to the effect that changes in law never do more than
reflect changes in the economic base. The various statements
treating law as a *product* of the material relations of production also tend to favour this view, e.g. *Capital* and above all

the preface to the *Contribution to the Critique of Political Economy* (above pp. 196–7).

The second concept of economic determinism, namely the denial of the operation of factors other than the economic in influencing changes in law is not evident in Marx's writings. His views on such factors are best seen in the preface to the *Contribution to the Critique of Political Economy* (above p. 196) where he describes them as 'ideological forms' in which the conflict between old and the newly transformed relations of production takes place. Even in this text, however, the reduction of such factors to mere forms, with the material transformations as the content or substance, tends to minimise their importance.

All the statements treating law as a product of material factors tend also to favour the third version of economic determinism, the denial of the relative autonomy of the superstructure. The 'organic' relationship between law and the relations of production posited in the *Grundrisse* (see above p. 194) argues even more strongly in this direction.

On the other hand, there are several points at which Marx seems to have been on the verge of an explicit recognition of the relative autonomy of law. Thus, in the article 'Communal Reform and the *Kölnische Zeitung*' (above p. 191), the description of law as an expression of the vital forces 'made independent' could easily be developed into a fully articulated theoretical treatment of the autonomy of law if a suitable development were given to the ideas of 'independence'. Similarly, in *The Poverty of Philosophy* (above p. 192) and the *Contribution to the Critique of Political Economy* (above p. 196), the assertion that changes in the superstructure follow 'before long' (in the former) or 'sooner or later' (in the latter) equally leaves room for a relative autonomy, as does the statement in volume I of *Capital* that 'The Labour Statutes . . . were first formally repealed in England in 1813, long after changes in methods of production had rendered them absolete' (p. 257 n3). The nearest to an express statement of the relative autonomy is the terse note from the

Gundrisse (above, p. 195), but it is a pity that the point was not taken up and developed more fully.

The empirical treatments of law consider both the economic interests behind the passing of laws and the economic effects resulting from them. In regard to the Corn Laws, for example, the main treatment of their effects is in volume III of *Capital*, whilst explanations of the class alignments behind their repeal are widespread — compare pp. 69–71 above with pp. 75–9 above. With the Factory Acts the picture is somewhat different; here it is the class interests behind the legislation that receive less attention while the economic effects are fully examined (above pp. 97–101). With the treatment of the Factory Acts in volume I of *Capital* there is also an extensive consideration of the actual operation of the Acts and their enforcement. The treatment of early legislation against machines leaves the effect on the development of the economy unstated (see above p. 169), whilst in regard to the Tudor Vagrancy Laws and the Statute of Labourers 1349 the treatment tends to suggest that the economic objective of compelling people to become wage-labourers was the motive for the passing of the Acts and its achievements was their effect (see above pp. 41–3). The account of the Bank Acts of 1844 and 1845, in Chapter 24 of volume III of *Capital* virtually ignores the economic interests behind the passing of the Acts, using them rather as an argument against the Ricardian theory on which they were based (see above pp. 184–5).

What conclusion, then, is to be drawn from this survey of Marx's writings on law and the economy? The conclusion I would draw is that whilst in the empirical treatments Marx clearly recognised the influence of law on the economy, he never articulated that insight into his theoretical treatment of the relationship. Consequently, his theoretical view remained uni-directional and deterministic even though in certain passages a basis is laid which might have been developed into a full recognition of the relative autonomy of elements of the superstructure such as law.

II. ENGELS

Before examining the question of Engels' view of the relationship between base and superstructure, which is one of the
areas where he most clearly developed the ideas of Marx, it is
desirable to summarise what has already been said to Engels'
own views of law. He appears to waiver between two
different views of law. On the one hand in some texts he
adopts a political, almost common-sense, view of the growth
and operation of law, whilst, on the other hand, other passages clearly adopt a class explanation.

Political Interpretation

As we have seen, in dealing with the repeal of the Corn Laws
Engels regarded political parties in England as coinciding with
social ranks and classes (see above p. 72). This creates a
difficulty in deciding whether his explanation is sociological or
political. If it is decided that the class element is uppermost in
these explanations there is the further problem of determining
the exact significance to be attached to the concept of a 'class'
in these early writings.

In the later works, especially those written after 1880,
political parties cease to occupy the forefront of attention and
social classes become central in the explanation. In these
works the old problem of the significance of a 'class' arises in a
more acute form: not only does Engels distinguish between
the industrial and the commercial bourgeoisie but he also
refers to sub-divisions of the financial bourgeoisie, e.g. 'fund-
holders', 'stockjobbers', etc., so that the question is whether
Engels regarded these subdivisions as the acting units or
whether it was the whole capitalist class. If the latter is the
case, the existence of such subdivisions with conflicting interests within the class raises doubt as to the utility of the concept
of the 'class' as an instrument of analysis. If the former alternative is adopted, either the same difficulty as to the utility of

the concept 'class' arises or one must redefine the concept in such a way that each of these subdivisions is a class in itself, but this raises further problems as to the criteria to be adopted in defining a group as a 'class'.

In his treatment of factory legislation (see above pp. 86–7) Engels exhibits the same bias towards the political, particularly in the works written before 1850. Surprisingly, in his accounts of the Reform Bill the effects of the Bill on the various classes are much more prominently featured, though as we have seen (above pp. 49–53) the accounts are not always consistent, and even in this case the preoccupation with parliamentary politics is still very much in evidence.

Common-Sense Viewpoint

The common-sense approach is perhaps most evident in the early journalistic pieces on contemporary Germany. The earliest of these is an article on 'Frederick William IV' in *Einundzwanzig Bogen aus der Schweiz* in 1843 (MECW II, pp. 360–7). The article describes the use of legislation by Frederick William IV to alter the nature of the state. There is no theoretical viewpoint manifest and Engels appears to have been at least as much interested in the religious dimension of the King's actions as in their political effects and motivation. Indeed the only political motivation apparent in the analysis is the wishes of the king.

Similarly, the following year several items in *The Northern Star* (MECW III, pp. 515–34) give little evidence of any underlying theoretical position. Thus, in 'The Situation in Prussia' (pp. 515–16) some account is given of the use of the courts to repress the expression of liberal opinions and in 'News from Germany' (pp. 517–18) the prosecution by Prussian courts of a book criticising the Austrian monarchy is described, but in neither case is there any theoretical explanation.

The article 'News from Prussia' (pp. 530–1) and the following article 'Further Particulars of the Silesian Riots' (pp.

532–4) show the beginnings of an attempt to explain events in economic terms. The first of these two articles starts by describing how the king withdrew his proposed new divorce law in response to popular opposition, which is very much the same sort of common-sense explanation that I have referred to in the other articles, but the article continues by mentioning the riots that had just occurred in Silesia. Engels relates the distress of the work-people that caused the riots to three causes — competition, machinery and greedy manufacturers — and compares their situation with that of the English hand-loom weavers. In the secnd article he expands this by specifying the wages these workers received and citing their indebtedness to the manufacturers which gave the masters the upper hand completely, but the explanation remains identical with that in the earlier article.

Towards the end of 1844, in the article 'Rapid Progress of Communism in Germany' (MECW IV, pp. 229–42), after describing the spread of socialism in spite of legal repression, Engels states that in the space of a year a strong socialist party had grown up in Germany but admits that 'up to the present time our stronghold is the middle class' though he expresses a hope that in a short time the working class will join them. This explanation treats socialism as a political party rather than as the political expression of a social movement that has been produced by developments in the economic base; it would require a modification of Marxian thought to reconcile this view of socialism with Marx's view of the roles of the bourgeoisie and the proletariat.

With the possible exception of the accounts of the Poor Law (see above pp. 62–5), where Engels links the changes in the law to a specific economic theory, i.e. that of Malthus, all the other early references to law exhibit a certain ambivalence even when social classes are mentioned. Thus, in the treatments of crime (see above pp. 155–7), and of English law in practice (see above pp. 157–9), one cannot escape the feeling that the important distinction was that between rich and poor rather than, for example, that between bourgeoisie and proletariat. By contrast, in the works written after 1850 the class element in the explanations is much more prominent. Even in the later works, however, the interest in the political process is by no means entirely absent as may be seen from the articles on 'The English Elections' and 'England in 1845 and in 1885' (On Britain, pp. 364–70 and 386–92).

Law and Economy

Engels' treatment of the relationship between law and the economy falls into two quite distinct periods. The works written between 1843 and about 1847 disclose an approach that tends to use expressions such as 'historical necessity', indicative perhaps of the continuing influence of Hegel on Engels at this period. The works written after 1875 show far more clearly the influence of Marx, but here again there seems to be a distinction to be made: in works and even more in letters written after 1885 Engels regularly advances explanations that expressly posit a reciprocal action between base and superstructure.

Early works

In addition to the Hegelian view of the development of society, the early works occasionally comment on the relationship between law and society in terms that indicate that Engels viewed the 'laws' of economics in much the same way as the 'laws' of physics, i.e. as descriptions of inevitable sequences of events. The 'Outline of a Critique of Political Economy' (MECW III, pp. 418–43) contains both types of statements. In considering the tendency towards the centralisation of property Engels says:

> This law of the centralisation of private property is as immanent in private property as all the others. The middle classes must increasingly disappear until the world is divided into millionaires and paupers, into large landowners and poor farm labourers. All the laws, all the dividing of landed property, all the possible splitting up of capital, are of no avail:

> this result must and will come, unless it is anticipated by a total transformation of social conditions, an abolition of private property. [p. 441]

Clearly the thought here is of the laws of economics as operating in the same way as the laws of physics. It is doubtful whether the reservation expressed in the last clause really mitigates this, since in positing the 'total transformation of social conditions' the very basis of existing laws is removed. The passage continues by considering free competition and monopoly, and concludes:

> Monopoly produces free competition, and the latter, in turn, produces monopoly. Therefore, both must fall, and these difficulties must be resolved through the transcendence of the principal which gives rise to them. [p. 442]

Although the terms 'thesis', 'antithesis' and 'synthesis' are not used, the passage shows a line of thought that is patently dialectical.

Throughout the years 1844–7 one finds in Engels' writings references to the inevitability of a revolution in society, but it is not clear to what extent Engels was committed at this time to the economic explanation of such a necessity. Thus, at the end of 'The Condition of England. The English Constitution' MECW III, pp. 489–513 at pp. 512–13), he asserts that the struggle of the poor against the rich must result in the victory of the poor, a victory that will produce democracy in England as a stage from which must develop the principle of socialism. Again in 'Rapid Progress of Communism in Germany' (MECW IV, pp. 229–42) he reports a speech of his own in which he proved that 'the present state of Germany was such as could not but produce in a very short time a social revolution' (pp. 238–9), unless perhaps communism were introduced volunarily.

In the second of the 'Speeches in Elberfeld' (MECW IV, pp. 265–54) Engels gives an indication of the relationship between economic and historical necessity. Referring to criticisms of the previous speech, he says:

We were likewise accused of not having sufficiently demonstrated the historical necessity of communism in general. This
is quite correct and it was not possible to do otherwise. A
historical necessity cannot be demonstrated in as short a time
as the congruence of two triangles. It can only be done by
study and inquiry into all kinds of far-reaching presuppositions. I will, however, today do my best to answer these two
accusations. I will try to show that communism is, if not a
historical at any rate an *economic necessity* for *Germany*. [p.
256]

The overall tenor of the passage suggests than Engels' own
opinion was that communism was a historical necessity for
Germany even though, as he admits, he could not prove this.
The implication of this treatment is not only that there are
such things as 'economic necessities' but that they are demon-
strable, which seems to indicate that Engels was not thinking
of necessity as necessity in the light of desired objectives.

The speech continues by analysing the outlook for
Germany under the alternative suppositions of free trade and
of protective tariffs. Under either possibility Engels thought
the result would be a concentration of capital and a growth in
the proletariat, with the unavoidable result of social revolution to implement the principles of communism. The weakness of the argument lies in the assumptions (a) that the
growth in the size of the proletariat must mean a corres-
ponding growth in its power, and (b) that the power *must* be
used to effect a social revolution. In fact this latter necessity is
nowhere demonstrated in the speech; it is merely assumed.

The most important work of this period to be considered is
The Condition of the Working Class in England (MECW IV,
pp. 295–583). Two passages in this work call for attention. In
describing the activities of trades unions, Engels observes:

The history of these Unions is a long series of defeats of the
working men, interrupted by a few isolated victories. All these
efforts naturally cannot alter the economic law according to
which wages are determined by the relation between supply
and demand in the labour market. Hence the Unions remain
powerless against all *great* forces which influence this relation.
In a commerical crisis the Union itself must reduce wages or

dissolve wholly; and in a time of considerable increase in the demand for labour, it cannot fix the rate of wages higher than would be reached spontaneously by the competition of the capitalists among themselves. But in dealing with minor, single influences they are powerful. [p. 505]

He continues by showing how the collective opposition of the workmen prevents the individual employer from reducing wages to the minimum, which his competition with other capitalists would otherwise compel.

The inadequacy of this explanation derives from the failure, understandable in the historical circumstances, to appreciate that trades unions achieve their results precisely by restricting the supply of labour on the market and that this is possible in regard to the labour market for a whole industry just as much as for the labour market for an individual employer. An appreciation of this possibility other than as a purely theoretical one would have required a degree of far-sightedness that it is unreasonable to demand. The distinction between 'great' and 'minor' economic forces is not without difficulty: inherent in it seems to be the view of economic laws we have already mentioned, i.e. that these laws operate with an inevitability that cannot be surmounted by human effort.

The second passage comes from the very end of the book:

Besides, it does not occur to any Communist to wish to revenge himself upon individuals, or to believe that, in general, the single bourgeois can act otherwise, under existing circumstances, than he does act. English Socialism, i.e. Communism, rests directly upon the irresponsibility of the individual. [p. 582]

The view stated here of the non-responsibility (surely a more appropriate translation than 'irresponsibility') of the individual sums up precisely the view of the economic laws we have been considering.

The clearest statement of this tendency is in the *Principles of Communism* (MECW VI, pp. 341–57), written in 1847, where, in answer to the question whether it will be possible to bring about the abolition of private property by peaceful methods, Engels says that the communists,

> . . . know only too well that revolutions are not made deliberately and arbitrarily, but that everywhere and at all times they have been the necessary outcome of circumstances entirely independent of the will and leadership of particular parties and entire classes. [p. 349]

This passage leaves no room for doubt that, in these early years, Engels' position was one of unmitigated economic determinism.

Works written after 1875

The tendency of the works written between 1875 and 1885 is towards a simple materialistic explanation, which may be due in part at least to a polemic objective of exorcising the idealist approach from the field of social explanation. The tendency is already evident in *The Part played by Labour in the Transition from Ape to Man* (ME Sel W, pp. 385–68), where the idea is put across in terms of the primacy of the works of the hand over those of the mind in the development of the human species (pp. 363–4).

A far more important treatment, however, is in the article 'Karl Marx' (ME Sel W, pp. 369–78). As the title would suggest, in this article Engels was expounding not his own thought but that of Marx, as he saw it. He cites Marx as having proved that the whole of previous history is a history of class struggles, and asks:

> To what, however, do these classes owe their origin and their continued existence? They owe it to the particular material, physically sensible conditions in which society at a given period produces and exchanges its means of subsistence. [p. 375]

After illustrating this point by reference to the feudal Middle Ages, the rise of the urban bourgeoisie and the rise of the industrial bourgeoisie, he concludes:

From this point of view all the historical phenomena are explicable in the simplest possible way — with sufficient knowledge of the particular economic condition of society, which it is true is totally lacking in our professional historians, and in the same way the conceptions and ideas of each historical period are most simply to be explained from the economic conditions of life and from the social and political relations of the period, which are in turn determined by these economic conditions. [pp. 375–6]

He ends the passage with an idea he was to develop more fully in the following passage of his 'Speech at the Graveside of Karl Marx' (ME Sel W, pp. 435–6):

Just as Darwin discovered the law of development of organic nature, so Marx discovered the law of development of human history: the simple fact, hitherto concealed by an overgrowth of ideology, that mankind must first of all eat, drink, have shelter and clothing, before it can pursue politics, science, art, religion, etc; that therefore the production of the immediate material means of subsistence and consequently the degree of economic development attained by a given people or during a given epoch form the foundation upon which the state institutions, legal conceptions, art, and even the ideas on religion, of the people concerned have been evolved, and in the light of which they must, therefore, be explained, instead of *vice versa*, as had hitherto been the case. [p. 435]

In his account of his own intellectual development in *On the History of the Communist League* (ME Sel W, pp. 437–54), Engels tells how the decisive force of economic facts in history was brought home to him and how they form the basis of class antagonisms and hence of political parties. He then states:

Marx had not only arived at the same view, but had already in the 'German-French Annals' [1844] generalised it to the effect that, speaking generally, it is not the state which conditions and regulates civil society, but civil society which conditions and regulates the state, and, consequently, that policy and its history are to be explained from the economic relations and their development, and not vice versa. [p. 442]

The primacy attributed to economic factors in these passages is indisputable and the rejection of the reciprocal explanation, i.e. of economics in terms of politics, favours the view that Engels' interpretation of Marx regarded Marx as holding a uni-directional view of the relationship between the economic base and the superstructure. This tends to support the view adopted above. On the other hand, however, it might be maintained that the rejection of the reciprocal explanation was purely a piece of polemic against the approach of the majority of their contemporaries and, as such, should not be taken as representing an integral part of the authors' views on the substance of the question.

After the death of Marx the beginnings of a modification of this uni-directional approach appear. In the passage quoted above from *On the History of the Communist League* the expression 'speaking generally' already suggests a reservation, and the preface to the first edition of *The Origin of the Family, Private Property and the State* is even more explicit: 'According to the materialist conception, the determining factor in history is, *in the last report*, the production and reproduction of immediate life (ME Sel W, p. 455; emphasis). Here, quite clearly, Engels sees the possibility of chains of intermediate factors between the mode of production and the specific occurrences that constitute any particular segment of history.

There is a possibility that this change may have been prompted at least in part by Engels' re-examination of the role of legal systems and codes of law and certainly the change is particularly well illustrated in his treatments of these topics. The first area in this reconsideration of the role of law was Engels' attempts to explain the role of Roman law in the relationship between burghers, princes and peasants in medieval Germany. At a slightly later date he encountered and investigated the problems arising out of the differences between the English legal system, the French Code Napoléon and the German Civil Code: the mode and relations of production in the three countries were substantially the same but the legal systems were significantly different or, even more contrarily from the simple materialist viewpoint, the mode and relations of production were the most advanced in England but it was precisely the English legal system that was the most medieval.

Engels' references to Roman law in medieval Germany occur in the contexts of the transition to feudalism or of the transition from feudalism to bourgeois/burgher society. The first of his works to look at these areas was 'The Mark' (PW, pp. 135–53) written in 1882, i.e. before the death of Marx. In both that work and 'On the History of the Prussian Peasantry' (PW, pp. 154–65), written in 1885, Engels states that the Roman jurists helped the princes and the nobles to exact services from the peasants. In the former work it is suggested that the need for this arose from the nobles' increasing need for money and the way it was done was by creating confusion of a sort from which the lord gained at the expense of the peasant, whilst in the latter, although the need for money is retained as the reason for the practice, the means is given more specifically as the reduction of the peasant to a serf and the use of an analogy between the serf and the Roman law concept of a slave.

A slightly different explanation is given in the manuscript on 'The Decay of Feudalism and the Rise of National States' (PW, pp. 178–88). The date of this work is uncertain but can be no earlier than 1874 since Engels refers in a footnote to Menke's atlas, which was published in that year. In the manuscript he admits that the Roman law offered pretexts for greater oppression of the peasants but dismisses this on the ground that the nobles could and did find such pretexts without the aid of Roman law (p. 184). This observation comes in the paragraph immediately following one in which he describes the new jurists as a burgher estate. He then continues:

> Moreover, the justice they studied, advanced and applied was essentially anti-feudal and, in a certain respect, bourgeois. Roman Law is so much the classical juridical expression of the living conditions and collisions in a society ruled by pure private property that all later legislation was unable to improve on it to any substantial extent. Medieval burgher ownership, however, was still strongly hemmed in by feudal

limitations and, for instance, consisted mostly of privileges. Roman law, therefore, was in this far ahead of the bourgeois relations of the time. But all further historical development of bourgeois ownership could only, as was the case, advance towards pure private ownership. This development was bound to spot a mighty lever in Roman law, which contained in ready form everything that the burgherdom of the later Middle Ages still unconsciously sought. [p. 184]

Here the emphasis is on Roman law as an answer to the needs of burgherdom rather than those of the nobility, which accords better with the general Marxian view of the influence of rising classes at the expense of classes that are in decline.

Engels' first examination of the problem of explaining how the same economic relations could give rise to widely differing legal systems occurs in 'Ludwig Feuerbach and the End of Classical Germany Philosophy' (ME Sel W, pp. 594–632), written in 1886. The passage in question calls for extensive quotation since it not only considers the relationship between the French Civil Code and Roman law but also makes comparisons with English and Prussian law and develops from these to a more general account of the relationship between law and economic relations.

If the state and public law are determined by economic relations, so, too, is private law, which indeed in essence only sanctions the existing economic relations between individuals which are normal in the given circumstances. The form in which this happens can, however, vary considerably. It is possible, as happened in England, in harmony with the whole national development, to retain in the main the forms of the old feudal laws while giving them a bourgeois content; in fact, directly reading a bourgeois meaning into a feudal name. But also, as happened in western continental Europe, Roman law, with its unsurpassably fine elaboration of all the essential legal relations of simple commodity owners (of buyers and sellers, debtors and creditors, contracts, obligations, etc.) can be taken as the foundation. In which case, for the benefit of a still petty-bourgeois and semi-feudal society, it can either be reduced to the level of such a society simply through juridical practice (common law) or, with the help of allegedly enlightened, moralising jurists, it can be worked into a special code of law to correspond with such social level — a code which in these circumstances will be a bad one also from the legal standpoint (for instance Prussian Landrecht). In which case, however, after a great revolution it is also possible for such a classic law code of bourgeois society as the French *Code Civil* to be worked out upon the basis of this same Roman Law. If, therefore, bourgeois legal rules merely express the economic life conditions of society in legal form, then they can do so well or ill according to circumstances. [p. 627]

The recognition that factors other than the economic may determine whether a code of law is well adapted to the economic circumstances entails the possibility of a relative autonomy of the superstructure.

Two paragraphs later Engels offers an explanation of how this relative autonomy occurs. The explanation is, in effect, a rediscovery or a resurrection of ideas that had been put forward in *The German Ideology* forty years earlier (see above p. 37) but not drawn on much in the intervening period:

> But once the state has become an independent power *vis-a-vis* society, it produces forthwith a further ideology. It is indeed among professional politicians, theorists of public law and jurists of private law that the connection with economic facts gets lost for fair. Since in each case the economic facts must assume the form of juristic motives in order to receive legal sanction; and since, in so doing, consideration of course has to be given to the whole legal system already in operation, the juristic form is, in consequence, made everything and the economic content nothing. Public law and private law are treated as independent spheres, each having its own independent historical development, each being capable of and needing a systematic presentation by the consistent elimination of all inner contradictions. [pp. 627–8]

From here Engels goes on to examine the development of still higher ideologies and thence to religion.

In 1887–8 Engels pursued this interest in the differences between English, French and German law in *The Role of Force in History*. The context is a discussion of the contemporary movement in Germany for a unified code of law. Engels introduces references to English and French law for the purpose of setting up a comparison in which German law is seen as failing to give adequate protection against police despotism. To this end he says that English law does not know the police state since it was nipped in the bud by the two revolutions of the seventeenth century, with the result that English law 'culminated in two centuries of uninterrupted development of civil liberty' (pp. 101–2). (This is a somewhat more favourable assessment than he had made of the English legal system in his early works, e.g. see above pp. 157–9.)

In 1892, in the 'Special Introduction' to the English edition of *Socialism: Utopian and Scientific* (ME Sel W, pp. 379–98), Engels combined both elements of his later view of English law, namely its protection of the liberty of the individual and its expression of bourgeois relations in feudal terminology, in one passage:

> Let us, however, not forget that if English law contines to express the economic relations of capitalistic society in that barbarous feudal language which corresponds to the thing expressed, just as English spelling corresponds to English pronunciation — vous écrivez Londres et vous prononcez Constantinople, said a Frenchman — that same English law is the only one which has preserved through the ages, and transmitted to America and the colonies, the best part of that old Germanic freedom, local self-government and independence from all interference but that of the law courts which on the Continent has been lost during the period of absolute monarchy, and has nowhere been as yet fully recovered. [pp. 391–2]

What is interesting both in this passage and the one from *The Role of Force in History* is the absence of any suggestion that the civil liberty protected by English law is the privilege of any particular class. On the other point, the analogy with English pronunciation, it can be said that the very minimum this entails an abandonment of any *necessary* correlation between legal concepts and economic relations.

The correspondence

The development of this more complex model of the action and reaction between base and superstructure is revealed particularly well in Engels' correspondence. To highlight the point one may contrast his statement on the subject in a letter to Kautsky of 26 June 1884 (ME Sel Cor, pp. 355–7) with the more comprehensive account in letters to Schmidt, Blockh, Mehring and Borgius in the period 1890–4. In the letter to Kautsky he says:

> As soon as you speak of means of production you speak of society, and of society that is also determined by these means of production. [p. 356]

(It must be admitted that the context in which this statement occurs is a criticism of Kautsky's failure to appreciate that the means of production *always* condition society and not merely in capitalist society as Kautsky had suggested.) On the other hand, in his letter to Schmidt of 5 August 1890 (ME Sel Cor, pp. 392–4), he states:

> . . . although the material mode of existence is the *primum agens* this does not prevent the ideological spheres from react-ing upon it and influence it in their turn, but this is a secondary effect. [p. 393]

In another letter to Schmidt later than same year, 27 October 1890 (ME Sel Cor, pp. 396–402), he develops at much greater length a theoretical view of the reaction of the various ideological spheres on the base. The exposition starts with the recognition that once trade becomes independent of production proper it acquires a movement of its own. He continues by explaining that the money market similarly be-comes independent of both trade and production. He then puts forward a generalised explanation of how this happens:

> The thing is easiest to grasp from the point of view of the division of labour. Society gives rise to certain common func-tions which it cannot dispense with. The persons appointed for this purpose form a new branch of the division of labour *within society*. This gives them particular interests, distinct, too,

from the interests of their mandators; they make themselves independent of the latter and — the state is in being. And now things proceed in a way similar to that in commodity trade and later in money trade: the new independent power, while having in the main to follow the movement of production reacts in its turn, by virtue of its inherent relative independence — that is, the relative independence once transferred to it and gradually further developed — upon the conditions and course of production. It is the interaction of two unequal forces: on the one hand, the economic movement, on the other, the new political power, which strives for as much independence as possible, and, which, having once been set up, is endowed with a movement of its own. [pp. 398–9]

After examinining the ways in which political power can react upon the economy, he applies the analysis specifically to the field of law:

As soon as the new division of labour which creates professional lawyers becomes necessary, another new and independent sphere is opened up which, for all its general dependence on production and trade, has also a specific capacity for reacting upon these spheres. In a modern state, law must not only correspond to the general economic condition and be its expression, but must also be an *internally coherent* expression which does not, owing to internal conflicts, contradict itself. And in order to achieve this, the faithful reflection of economic conditions suffers increasingly. All the more so the more rarely it happens that a code of law is the blunt, unmitigated, unadulterated expression of the domination of a class — this in itself would offend the 'conception of right'. [pp. 399–400]

He illustrates this by pointing out that even the Code Napoléon daily has to undergo all sorts of attenuations of its original purely bourgeois conception owing to the rising power of the proletariat. He then makes an important observation:

Thus to a great extent the course of the 'development of law' simply consists in first attempting to eliminate contradictions which arise from the direct translation of economic relations into legal principles, and to establish a harmonious system of law, and then in the repeated breaches made in this system by

the influence and compulsion of further economic development, which involves it in further contradictions. [p. 400]

He concludes the treatment of law by explaining how law is an
ideological outlook: the jurist imagines he is dealing with *a
priori* propositions, whereas these are in fact merely the reflection of the economic realities. The inverted viewpoint thus
reached is consequently ideological.

At the end of this paragraph Engels considers the right of
inheritance. The basis of the right is economic but obviously
this right exerts a great influence on the economic sphere by
influencing the distribution of property. He contrasts the
liberty enjoyed by testators in England with the detailed
restrictions imposed in France and notes that it would be
difficult to prove that these differences are due solely to
economic causes. It is a pity that Engels did not investigate the
other causes he thought might be responsible, since it is by no
means clear that the only other causes he mentions, i.e. a
desire of the professional lawyers to have a harmonious system of law, are adequate either by themselves or in con-
junction with economic ones to explain such differences.

This raises the possibility that the model of the relationship
between law and society that Engels was developing was an
even more complex one, embracing the prospect not only of a
reciprocal action between the base and the various superstructures but also between the superstructures themselves
independent of the base. The difficulty with such a model is,
of course, that it goes a long way towards abandoning completely the primacy of the economic base. In fact he had
already put forward an undeveloped version of such a view in
a letter to Bloch of 21 September 1890 (ME Sel Cor, pp.
394–6), where he stated that the elements of the superstructure such as political and legal forms, and political, religious,
legal or philosophical theories also influenced the course of
historical struggles and might even determine the particular
form the struggle took. He continues:

> There is an interaction of all these elements in which, amid all
> the endless host of accidents (that is, of things and events

whose inner interconnection is so remote or so impossible of proof that we can regard it as non-existent and neglect it), the economic movement is finally bound to assert itself. [p. 395]

By 1894 he was even clearer in this view. In a letter to Borgius of 25 January 1984 (ME Sel Cor, pp. 441–3), he put it thus:

Political, legal, philosophical, religious, literary, artistic, etc., development is based on economic development. But all these react upon one another and also upon the economic basis. One must not think that the economic situation is *cause, and solely active* whereas everything else is only a passive effect. On the contrary, interaction always takes place on the basis of economic necessity, which ultimately always asserts itself . . . The economic situation therefore does not produce an automatic effect as people try here and there conveniently to imagine, but men make their history themselves, they do so, however, in a given environment, which conditions them, and on the basis of actual, already existing relations, among which the economic relations — however much they may be influenced by other, political and ideological relations — are still ultimately the decisive ones, forming the keynote which alone leads to understanding. [p. 442]

A feature that is common to all these formulations is the emphasis they place on the participating actor. Perhaps the clearest illustration of this is the use of the division of labour in explaining the independence of the various areas of the super-structure. Such an approach inevitably throws the focus of attention onto the ideas, objectives and ideals of the persons involved in the particular specialised sub-division of labour. The concept of 'ideology' reinforces this, since the concept essentially attempts to explain and account for the difference between the actualities in question and the participating actors' views of those actualities. In view of the importance that Engels attached to 'ideology', particularly in the letter to Schmidt of 27 October 1890 (see above pp. 216–18), it would seem a sounder conclusion to interpret the references to 'elements', e.g. political, also in an interactionist sense rather than as elements of a 'system' type of explanation.

Although he had developed this more complex model of the relationship between the economic base and the various elements of the superstructure, Engels did not abandon the view that the development of society was subject to 'necessity'. In fact, in the same letter to Borgius he makes precisely this point as the second of the two points in his explanation of the Marxist view that economic conditions ultimately determine historical development (the first being the one already quoted on the reciprocal effect of ideological etc. factors on the base):

> Men make their history themselves, but not as yet with a collective will according to a collective plan or even in a clearly defined given society. Their aspirations clash and for that very reason all such societies are governed by *necessity*, whose complement and manifestation is *accident*. The necessity which here asserts itself through all accident is again ultimately economic necessity. [p. 442]

He then deals with the difficulty raised by so-called 'great men'. Whilst pure chance determines which particular individual is cast in the role, if the necessity for such a person existed a substitute would have been found had that particular individual not been available. To prove this he cites as a fact that 'a man has always been found as soon as he became necessary'. This is more than a little questionable inasmuch as it assumes that there are clear criteria by which one could recognise the negative instance, i.e. the situation where the presence of a 'great man' would have altered the course of events but where, for the lack of such a person, the development continued in an unaltered course. The assertion that such individuals arose 'as soon as' the necessity was present is also open to question: either it is a mere truism depending on the definition of 'necessity' or it posits a more direct influence of the economy than that envisaged in the immediately preceding paragraph.

The continuation of the letter clarifies the matter somewhat:

> So with all the other contingencies, and apparent contingencies, of history. The further the particular sphere which we are investigating is removed from the economic sphere and

approaches that of pure abstract ideology, the more we shall find it exhibiting accidents in its development, the more will its curve run zigzag. But if you plot the average axis of the curve, you will find that this axis will run more and more nearly parallel to the axis of the economic development the longer the period considered and the wider the field dealt with. [pp. 442–3]

Even this explanation is not entirely free from difficulty. First, the approach suggested is of a statistical kind and like any statistical law/regularity is explanatory capabilities are restricted by the existence of the empirical residue: such a law may explain cases that have occurred in conformity with the law but it cannot be used to predict the outcome of the specific empirical instance. Secondly, which is perhaps merely another way of highlighting the difference between the statistical generalisation and the empirical instance, the choice of scale may affect the apparent importance of discrepancies — if one is considering a period of 10,000 years a delay of 50 years may appear unimportant whereas in a period of 200 such a delay appears far more significant.

The third difficulty not only gives rise to the necessity to make such a selection of time-scales but also raises the question of whether the belief that in the long run the economic development is the leading factor is verifiable/falsifiable at all or whether it is rather a value-judgement that one brings to the examination of the evidence. The difficulty is that the longest period and the widest area that could be considered would embrace the whole of human history throughout the entire world; the examination of this, the limiting case, is impossible simply for lack of the relevant evidence, if for no other reason. Such being the case, a selection must be made and there is no way of guaranteeing that the selection does not predetermine the conclusion.

A further point that deserves some attention is the issue of what Engels though he was doing in presenting this developed model of the relationship between base and superstructure. On this point the letters are again most helpful. At the beginning of the extract from the letter to Bloch (p. 394) Engels claims that neither he nor Marx ever asserted more than that the production and reproduction of life were the *ultimately* determining factor in the history, but towards the end of the letter he admits that:

> Marx and I are partly to blame for the fact that the younger people sometimes lay more stress on the economic side than is due to it. We had to emphasise the main principle *vis-a-vis* our adversaries, who denied it, and we had not always the time, the place or the opportunity to give their due to the other factors involved in the interaction. But when it came to presenting a section of history, that is, to applying the theory in practice, it was a different matter and there no error was permissible. [p. 396]

In the letter to Mehring of 14 July 1893 (ME Sel Cor, pp. 433–7) the admission is even more comprehensive:

> Otherwise only one more point is lacking, which, however, Marx and I always failed to stress enough in our writings and in regard to which we are all equally guilty. That is to say, in the first instance we all laid, and *were bound to lay*, the main emphasis on the *derivation* of political, juridical and other ideological notions, and of actions arising through the medium of these notions, from basic economic facts. But at the same time we have on account of the content neglected the formal side — the manner in which these notions, etc., come about. [pp. 433–4]

There is some difficulty in reconciling the assertions. On the one hand, in the letter to Mehring Engels admits to having neglected the 'formal' side, whilst to Bloch he claims that when it came to presenting a section of history 'no error was permissible'. Some light may be thrown on the matter by the previous paragraph of the letter to Bloch where Engels cites 'The Eighteenth Brumaire' as a 'most excellent example' of the application of the theory in practice. As we have seen, however, (above pp. 128–52) the validity of this particular attempt to explain political events by reference to economic factors is by no means beyond dispute.

Conclusion

In conclusion of this examination of Engels' writings it may be said that this intellectual development reveals far greater changes than does that of Marx. The change from the pure, idealistic Hegelianism of 'The Internal Crises' to the materialism of the later works in itself entails a greater distance travelled to reach what was, for Marx, almost the starting-point. The development in the final years of a model of the reciprocal action between base and superstructure indicates perhaps a further change of direction. The other major changes in Engels' approach, the inclusion of an increasingly economic approach and the reduction of the emphasis on the political, is probably due to the influence of Marx. It is a matter for conjecture whether the economic determinism of the early works such as the *Principles of Communism* of 1847 was the result of an attempt by Engels to make his own the approach of Marx. If this conjecture is true, however, then the later formulation of the more complex model of the relationship between base and superstructure could be seen as the re-emergence of his own ideas, now modified by the experience of years in contact with actual political praxis. Finally, the difference between the early presentation of the 'juridical mendacity' of English law and the later presentation of English law as preserving the old Germanic freedom may be symptomatic of a more extensive revision of his opinion of the role of law, as part of this same development.

Chronological List of Works of Marx and Engels Cited

In the following list preference has generally been given to the year of writing rather than the year of first publication of a work. Thus, for example, *Capital* vol. III is listed under 1867 as this gives a closer indication of the period to which the work belongs.

1837   (M) Letter to his Father; MECW I pp. 10–21.

1840–1   (M) The Difference between the Democritean and the Epicurean Philosophy of Nature; MECW I pp. 25–105.

1842   (M) Debates on Freedom of the Press; RhZ May 1842, MECW I pp. 132–81.

           (E) The Liberalism of the *Spenersche Zeitung*; RhZ June 1842, MECW II pp. 300–1.

           (E) The End of the *Criminalistische Zeitung*; RhZ June 1842, MECW II pp. 302–3.

           (E) On the Critique of the Prussian Press Laws; RhZ July 1842, MECW II pp. 304–11.

           (E) Centralisation and Freedom; RhZ Sept. 1842, MECW II pp. 355–9.

           (E) Frederick William IV; *Einundzwanzig Bogen aus der Schweiz*, 1843, MECW II pp. 360–7.

           (M) Debates on the Law on Thefts of Wood; RhZ Oct. 1842, MECW I, pp. 224–63.

(M) Communal Reform and the *Kölnische Zeitung*; RhZ Nov. 1842, MECW I pp. 266–73.

(E) The Internal Crises; RhZ Dec. 1842, MECW II pp. 370–4.

(E) The Position of the Political Parties, RhZ Dec. 1842, MECW II pp. 375–7.

(E) The Corn Laws; RhZ Dec. 1842, MECW II, pp. 380–2.

1843

(M) The Ban on the *Leipziger Allgemeine Zeitung*; RhZ Jan. 1843, MECW I pp. 311–30.

(M) Justification of the Correspondent from the Mosel; RhZ Jan. 1843, MECW I pp. 332–58.

(M) Marginal Notes to the Accusation of the Ministerial Rescript; Feb. 1843, MECW I pp. 361–5.

(M) *Contribution to the Critique of Hegel's Philosophy of Law*; MECW III pp. 3–129.

(E) Letters from London; *Schweitzerischer Republikaner* May/June 1843, MECW III pp. 379–91.

(E) Progress of Social Reform on the Continent; *New Moral World* Nov. 1843, MECW III, pp. 392–408.

1844

(E) Outline of a Critique of Political Economy; DFJ 1844, MECW III pp. 418–43.

(E) The Condition of England. *Past and Present* by Thomas Carlyle; DFJ 1844, MECW III pp. 444–68.

(M) On the Jewish Question; DFJ 1844, MECW III pp. 146–74.

(M) Critical Marginal Notes on the Article 'The King of Prussia and Social Reform' by a Prussian; *Vorwärts*, Aug. 1844, MECW III pp. 189–206.

(E) The Condition of England. The Eighteenth Century; *Vorwärts*, Aug/Sept 1844, MECW

III pp. 469–88.

(E) The Condition of England. The English Constitution; *Vorwärts* Sept/Oct, 1844, MECW III pp. 489–513.

(E) The Situation in Prussia; NS May 1844, MECW III pp. 515–16.

(E) News from Germany; NS May 1844, MECW III pp. 517–18.

(E) News from France; NS June 1844, MECW III pp. 527–9.

(E) News from Prussia; NS June 1844, MECW III pp. 530–1.

(E) Further Particulars of the Silesian Riots; NS June 1844, MECW III pp. 532–4.

(M) Comments on James Mill: MECW III pp. 211–28.

(M) Economic and philosophic manuscripts; MECW III pp. 229–346.
    Estranged (Alienated) Labour
    The Antithesis of Capital and Labour
    Critique of the Hegelian Dialectic and Philosophy as a Whole.

1844–5   (E) Rapid Progress of Communism in Germany; *New Moral World* Dec. 1844, March/May 1845, MECW IV pp. 229–242.

1845 (M&E) *The Holy Family*; MECW IV pp. 3–211.

(E) Speeches in Elberfeld; *Rheinische Jahrbücher für gesellschaftlichen Reform* 1845, MECW IV pp. 243–64.

(M) On Friedrich List's book *Das Nationale System der Politischen Oekonomie*; MECW IV pp. 265–93.

(E) *The Condition of the Working Class England*; MECW IV pp. 295–583.

(E) History of the English Corn Laws; *Telegraph für Deutschland* Dec. 1845, MECW IV pp. 656–61.

1845–6 (M&E) *The Germany Ideology*; MECW V pp. 19–539.

1846   (E) Government and Opposition in France; NS Sept. 1846, MECW VI pp. 61–3.

  (M) Letter to Annenkov, 28 Dec. 1846; ME Sel Cor pp. 29–39.

1847   (M) *The Poverty of Philosophy*; MECW VI pp. 105–212.

  (E) The Decline and Approaching Fall of Guizot; NS July 1847, MECW VI pp. 213–19.

  (E) *Principles of Communism*; MECW VI pp. 341–57.

  (E) The Reform Movement in France; NS Nov. 1847, MECW VI pp. 375–82.

  (E) Split in the Camp; NS Dec. 1847, MECW, VI pp. 385–7.

  (E) The *Réforme* and the *National*; *Deutsche-Brüsseler-Zeitung* Dec. 1847, MECW VI pp. 406–8.

1848   (E) The 'Satisfied' Majority; NS Jan. 1848, MECW VI pp. 438–44.

  (M) Speech on the Question of Free Trade; MECW VI pp. 450–65.

  (E) Extraordinary Revelations; *La Réforme* Jan. 1848, MECW VI pp. 469–75.

  (M&E) *Manifesto of the Communist Party*; MECW VI pp. 477–519.

  (E) The Movements of 1847; *Deutsche-Brüsseler-Zeitung* Jan. 1848, MECW VI pp. 520–9.

  (M) Speech on the Polish Question; MECW VI pp. 545–9.

  (E) Speech on the Polish Question; MECW VI pp. 549–52.

  (E) Revolution in Paris; *Deutsche-Brüsseler-Zeitung* Feb. 1848, MECW VI pp. 556–8.

  (–) News from Paris; NRhZ June 1848, MECW VII p. 121.

(–) News from Paris; NRhZ June 1848, MECW VII p. 123.

(M) News from Paris; NRhZ June 1848, MECW VII p. 128.

(E) Details about the 23rd of June; NRhZ June 1848, MECW VII pp. 124–7.

(E) The 23rd of June; NRhZ June 1848, MECW VII pp. 130–3.

(E) The 24th of June; NRhZ June 1848, MECW VII pp. 134–8.

(E) The 25th of June; NRhZ June 1848, MECW VII pp. 139–43.

(M) The June Revolution; NRhZ June 1848, MECW VII pp. 144–9.

(E) The June Revolution; NRhZ July 1848, MECW VII pp. 157–64.

(–) Marrast and Thiers; NRhZ July 1848, MECW VII pp. 168–9.

(M) The Prussian Press Bill; NRhZ July, 1848, MECW VII pp. 250–2, PR1848 pp. 134–7.

(M) The Bill for the Abolition of Feudal Burdens; NRhZ July 1848, PR1848 pp. 137–43, MECW VII pp. 290–5.

(–) Proudhon's Speech against Thiers; NRhZ Aug. 1848, MECW VII pp. 321–4.

(M) The *Réforme* on the June Insurrection; NRhZ Oct. 1848, MECW VII pp. 478–9.

(M) The Paris *Réforme* on the Situation in France; NRhZ Nov. 1848, MECW VII pp. 493–5.

(E) The French Working Class and the Presidential Elections; Dec. 1848, MECW VIII pp. 123–8.

1849   (M) The Revolutionary Movement; NRhZ Jan. 1849, MECW VIII pp. 213–15.

(–) The Situation in Paris; NRhZ Jan. 1849, MECW VIII pp. 281–5.

(M) The Trial of the Rhineland District Comit-
tee of Democrats; NRhZ Feb. 1849, PR1848
pp. 245–64, MECW VIII pp. 323–39.

(M) Three New Bills; NRhZ March 1849,
MECW IX pp. 50–4.

(M) The Hohenzollern General Plan of Reform;
NRhZ March 1849, MECW IX pp. 65–9.

(–) The Milliard; NRhZ March 1849, MECW
IX pp. 79–83

(M) The Hohenzollern Press Bill; NRhZ March
1849, MECW IX pp. 125–32.

1850   (E) Letters from France; *Democratic Review*
Jan.-Aug. 1850, MECW X pp. 17–40.

(M) The Class Struggles in France; PSE pp. 35–
142, MECW X pp. 45–145.

(M) Review of Guizot's book *Why has the English
Revolution been Successful?*; On Britain
pp. 89–95, MECW X pp. 251–6.

(M&E) Review; NRhZ POR nos. 2, 4, 5–6 1850,
MECW X pp. 257–70, 338–41, 490–532.

(E) The English Ten Hours Bill; NRhZ POR no.
4 1850, On Britain pp. 96–108, MECW X
pp. 288–300.

1851   (M) The Constitution of the French Republic;
Notes to the People June 1851, MECW X
pp. 567–80.

1852   (M) The Eighteenth Brumaire of Louis Bonaparte;
PSE pp. 143–249, MECW XI pp. 99–197.

(M) The Elections in England – Tories and
Whigs; NYDT Aug. 1852, On Britain pp.
109–15, MECW XI pp. 327–32.

(M) The Chartists; NYDT Aug. 1852, On Britain
pp. 116–24, MECW XI pp. 333–41.

1853   (M) Capital Punishment; NYDT Feb. 1853, On
Britain pp. 149–52, MECW XI 495–501.

(M) Parliamentary Debates — The Clergy and the
Struggles for the Ten Hour Day; NYDT

March 1853, On Britain pp. 153–9, MECW XI pp. 522–7.

(M) The Indian Question — Irish Tenant Right; NYDT July 1853, Ireland pp. 59–65, MECW XII pp. 157–62.

(M) The War Question — Doings of Parliament; NYDT Aug. 1853, Ireland pp. 67–9, MECW XII pp. 209–16.

1855   (M) The British Constitution; *Neue Oder_Zeitung* March 1855, On Britain pp. 219–22.

(M) From Parliament; *Neue Oder-Zeitung* July 1855, Ireland pp. 77–8.

1857–8   (M) *Grundrisse*; London: Penguin, 1873.

1859   (M) *Contribution to the Critique of Political Economy*; London: Lawrence and Wishart, 1971.

(M) Population, Crime and Pauperism; NYDT Sept. 1859, Ireland pp. 92–4.

1861   (M) The Crisis in England; *Die Presse* Nov. 1861, Ireland pp. 95–6.

1862   (M) A London Workers' Meeting; *Die Presse* Feb. 1862, On Britain pp. 311–4.

1861–3   (M) *Theores of Surplus Value*; parts I and II; London: Lawrence and Wishart, 1969.

1865   (M) *Wages, Price and Profit;* ME Sel W pp. 186–299.

1867   (M) *Capital* I; London: Lawrence and Wishart, 1974.

(M) *Capital* III; London: Lawrence and Wishart, 1974.

(M) Outline of a Report on the Irish Question; Ireland pp. 126–39.

(M) Speech on the Irish Question; Ireland pp. 140–2.

1874   (E) The English Elections; *Der Volksstaat* March 1874, On Britain pp. 364–70.

1875   (E) The Decay of Feudalism and the Rise of National States; PW pp. 178–88.

1876   (E) The Part played by Labour in the Transi-from Ape to Man; ME Sel W pp. 358–68.

1877   (E) Karl Marx; *Volkskalender* 1878, ME Sel W pp. 369–78.

1880   (E) Socialism — Utopian and Scientific; *La Revue Socialiste* March, April, May 1880, ME Sel W pp. 399–434.

1881   (E) Social Classes — Necessary and Superfluous; *Labour Standard* Aug. 1881, On Britain pp. 382–5.

1882   (E) The Mark; PW pp. 135–53.

1883   (E) Speech at the Graveside of Karl Marx; ME Sel W pp. 435–6.

1884   (E) *The Origin of the Family, Private Property and the State;* ME Sel W pp. 455–593.

         (E) Letter to Kautsky, 26 June 1884; ME Sel Cor pp. 355–7.

1885   (E) On the History of the Prussian Peasantry; PW pp. 154–65.

         (E) *On the History of the Communist League*; ME Sel W pp. 437–54.

     (M) England in 1845 and in 1885; *Commonseal* March 1885, On Britain pp. 386–92.

1886   (E) Ludwig Feuerbach and the End of Classical German Philosophy; *Die Neue Zeit* 1886, ME Sel W pp. 594–632.

1888   (E) *The Role of Force in History*; London: Lawrence and Wishart, 1968.

1890   (E) Letter to Schmidt, 5 Aug. 1890; ME Sel Cor pp. 392–4.

         (E) Letter to Bloch, 21–2 Sept. 1890; ME Sel Cor pp. 394–6.

         (E) Letter to Schmidt, 27 Oct. 1890; ME Sel Cor pp. 396–402.

1892   (E) Special Introduction to the English edition of *Socialism: Utopian and Scientific*; ME Sel W pp. 379–98.

1893   (E) Letter to Mehring, 14 July 1893; ME Sel Cor
              pp. 433–7.
1894   (E) Letter to Borgius, 25 Jan. 1894; ME Sel Cor
              pp. 441–3.

Alphabetical List of Works Cited

History of the English Corn Laws, The (E) 1845; 51, 67, 69, 75, 84

Hohenzollern General Plan of Reform, The (M) 1849; 13

Hohenzollern Press Bill, The (M) 1849; 13

Holy Family, The (M&E) 1845; 160, 162–4, 165

Indian Question — Irish Tenant Right, The (M) 1853; 171, 188–9

Internal Crises, The (E) 1842; 23, 223

June Revolution, The (M) 1848; 115

Justification of the Correspondent from the Mosel, (M) 1843; 12

Karl Marx (E) 1877; 209–10

Letter to Annenkov (M) 1846; 172

Letter to Bloch (E) 1890; 216, 218–9, 221–2

Letter to Borgius (E) 1894; 216, 219, 220

Letter to his Father (M) 1837; 4–5, 8, 10, 17

Letter to Kautsky (E) 1884; 216

Letter to Mehring (E) 1893; 216, 222

Letter(s) to Schmidt (E) 1890; 216–18, 219, 222

Letters from France (E) 1850; 121, 145, 146–7, 149

Letters from London (E) 1843; 72, 86, 89

Liberalism of the *Spenersche Zeitung,* The (E) 1842; 25

London Workers' Meeting, A (M) 1862; 78

Ludwig Feuerbach and the End of Classical German Philosophy (E) 1886; 2, 213–4

Manifesto of the Communist Party, The (M&E) 1848; 34, 40

Marginal Notes to the Accusation of the Ministerial Rescript (M) 1843; 12, 21

Mark, The (E) 1882; 177, 212

Marrast and Thiers (—) 1848; 115

Milliard, The (—) 1849; 119

Movements of 1847, The (E) 1848; 114

News from France (E) 1844; 110

News from Germany (E) 1844; 203

News from Paris (M) 1848; 115

News from Prussia (E) 1844; 203

On Friedrich List's Book, *Das Nationale System der Politischen Oekonomie,* (M) 1854; 69–70

'Satisfied' Majority, The (E) 1848; 113

Situation in Paris, The (—) 1849; 119

Situation in Prussia, The (E) 1844; 203

Social Classes — Necessary and Superfluous (E) 1881; 83

Socialism: Utopian and Scientific (E) 1892; 51, 83, 215

Speech at the Graveside of Karl Marx (E) 1883; 210

Speech on the Irish Question (M) 1867; 80

Speech on the Polish Question (M) 1848; 53–4

Speech on the Question of Free Trade (M) 1848; 76–7, 82, 85

Speeches at Elberfeld (E) 1845; 155, 206–7

Split in the Camp (E) 1847; 113

Theories of Surplus Value I, (M) 1861–3; 160, 161–2

Theories of Surplus Value II (M) 1861–3; 48, 76

Three New Bills, (M) 1849; 13

Trial of the Rhineland District Committee of Democrats, The (M) 1849; 187, 193, 199

Twenty Fifth of June, The (E) 1848; 115

Twenty Fourth of June, the (E) 1848; 115

Twenty Third of June, The (E) 1948; 115

Wages, Price and Profit, (M) 1865; 100.

War Question — Doings of Parliament, The (M) 1853; 171